THE GWR STARS, CASTLES & KINGS

David & Charles Locomotive Monographs

General Editor:
O. S. NOCK, B.Sc., C.Eng., M.I.C.E., M.I.Mech.E., M.I.Loco.E.

Published titles
The Midland Compounds, by O. S. Nock
The Stirling Singles of the Great Northern Railway, by Kenneth H. Leech and Maurice Boddy
The LNWR Precursor Family, by O. S. Nock
The GWR Stars, Castles & Kings, Part 1, by O. S. Nock

In preparation
The Caledonian Dunalastairs, by O. S. Nock
The GWR Stars, Castles & Kings, Part 2, by O. S. Nock
The Gresley Pacifics, by O. S. Nock

One of the first batch of 'Stars' as built in 1907: No. 4009 'Shooting Star',
with non-superheater boiler and smaller diameter chimney

DAVID & CHARLES LOCOMOTIVE MONOGRAPHS

THE GWR STARS, CASTLES & KINGS

Part I : 1906 - 1930

O. S. NOCK, B.Sc.C.Eng., M.I.C.E., M.I.Mech.E., M.I.Loco.E.

DAVID & CHARLES   :   NEWTON ABBOT   :   DEVON

First Published in 1967 by
David & Charles (Publishers) Ltd
Newton Abbot Devon

Printed in Great Britain by
W. J. Holman Ltd Dawlish Devon

CONTENTS

PREFACE

WHEN the Locomotive Monograph series was first considered the Churchward dynasty of four-cylinder 4—6—0 locomotives of the GWR was an obvious choice for early attention, and Mr. David St. John Thomas asked me to inaugurate the series by dealing with these engines. It so happened that I was then engaged on other literary work concerning the GWR, and in view of the research work involved I felt that 'Stars, Castles & Kings' should be embarked upon as a longer-term project.

The research into the engineering development of these famous engines, and the collation of data regarding their performance has taken longer even than was at first expected and such is the volume of material that has come to hand that after due consideration it was decided that this monograph would have to extend into two volumes. This first volume ends roughly at the year 1930, by which time the 'Kings' were at work. The second volume will deal with the subsequent development of the 'Castles' and 'Kings', at first under Hawksworth, and later under the auspices of the nationalised British Railways.

I owe a debt of gratitude to many men of the old GWR for their help over the years, because a book of this kind is not the result of some quick and intense 'homework'. I must mention particularly the distinguished engineers who successively have held the office of Chief Mechanical Engineer at Swindon: F. W. Hawksworth, Kenneth J. Cook and R. A. Smeddle. To Hawksworth in particular I am indebted for the privileges he accorded to me, now more than 20 years ago, for seeing Great Western locomotives at work and on test. Furthermore, in his retirement his interest is as keen as ever, and he was kind enough to give me his own clear recollections of the designing of *The Great Bear*, of which engine he himself made the general arrangement drawing.

I am also very much indebted to S. O. Ell, who was in charge of dynamometer-car testing and experimental development since World War II. There is also W. H. Pearce, the senior draughtsman who worked out the valve gears of the Churchward 4—6—0 locomotives.

On the 'running' side, my thanks are due to W. N. Pellow and H. E. A. White, successively Locomotive Running Superintendents, and to the many inspectors who have been my guide and philosopher over thousands of miles of footplate travel. My special thanks are due to A. Cameron, C. J. Pullen, W. Andress, A. Jenkins, W. Button, H. Price and J. Hancock.

My thanks are also due to the present Chief Engineer, Rolling Stock, of the British Railways Board, Mr. A. E. Robson, for his help in supplying drawings and photographs, and in particular for loaning many original tracings. It is this latter help that has enabled these historic drawings to be reproduced in so splendid a form.

The literature of Great Western locomotives is already considerable and I have referred to many of the existing works. Books and papers I have found particularly useful are listed in the bibliography on page 160.

O. S. NOCK

Silver Cedars,
High Bannerdown,
Bathcaston,
Bath
April, 1967

9

*A GWR poster showing how the majestic proportions of the
'Kings' were used in pictorial advertising effect*

*The presentation bell mounted upon
engine No. 6000 after the visit to the
U.S.A. in 1927*

CHAPTER 1

THE PRELUDE
'By Frenchman out of Albion'

IN the closing years of the nineteenth century the management of the Great Western Railway, finally rid of the encumbrance of the broad gauge, hammered out a policy of such widespread expansion as to constitute a positive resurgence of the spirit of Brunel. New cut-off lines were to be constructed, shortening the main lines to the West of England, to South Wales, and to Birmingham; train schedules faster than ever before were planned, and a new enthusiasm, drive, and sense of renewed purpose was fostered in the staff from end to end of the line. With the passing of the broad gauge there were many older servants of the company who felt that a little 'something' which other railways did not possess had been jettisoned; out of necessity maybe, but a little sadly. But the tremendous upsurge that followed restored, and emphasised to an extent perhaps never previously touched, that inherent Great Western 'pride in the job'.

Nowhere was this spirit more clearly manifested than in the Locomotive Department at Swindon Works. William Dean, Locomotive, Carriage and Wagon Superintendent, was a true industrial autocrat of the late Victorian era. His engines were beautiful to see, and economical to run. Dean on the Great Western, together with S. W. Johnson on the Midland, produced some of the most graceful, exquisitely-styled locomotives ever to run on rails. But then, towards the end of their careers, both engineers began to break with tradition and give their products an entirely new look. Dean began it with the 'Atbara' class of 4—4—0s, dating from 1898, and Johnson followed with his celebrated 'Belpaire' 4—4—0s of 1901. At Swindon, however, the change was undoubtedly due to the rising influence and stature of Dean's principal assistant, George Jackson Churchward, and in the 'Atbara' class 4—4—0s can be seen the first steps towards the great development that was to make

Swindon Works forever famous in the history of steam locomotive engineering.

Churchward was a man of immense vision. Even before he was called upon to take charge of the department he conceived a vast project of standardisation. He looked ahead to the great increases in traffic that were expected to come from the modernisation plans that were being launched by the Board; and just as Daniel Gooch had done when the Battle of the Gauges was at its height he planned to provide the GWR with locomotives, for all classes of traffic, that would be in advance of their time. Standardisation can lead to stagnation, and never more so than in locomotive engineering. But Churchward was looking at least 20 years ahead, when he formulated his historic proposals for no more than six standard classes to work the great bulk of the traffic on the line.

His first approaches to the practical task of setting this plan in action were made while Dean was still in full harness, and were concentrated entirely upon the development of a new design of boiler. Throughout his career Churchward attached an over-riding importance to boiler design, for without a free-steaming boiler a locomotive could not do its work on the road; and equally from the maintenance point of view the boiler could be the most expensive and troublesome part of the locomotive. To those who had delighted in the artistic appearance of Dean's express passenger engines, particularly the 7 ft. 8 in. 4—2—2 singles, the 'Atbaras' with their severe lines, came as something of a shock.

About the turn of the century the directors began to observe with great sadness that Dean's brilliant mind was beginning to give way, and with the utmost discretion they began to place more and more reliance upon Churchward for the management of the department. Never was the greatness of his personal character more finely shown than in those difficult years 1900, 1901 and 1902. He was on the threshold of attaining his life's ambition, in the complete confidence of the directors, yet exercising his delicate assignment with such kindliness and tact that Dean never felt that he was very gradually being superseded. It was in 1901 that the drawing was prepared showing the six standard classes for the future, and the first prototype, the 4—6—0 express passenger engine No. 100, was built in 1902 while Dean was still in office.

One feature was common to all these proposed standard classes. They were all to have two outside cylinders, with Stephenson's link motion inside, and those cylinders were to have the same diameter and stroke on every one of the six classes. All were to have domeless boilers, of varying sizes according to the duties for which the engines were designed, and only three diameters of coupled wheels were proposed. It was a magnificent conception, wholeheartedly endorsed by the Board, and eventually carried through in its entirety, and developed further in later years. Yet within five years of the preparation of that historic outline drawing of the six standard classes another had been introduced that cut right across the policy of standardising the machinery of all GWR main-line locomotives. Churchward had built his first four-cylinder simple express engine, the *North Star,* and this remarkable prototype founded the parallel dynasty of four-cylinder 4—6—0 locomotives that is the subject of this monograph.

Before coming to the locomotives themselves it is extremely interesting and important to recall the events that led Churchward to diverge from the very simple policy he had laid down in 1901, and which could in actual fact have been completely adequate to meet all the motive power needs of the GWR up to the time of his retirement, at the end of 1921. In terms of tractive ability the two-cylinder express passenger 4—6—0s of the 'Saint' class could, until that time, have equalled anything achieved by the four-cylinder 'Stars'; but the development of the four-cylinder engine, from 1906 onwards, was yet another example of Churchward's breadth of vision, and it does not need much consideration to appreciate how difficult it would have been to enlarge the 'Saint' to the tractive capacity ultimately represented by the 'Kings' of 1927.

Two basic features of future Great Western practice had nevertheless been established before consideration was given to a four-cylinder engine. The beginnings of the great development in boilers have already been mentioned; the second basic feature was the evolution of the long-lap, long-travel piston valve. Both these features, in their earliest form, were incorporated in the first express passenger 4—6—0, No. 100, completed at Swindon in February 1902. In his own mind Churchward had established a yardstick of express locomotive performance that was to be a guide to Swindon design for many years, namely the ability to sustain a drawbar pull of 2 tons at 70 m.p.h. on level track. At the time this was considerably in advance

William Dean: Locomotive, Carriage and Wagon Superintendent from 1877 to 1902

G. J. Churchward: succeeded Dean in 1902. His title was changed to that of Chief Mechanical Engineer, in 1916

The first evidence of the Churchward boiler development. The 'Badminton' class of 1897, with raised Belpaire firebox

of anything demanded elsewhere in Great Britain, and in addition to developing a range of boilers that would steam freely Churchward set out to obtain greater efficiencies in the cylinders, and so to obtain greater power from a given volume of steam passing through.

A prolonged study of the characteristics of valves, supported by experimental work on a single-cylinder stationary engine, had taught Churchward that the admission of steam to a cylinder without excessive loss of pressure, and its subsequent release without excessive back-pressure on the piston, could only be attained by the use of large piston valves. These valves must have a lap and travel about 50 per cent larger than was customary in British locomotives. Furthermore, to give a high expansion ratio, the clearance volume at the end of the cylinder when the piston was at the end of its stroke must be as small as possible, and to reduce to a minimum the condensation of steam as it entered a comparatively cold cylinder the surfaces of the piston and of the ends of the cylinder must be flat, and the steam ports must be short and straight.

Engine No. 100 was no more than a first prototype, and it went into traffic at the time when Dean's days at Swindon were ending. He retired in June 1902, and Churchward, succeeding him at the relatively early age of 45, could expect to continue in office for 20 years at least. At that time the passenger traffic of the GWR did not immediately need much larger and more powerful locomotives.

A further development: 'Waterford' of the Badminton class, with domeless boiler, built at Swindon 1899

The flowing curves of the Dean era vanish in the 'Atbara' class of 1900. Engine No. 3373 'Atbara', built at Swindon, temporarily renamed 'Britannia' for a Royal Train working

There was no motive power crisis facing Churchward in 1902, such as faced George Whale on the London & North Western Railway, when he succeeded Webb in 1903. The Dean 7 ft. 8 in. 4—2—2s and the 'Atbaras' were entirely adequate for the job, and indeed while his 'big engine' policy was gradually evolved Churchward built more inside-cylinder 4—4—0s, in 1903. These engines, the 'City' class, significantly equipped with tapered boiler barrels, did such brilliant work in the years 1903 and 1904 that not a few experienced observers questioned the need for the large ten-wheeled express passenger engines that were emerging from Swindon in ones and twos in those years.

Nine months after Churchward became Chief his second 4—6—0 appeared—No. 98, later 2998 *Ernest Cunard*. In the year which had elapsed since the completion of No. 100, all the main features of the future Great Western outside-cylinder locomotive had been worked out. The boiler and the firebox had acquired tapers, and the cylinder layout and valve gear had reached the form which they were to retain until the construction of GWR locomotives ceased. There were refinements still to come—extended smokeboxes, superheating, top-feed, improved piston valves, and other details—but here was a locomotive which, with no change in its basic layout and proportions, was still to be engaged on express work fifty years later.

It has often been said that the principles under-lying the design of Churchward's locomotives were not revealed to his contemporaries. But for those who could combine a period of observation at Paddington with a study of such dimensions as were published in the technical press, and with the contributions made by Churchward to the discussions of the Institutions of Mechanical and Civil Engineers, there was little mystery. Furthermore, in the privacy of meetings of the Association of Railway Locomotive Engineers there emerged more detailed information than ever appeared in print. The reluctance of his contemporaries to adopt Churchward's ideas was not due to ignorance of the motives behind them, but to lack of conviction that there was justification for the complication and expense of the distinctive Churchward features.

It is interesting to follow the lines of Churchward's arguments as recorded by his own contributions to the proceedings of the engineering institutions. On 2 February 1906, Churchward read his only paper to one of these bodies—'Large Locomotive Boilers'—presented to the Institution of Mechanical Engineers. The opening words of this paper summarise the aims of his sequence of boiler experiments.

'The modern locomotive problem is principally a question of boiler. . . The higher temperatures incidental to the higher pressures have required . . . much more liberal water spaces and better provision for circulation.'

The pioneer GWR passenger 4—6—0 No. 100 as originally built 1902. Later named 'William Dean' and numbered 2900

He considered that the troubles which many engineers were having with large boilers were caused mainly by poor circulation between the inner and outer fireboxes, particularly adjacent to the rear tubeplate. As the 'main mass of the fire is nearer the tubeplate', it is here that the greatest circulation of water is required to absorb the heat. In many large boilers the water space for circulation round the inner firebox had not increased in proportion to the greater quantity of heat produced in the firebox, and this led to local overheating, damaged plates, and leaking stays and tubes. Insufficient water circulated around the front of the firebox for the water spaces at the sides of the firebox to be kept fully supplied, with consequent damage to the rear of the firebox.

Churchward discussed various methods for improving the circulation between the firebox itself and its outer casing, such as circulating pipes outside the boiler to bring the water to each side of the firebox, and the introduction of the feed water into the spaces between the inner and outer fireboxes. His own solution was to increase the space between the fireboxes where the need was greatest, that is,

at the front. At this section of the boiler he left a clear space between the tubes and the sides of the barrel equal to the combined area of the vertical spaces between the tubes, so ensuring that as water rose between the tubes and between the fireboxes an adequate down-flow was maintained to feed the water space in front of the throat plate. The effect of these proportions was to produce the tapered barrel and tapered firebox. Between the inner and outer fireboxes the water space increased in width from bottom to top, to allow for the greater volume of the water as bubbles of steam formed.

He had found that less trouble was experienced with the flat-topped firebox than with the round-topped. In a flat-topped firebox the surface area of the water is greater than in a round-topped, and there is thus more surface for the release of bubbles of steam. This had been found to reduce foaming, and had enabled him to take steam from the front of the firebox casing. He could then dispense with the dome—'always a source of weakness'. He had tried two identical boilers, one domed and the other domeless, and had found the domeless boiler 'decidedly freer from priming'. The 'liberal dimen-

The second express 4—6—0, No. 98, built 1903 in which all the standard features of the two-cylinder stud were incorporated

sion' of 2 ft. between the top of the firebox and the casing no doubt contributed to this.

Churchward's reasons for using high pressures were then given: 'Higher pressures have produced more efficient locomotives, both in respect of hauling power and coal consumption. The improvement was marked with every increment right up to 227 lb. per sq. in. By employing 225 lb. per sq. in. in the simple engine, and making the necessary improvements in the steam distribution, enabling higher [i.e. earlier] cut-offs to be used, corresponding improvements in efficiency and economy of fuel have been obtained. A great increase in drawbar pull has also resulted. Of course, a price for these improvements has to be paid in firebox repairs, but it is probably better to submit to this expense than to employ the very much heavier and more costly machines which would be necessary to give the same hauling power at high speeds' [that is, with lower pressures].

A sideline on the Churchward locomotives appeared in James Stirling's contribution to the discussion. He said: 'Many of the very interesting diagrams the author has shown are novel in shape and expensive in construction; they may be good, but they are certainly not "bonnie", to use a Scottish expression.'

In his reply, Churchward expressed his views on locomotive aesthetics: 'I feel really hurt that Mr. Stirling should have said that I have so disgracefully spoiled the appearance of the British locomotive. I know that I have been accused of spoiling the appearance of the British locomotive as much as any man in the country, but I take exception to the statement. In my opinion there is no canon of art in regard to the appearance of the locomotive as a machine except that which an engineer has set up for himself, by observing from time to time types of locomotive which he has been led from his nursery days upwards to admire.'

Which of the broad-gauge locomotives that Churchward must have seen in his native Devon had inspired the gaunt lines of No. 100 is not clear, but it is interesting to note that just a year after the reading of this paper 'Star' No. 4001 appeared with curved footplating at the front and rear. This simple change, the details of which were worked out by H. Holcroft, made a striking improvement in the appearance of Churchward's 4—6—0 locomotives, and was a standard feature of all subsequent Swindon 4—6—0s.

At a very early stage in his career it became evident that much of Churchward's genius lay in the ability to appreciate existing work, and to apply

The French-built four-cylinder compound 4—4—2 No. 102 'La France', introduced 1903; at Bristol, at the time when she was painted black

The Second French compound No. 103, after receiving the name 'President'; purchased 1905

it by adaptation and development to the needs of the GWR. He was not the isolationist inventor, working in the back room as it were with no heed of what was going on in the world at large; neither was he in the slightest degree a copyist. His development of the tapered boiler originated from his interest in American practice; but the final Swindon design, exemplified in the Standard No. 1 Boiler, and the progenitor of more than 2,000 boilers on the GWR, the LMS and the nationalised British Railways, was entirely his own. And from American ideas in the form of the so-called wagon-top boilers, bar frames and other detail features, he turned to France, where the four-cylinder compound 'Atlantics' of Alfred de Glehn's design were compelling the attention of all locomotive engineers, by their magnificent performances on the boat expresses running between Paris, Boulogne and Calais, and on other fast services of the Northern Railway.

Churchward's interest in these locomotives went to the extent of his obtaining permission to order one for trial in England. The French loading gauge was sufficiently near to that of the GWR for it to be possible to order a de Glehn compound 4—4—2 which was almost a replica of the Nord "2641" class. A few fittings were modified to suit Great Western requirements, notably the chimney, smokebox door, and brake equipment, and the rear end was made suitable for attaching to a standard tender. The locomotive was built by the Société Alsacienne des Constructions Mechaniques at Belfort in France, and was received by the GWR in October 1903. It was numbered 102 and named *La France*.

The design followed the normal lines of a de Glehn compound. The high-pressure cylinders were outside, and drove the trailing coupled wheels, and the low-pressure cylinders drove the leading coupled wheels. The locomotive could be worked as a simple by allowing the exhaust from the high-pressure cylinders to pass to atmosphere, and by admitting boiler steam to the low-pressure cylinders through a reducing valve. There were separate sets of Walscheart's valve gear for the inside and outside cylinders, with provision for varying the cut-off in the two sets of cylinders independently or together. The firebox was 10 in. longer than that of the GWR 4—6—0s, giving a grate area of 29.5 sq. ft. instead of 27.1 sq. ft. The firebox heating surface was greater, and the use of Serve tubes made the tube heating surface greater despite a shorter barrel. The boiler pressure was 227 lb. per sq. in.

The fame of the de Glehn compounds came from their high power output at speed, and from their economy. In buying this locomotive Churchward intended to find by direct comparison whether or not the benefits of compounding could equal the improvements which he had made in the simple engine. His views on the experiment were expressed publicly in the discussion on a paper entitled 'Compound Locomotives' read on 18 March 1904 to the Institution of Mechanical Engineers by M. Edouard Sauvage, Chief Consulting Engineer to the Western Railway of France. The paper reviewed the development of the modern compound locomotive in France, and in his conclusions the author said that: '. . . by their use the French railways have been enabled to increase largely the weight and speed of their trains . . . without any large increase of coal consumption. . . . A complete solution of the problem would require proof that the same results might not be obtained in some other

17

way. Available data are not sufficient to give such a proof in an indisputable manner; still, it seems difficult to build an ordinary locomotive quite equal in every respect to the latest compounds.' It might have the same boiler, but 'with the ordinary valve gear of the locomotive, steam at such a high pressure cannot be as well utilised (in a simple locomotive) as by compounding'. The simple locomotive would require more steam for the same work.

These remarks gave Churchward the opportunity to outline the work which he had done to improve the performance of his locomotives, and at the same time to pay a tribute to his staff. After saying that the compound had been brought to a point of greater perfection in France than in any country—which explained his purchase of *La France*—he said that in his judgment 'no really fair and square tests between the advantages of compound and simple have ever been made'.

Some of the earliest trials had been between compounds working at 200 lb. per sq. in. and simple locomotives working at 175 lb. per sq. in. He then came to the crux of the matter: 'I shall no doubt be told that high pressures were used in the compound in the belief that it was impossible by any known valve gear to use the same pressures to advantage in a simple cylinder. I thought that that had yet to be proved, and I have had the courage to fit a simple engine with 18 in. by 30 in. cylinders, and with a boiler carrying 225 lb. per sq. in. I have done that with the deliberate idea of finding whether such improvements can be made in the valve gear, and consequent steam distribution, as to enable the simple cylinder to use steam of that pressure as efficiently as the compound engine.'

He had made the powers at high speed nearly equal. In the compound he used the recommended cut-offs of 55 per cent and 65 per cent in the h.p. and l.p. cylinders, and in the simple he used 20-25 per cent cut-off. He continued: 'It would seem no doubt ambitious to expect such power as was developed at 55 per cent and 65 per cent by the compound out of a cylinder cutting off at 20-25 per cent, but I am pleased to say that with the assistance of an efficient staff, a good deal of very hard work, and a determination to see what could be done with the valve gear, I believe such improvements have been made in the steam distribution that a satisfactory result can be ensured from as high a cut-off as 15-20 per cent.'

He had obtained a 2-ton drawbar pull at 70 m.p.h. both from *La France* and from his simple locomotive with 200 lb. per sq. in. working at 25 per cent cut-off. From the 225 lb. per sq. in. locomotive he expected to get 2 tons at 75 m.p.h.

on a shorter cut-off. Theoretically the steam consumption of the compound working at 55 per cent and 65 per cent was the same as that of the simple working at 25 per cent, so that he had the means for a more equal trial than ever before. He then said that although *La France* had not yet worked sufficient mileage to give reliable figures of coal consumption, it was doing 'very first class work indeed on the GWR', and had entirely fulfilled his expectations'.

Further remarks of Churchward's, later in the discussion, gave the first hint of his thoughts on four-cylinder locomotives. The author had stressed that the division of the drive between two axles on the de Glehn compounds reduced the loads on the coupling rods and axleboxes. Of this Churchward said: 'I am not sure that at present we have arrived at the point at which we must divide the engine, but we shall soon do so if the engine grows much bigger.' He further remarked that it had been suggested that a divided engine with four cylinders gave a more even torque, but he could not see this.

It is thus clear that in March 1903 Churchward was satisfied that his two-cylinder 4—6—0 was the equal of the French compound in power output at speed, and that as yet he saw no advantage to be derived from a four-cylinder locomotive. Tests soon showed that the fuel consumption of the compound was only slightly better than that of the GWR locomotives and there seemed to be no reason to expect that a departure from the two-cylinder locomotive would be deemed necessary in the foreseeable future—either for the possible fuel economy of a compound or for the mechanical advantages inherent in any four-cylinder locomotive with divided drive.

Churchward's remarks show that he believed that he had made a fair and square comparison of compound and simple working. The equality of his own locomotives with the compound came from the improvements which he had made in the valve gear and steam distribution compared with what he termed the 'old-fashioned simple engine'. It seems surprising that he did not incorporate these same improvements in a compound, to give an even fairer comparison with the simple. That he did not do so was not because he had finally rejected the compound from his plans, for two years later he ordered two more French compounds of another type. It can only be assumed that, as his own cylinder improvements were aimed at producing high power at short cut-offs, he did not expect them to produce a marked difference in a compound, which necessarily works at longer cut-offs than a simple engine giving the same power output.

For the tests against *La France*, Churchward had built a further 4—6—0, No. 171, later 2971 *Albion*. This differed from No. 98 in having the boiler pressure raised from 200 to 225 lb. per sq. in. This achieved the double effect of making the pressure almost equal to that of *La France,* and of making the nominal tractive effort of the two locomotives almost equal—23,710 lb. for *La France* and 23,090 for *Albion*. After the Frenchman had run for a year, the comparison was made even closer by the conversion of No. 171 to a 4—4—2. In retrospect this conversion seems surprising for, despite the easy gradients on many parts of the GWR, there were a number of stretches where the loss of adhesive weight would seriously prejudice the performance of the 'Atlantic'. Even more surprising was the construction of fourteen more 'Atlantics', thirteen with two cylinders and one with four. The two-cylinder engines appeared in 1905, and in the same year six more two-cylinder 4—6—0s were built. In later years these were all assimilated into the 'Saint' class, and it will be convenient to refer to them by that name.

In 1905 there also appeared the additional French compounds, Nos. 103 and 104. These locomotives were similar to the Paris-Orleans 3001 class, modified to suit the GWR loading gauge. They were larger than No. 102 in most of their leading dimensions, the most notable figure being the grate area of 33.4 sq. ft.

The trials of the new Frenchmen showed that there was again little difference in the fuel consumption from the Churchward locomotives; indeed, the larger Frenchmen were slightly inferior. The duplication of cylinders made their oil consumption greater. Against this it was expected that the division of drive between two axles, which reduced the loading on the axleboxes due to piston thrust, would enable the locomotives to run greater mileages between general repairs. The improved balance of the four-cylinder layout also made the riding better than that of the two-cylinder engines. The advantages of the Frenchmen were therefore mechanical rather than thermal, and Churchward finally abandoned any idea of compounding. The mechanical advantages, however, were not yet fully investigated.

But the French influence at Swindon was nevertheless profound. The compound 'Atlantics' ran with exceptional smoothness, and as mileage increased they were not subject to the roughness that develops almost inevitably in a locomotive with two outside cylinders. One can think of many other famous designs outside the GWR that were rough and uncomfortable to ride upon, such as 'King Arthurs' of the Southern, Stanier 'Black-Fives' and the whole range of British standard locomotives. The two-cylinder engine is ideal for general-purpose work; but in long-distance express passenger traffic, such as was being actively developed on the GWR in the early 1900s, the desire for a smooth-riding engine was more than a mere question of comfort on the footplate. To lessen vibration and knocking enginemen will work with longer cut-offs and partly-opened regulator; and this, in limiting the range of expansion of the steam would defeat the very object on which Churchward had so fixedly set his sights, in his adoption of high boiler pressure, and long-lap, long-travel valves.

Thus, by Frenchman out of *Albion* was born the first Great Western four-cylinder *simple* express passenger locomotive, the famous prototype, No. 40, *North Star,* built originally as an 'Atlantic' in 1906.

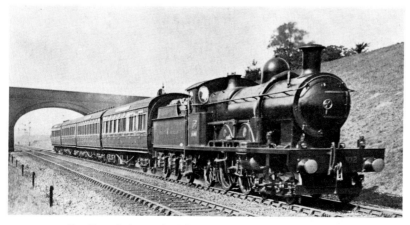

'La France', in standard GWR colours, working an up 2-hour Birmingham express near Denham

The third French compound, No. 104, as newly delivered, before the name 'Alliance' was added

By Frenchman out of Albion

'Albion' in later days, numbered 2971, and descending Dainton bank, near Newton Abbot, with the Penzance – Aberdeen express. The third and fourth coaches in the train are ex-North British Railway stock

CHAPTER 2

THE 'NORTH STAR'

CONSTRUCTION of the new and epoch-marking four-cylinder simple express locomotive was authorised by the Locomotive and Stores Committee of the Board on 19 July 1905, at an estimated cost of £3,600. This compared with £3,200 for the two-cylinder 'Atlantics' and £4,300 for the larger Frenchmen. The comparison of 4—4—2 and 4—6—0 locomotives had not yet convinced Churchward of the superiority of the 4—6—0, and as the inspiration of the four-cylinder design was the French 'Atlantic', the new design was therefore given this wheel arrangement. As on all the Churchward 4—4—2s, the trailing wheels were located in additional plate frames attached outside the main frames. The main frames had holes cut in them to reduce weight just where the trailing axle would fit if the engine were converted to a 4—6—0, but the holes were of such a size as to make it impracticable to use the same rear end of the frames in the conversion.

In less than two years from his statement that the time had not yet arrived at which 'we must divide the engine', Churchward had thus produced his first engine with divided drive, and in doing so

had evolved the prototype of 269 famous machines. It is clear that the move into four-cylinder engines was influenced not by any dissatisfaction with the existing two-cylinder engines, but by the new evidence produced by the experiences with the Frenchmen. This was the first sign of a decline in the American influence on Churchward, and of the rise of a French influence which was to affect a number of details of design in the coming years.

The design of No. 40, later named *North Star*, showed a marked regression from some of the extreme American influences apparent in Churchward's two-cylinder machines. The boiler was generally similar, and retained the working pressure of 225 lb. per sq. in. which had been introduced for comparison with the Frenchmen. The main difference in the boiler, and one which was quite noticeable, was that the taper of the barrel extended over its full length, whereas in the previous types of boiler on the ten-wheeled engines the taper extended along half the length only. The chassis showed marked differences from the two-cylinder types. Churchward considered that, for the full benefit to be derived from the improved balance

The 'North Star' as originally built, 1906, before receiving the name.   Note the small holes below the valve rocker for access to the inside motion

The 'fountain head': the locomotive drawing office at Swindon in GWR days

of the divided drive, the inside and outside connecting rods must be of equal length. This could only be achieved by setting the outside cylinders as far back as possible, and the inside cylinders as far forward as possible. The outside cylinders were thus opposite the rear bogie wheels, a position which limited the size of cylinder which could be attained in later developments of the type. The inside cylinders projected beyond the smokebox, so that the inside slidebars and much of the valve gear were enclosed between the smokebox and the bogie, and were thus relatively inaccessible.

The wheelbase of the locomotive was 8 in. greater than that of the 'Saints'. Of the increase 6 in. was in the distance from the rear coupled axle to the trailing wheels, and the remaining 2 in. between the rear bogie axle and the leading coupled axle. The bogie was of the then-standard swing-link type, with the same wheelbase as those of the 'Saints'.

The arrangement of cylinders made the use of plate frames almost inevitable. The American type of cylinder and bar frame construction could not be adapted to a layout in which there were two pairs of cylinders out of line with one another. The alternate thrust on the front and back covers of an outside cylinder tends to 'rock' the cylinder on the frames, and if bending of the frames is to be avoided, there must be massive bracing of the frame opposite the cylinders. In the Churchward two-cylinder locomotives, the combined smokebox

saddle and cylinders form a rigid box well able to resist the thrust in the cylinders. The inside cylinders of the four-cylinder locomotives also formed a rigid box, as do any inside cylinders, but the outside cylinders presented a difficult problem. They were attached at a point where the frames were weakened by the cut-out required to allow translation of the rear bogie wheels. It was thus necessary to stiffen the frames by a massive bracket which impeded access to the inside cylinders from above, and made the use of a pit for working on the inside motion almost a necessity. The frames were stepped in, or 'joggled' opposite the inside cylinders to leave clearance for the translation of the front bogie wheels.

The position of the outside cylinders made it impossible to use the same type of slidebar as on the two-cylinder 4—4—2s. These latter had the motion bracket ahead of the coupled wheels, and the slidebars were supported at about the middle of their length. On the four-cylinder machine the only convenient place for the motion bracket was between the coupled wheels. The slidebars had therefore to be extended beyond their normal length to reach the motion bracket, and at their outer ends they had to be tapered outwards to give clearance for the connecting rod. This produced the very distinctive slidebars which were a conspicuous feature of all the Great Western four-cylinder locomotives.

22

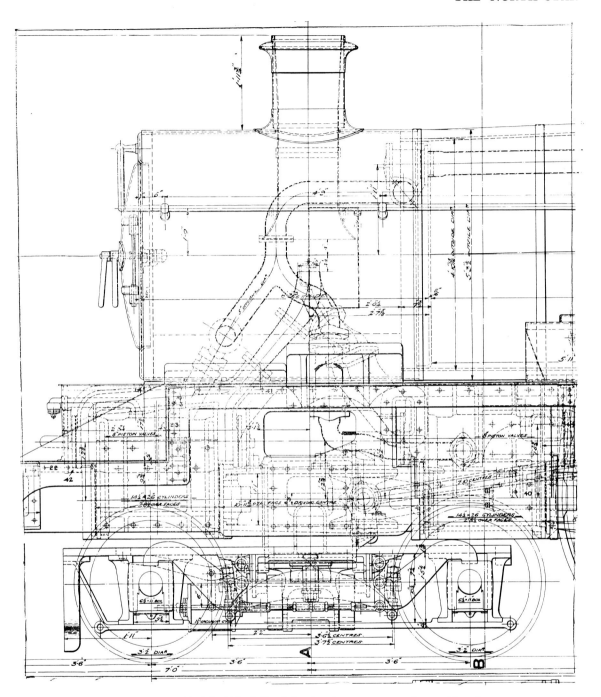

The 'Front end' of the 'North Star' showing the arrangement of steam pipes, the two-framed bogie, and the bogie brake linkage

The use of inside cranks, combined with the generous size of axlebox and crankpin which Churchward employed, left insufficient room for inside Stephenson valve gear. Churchward was impressed by the Walschaert's gear of the Frenchmen, but he thought it very light, and described it as a 'watchmaker's job'. In his two-cylinder engines he had used a massive valve gear with generous bearing surfaces. This gear would not deflect under the heaviest loads, and would suffer little wear between general repairs; it ensured that the valve setting was maintained with little deterioration, in sharp contrast to the behaviour of the locomotives of some other railways. As Churchward proposed to use two valve gears for four valves, the valve gear of the four-cylinder engine must therefore be at least as massive as that of the two-cylinder machines and he considered that there was insufficient room within the loading gauge for an outside gear with links of the requisite size.

Yet another objection to an outside valve gear was that Churchward's outside connecting rods had solid-bush big ends, so that an outside valve gear would have had to be partly dismantled to allow the removal of a connecting rod (this in fact has to be done on thousands of locomotives on other railways). It was thought that, provided that the valve gear could be made as durable as that of the two-cylinder engines, the big end would need to be taken down more frequently than the valve gear.

With an outside gear behind the cylinder and a rocking lever ahead of it, some part of the valve gear would have had to be disconnected before an outside valve could have been removed. On top of all these technical objections was Churchward's aesthetic objection to any unnecessary outside fittings. Whatever the critics might dislike in his early locomotives, they must have agreed that only the bare essentials of the mechanism were visible.

A study of the characteristics of Stephenson and Walschaert's gears, designed with the same steam lap, port size, and valve travel, showed that at short cut-offs, although the maximum opening of the valve to steam was the same for both gears, the tendency of the valve with Walschaert's gear to 'dwell' at the end of its movement caused it to admit more steam to the cylinder whilst it was open. As it was expected that the four-cylinder engine would be capable of doing much of its work at 15 per cent cut-off, which gave the maximum possible expansion ratio in the cylinder, the Walschaert's gear offered an advantage.

W. H. Pearce, the draughtsman who had designed the Churchward Stephenson gear, began to sketch a Walschaert's gear for the four-cylinder engine, and hit on the idea of simplifying this gear further by eliminating eccentrics altogether. He proposed to use the crosshead of one inside cylinder to provide the equivalent of the eccentric of the other inside cylinder. In the Walschaert's gear the

The wooden model of the proposed 'scissors' valve gear made by
W. H. Pearce, in June 1905

24

final drive to the valve is compounded of two motions, one taken from the crosshead of the cylinder concerned, and the other from an eccentric or return crank at 90 deg. to the crank of the cylinder. This second component can alternatively be taken from the crosshead of the other cylinder, since the cranks of the two cylinders are at 90 deg. There is some geometrical complication in fitting two gears of this type between the two sets of slide-bars, but the arrangement eliminates eccentrics, and leaves the crank axle unencumbered. This gave two advantages: it reduced the unsprung weight on the crank axle, and it also removed a weakness of all gears in which a drive is taken from an eccentric or return crank—that in any position of the axle in which the eccentric rod is inclined to the horizontal, movement of the axle on its springs causes a small displacement of the valve.

Pearce made a wooden model of this gear in June 1905, and submitted it to Churchward, who ordered the gear to be fitted to the engine. The wooden model is still in existence. This same idea had previously occurred to a number of other engineers, both locomotive and marine, but Pearce was quite unaware of this when the idea came to him. R. M. Deeley is said to have designed a gear of this type when he was an assistant to S. W. Johnson on the Midland Railway at Derby. He showed the scheme to Johnson, who would have nothing to do with it; but when Deeley himself succeeded Johnson he revived the idea for his large 4—4—0 No. 990. On 11 August 1905 he applied for a patent for the gear, which was granted in June 1906. In the meantime No. 40 had appeared from Swindon fitted with Pearce's gear, which from the shape of the expansion link levers earned the name of 'scissors' gear.

It was said at Swindon that a strong letter arrived from Deeley accusing Churchward of using the Deeley gear without acknowledgement. There was no difficulty in establishing that the Swindon gear was designed before Deeley applied for his patent, and that Churchward had every right to use it. In its characteristics, the scissors gear was similar to Walschaert's, that is, the lead was constant at all positions of cut-off. The Stephenson gear, as used in the two-cylinder locomotives, has the characteristic that the lead decreases as cut-off is increased, and it therefore makes an engine better at starting, and on hill climbing at low speed.

The gear fitted to No. 40 had a disadvantage. If a defect developed in one cylinder, motion, or valve gear of a two-cylinder locomotive, involving dismantling of the connecting rod, the locomotive had a good prospect of moving itself off the running

lines, or even of reaching a shed, on the surviving cylinder. With the cross-connected gear, the disconnection of one connecting rod automatically immobilised the valve gear of the other cylinder, and the locomotive could not move itself. For this reason the scissors gear was not used on subsequent four-cylinder engines, but it remained in No. 40 until 1929, when the engine was rebuilt as a 'Castle'. The valve gear of the subsequent Great Western four-cylinder locomotives incorporated a detail which made it easy to fasten one pair of valves in their mid-position in an emergency, so this requirement was evidently important to Churchward.

The rocking shaft for operating the outside valves was slightly cranked to allow for the angularity of the connecting rods. This design detail, which was due to Pearce, may be explained by mentioning that the inclination of the connecting rod causes the motion of the piston of a locomotive to be non-symmetrical, the piston being nearer to the rear of the cylinder at any instant (except at the dead-centres) than the position of the crank would suggest. The shorter the connecting rod in proportion to the throw of the crank, the greater is the inclination of the connecting rod. If the point of cut-off is to be the same at both ends of the cylinder, the movement of the valve must also be non-symmetrical to match the motion of the piston. In all well-designed valve gears there is a geometrical device for giving the valve the correct non-symmetrical motion. If, in a four-cylinder locomotive, the valve of one cylinder is driven by a rocker from the valve of another cylinder, the rocker has the correct motion for the valve from which it is driven, and this gives a 'correction' in the wrong direction to the valve which is driven by the rocker. The cranking of the rocker on the Great Western four-cylinder locomotives was cleverly arranged to cancel the correction given to the inside valves, and to apply the proper correction to the outside valves. Its success is proved by the clear, short beats which give no indication that two cylinders are exhausting simultaneously.

The gear contained another of Pearce's novel ideas. It was usual in Walschaert's gear of that time for the radius rod to be supported from the reversing crank by a vertical swinging link attached ahead of the expansion link. There was usually only a limited space above the valve gear for this swinging link, which had perforce to be short. The point of attachment to the radius rod therefore swung in a small arc, and there was significant rise and fall of the radius rod as it moved from one end of its travel to the other. This caused unnecessary slip of

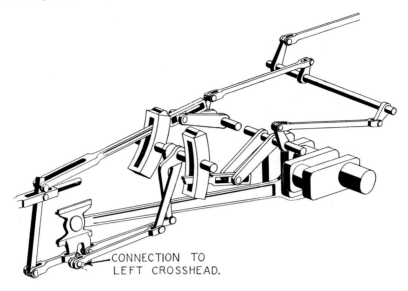

Pictorial drawing of the 'scissors' gear as applied to the 'North Star'

the die block in the expansion link, and consequent wear. With the long travel of the radius rod on the Great Western locomotives this slip would have been serious, and it was therefore reduced greatly by positioning the reversing crank behind the expansion link, and in line with the pivot of the link. The movement of the radius rod relative to the crank was accommodated by a die block working in a slot in the reversing crank. This die block introduced additional wearing surfaces, but slight wear at these surfaces does not affect the movement of the valve, whereas wear at the expansion link die block does. This method of supporting the radius rod was adopted by Gresley on his 2—6—0s, and later became a common arrangement.

One striking feature of the Churchward two-cylinder types was the use of 30 in. piston stroke. In a letter to Mr. A. V. Goodyear, dated 25 October 1909, Churchward wrote: 'It is correct that there are great advantages in the 30 in. stroke in the matter of expansive working. The long stroke in relation to the bore is the only way we know of making the simple engine equal in efficiency to the compound engine. You are correct in assuming that the adoption of the 4-cylinder design was not on account of any dissatisfaction with the 18 in. by 30 in. cylinders—the relation of stroke to bore is even greater in the 4-cylinder than in the 2-cylinder engines.'

The actual cylinder diameter was $14\frac{1}{4}$ in., an odd figure, but one which made the cylinder dimensions very close to those of the high-pressure cylinders of the larger Frenchmen ($14\frac{3}{16}$ in. by $25\frac{3}{16}$ in.). Whether this diameter was influenced by the French figure, or whether it was reckoned to be the largest which would safely be used with the boiler, is not recorded. Certainly there is no evidence that it made the nominal tractive effort identical with any other engine. The reduction of the stroke to 26 in. made a useful contribution towards improving the balance of the four-cylinder locomotive, compared with the two-cylinder, by reducing the inertia forces of the reciprocating parts. Even in the four-cylinder design these forces produced couples tending to sway the engine, and as the whole justification for the complication of the four-cylinder arrangement was better balance, this further contribution was welcome.

The four-cylinder layout involved some other changes in detail from the two-cylinder machines, but these were kept to a minimum. In accordance with prevailing Swindon practice, bogie brakes were fitted. There were compensating beams between the springs of the coupled wheels. There was further evidence of French influence in the use of a forked big-end for the inside connecting rod. The arrangement of the exhaust pipes from the cylinders to the blast pipe was a problem on all the GWR four-cylinder types because of the considerable distances from the cylinders to the blast pipe. In No. 40 the four branch exhaust pipes were formed from copper plate, beaten to shape and brazed.

The coupling rods were of I-section, which allowed them to be of lighter weight than rectangular section rods designed to withstand the same maximum thrust. Unfortunately, No. 40 several times bent its coupling rods, and this trouble was cured by replacing the I-section rods by rectangular

'North Star' as an 'Atlantic' and as yet unnamed passing Old Oak Common with the down Cornish Riviera Express

ones. The explanation of this apparent anomaly is that rectangular rods designed to withstand the same thrust as I-section ones are less stiff laterally, that is, against bending in a horizontal plane. They can withstand a greater lateral deflection than the I-section rods before the metal reaches its 'elastic limit'. A similar trouble was encountered with the British Railways 'Britannia' Pacifics, and an investigation showed that the cranks of the two wheels on certain axles were not set at exactly 90 deg. As a result, at each revolution of the wheels, the coupling rods tried to lengthen and shorten, and were thus subjected to an alternating stress. The combination of this stress with the normal effect of the piston thrust caused the rods to bend laterally. With the I-section rods this led to overstressing and ultimate failure, but when rectangular section rods were fitted the trouble was cured, as they could withstand the lateral deflection without distress.

Apart from two later experiments on small batches of engines with alloy steel rods, rectangular section coupling rods were used on all subsequent GWR ten-wheeled engines. It should be noted, however, that other railways used I-section rods without difficulty, and it is likely that with the high standards of accuracy which were later attained at Swindon they could have been used there also.

The general outline of the locomotive was in

The rear end of 'North Star,' showing back sanding gear and original brake gear

A later view of 'North Star' showing large diameter chimney, as later standardised

'North Star' as first rebuilt as a 4—6—0 in 1909 with half-cone superheated boiler, and de Glehn type bogie

accordance with the first phase of the Churchward 4—4—2s and 4—6—0s, that is, the footplating continued in an unbroken line under the cab, and there was a vertical rise in the footplating ahead of the cylinders. The external lines of the boiler were free from the various fittings which crept in over the next ten years. As already mentioned, the boiler had a taper extending over the full length of the barrel, but for the first time the length of the smokebox reached a figure of 6 ft. This increase in smokebox length was necessary to bring the smokebox over part of the inside cylinders, so that the steam and exhaust pipes could be connected directly from the cylinder casting to the smokebox. The same length of smokebox was subsequently adopted as standard for the No. 1 Standard Boiler, and was thus used on the two-cylinder 4—6—0s also. The chimney was of smaller diameter than that which later became standard.

No. 40 was completed in April 1906, and in September of the same year was named *North Star*. This revived a famous broad-gauge name, and gave the name 'Stars' to a class that was eventually to include not only the celestial bodies, but also male and female royalty, the nobility, and finally some monastic buildings. The appearance of No. 40 aroused great interest amongst Great Western enthusiasts, and many of them must have made journeys behind the engine to record its performance. It is therefore surprising and disappointing to find no record in the contemporary press of any notable running by it. The loading of most of the main-line trains was still moderate, 300-ton trains being uncommon; and Churchward does not seem to have conducted any tests with heavy loads despite the fact that the four-cylinder design was contemplated only for the heaviest express work. The engine was not tested on the Swindon testing plant, because the capacity of the plant was then insufficient to produce any useful information about a locomotive of this size.

The only run by No. 40 recorded by C. Rous-Marten was on the down 'Cornish Riviera Express' with a tare load of 290 tons to Westbury, 255 tons to Taunton, 220 tons to Exeter, and 185 tons to Plymouth. The train made a net time of 92 minutes

No. 40 with the later standard full-cone boiler and top feed, at Laira shed

'North Star' in wartime austerity livery, numbered 4000

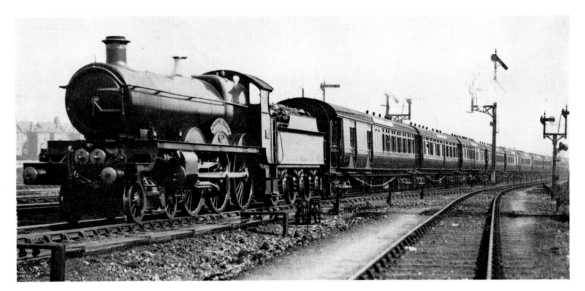

Another stage in the history of 'No. 40'; long cone boiler; small diameter chimney; no top feed. Shown passing Old Oak Common with the down Cornish Riviera Express in 1911

to Westbury, 142 minutes to Taunton, and 170 minutes to Exeter. The 32 miles from Reading to Savernake occupied 32 minutes. The maximum speed was 80 m.p.h. near Patney, and on Wellington bank speed fell to 45 m.p.h. before Whiteball and to 43 m.p.h. in the tunnel. The minimum on Dainton bank was 24 m.p.h. and on the climb to Rattery 25 m.p.h. Rous-Marten commented that this run was 'on the whole creditable, but there were indications that with heavier load, and less favourable weather, greater adhesion would be needed'. The performance was well within the capacity of a 'Saint'.

The later history of *North Star* can be summarised briefly here. In November 1909 it was rebuilt as a 4—6—0, with the wheelbase shortened by 6 in. to conform with the later 'Stars'. New frames were provided, but the footplate remained 2½ in. higher than on the other 'Stars'. The casing over the inside cylinders was replaced by the more elegant pattern which had been introduced with No. 4021. By this time the exchange of boilers at general repairs had become normal, and *North Star* received one of the half-cone boilers originally fitted to 'Saints'. In June 1911 another long-cone boiler was fitted, and the engine ran in this condition—although not with the same boiler—for eighteen years. In November 1929 it emerged from its second rebuilding as a 'Castle'. This involved lengthening of the frames to take the larger firebox. The scissors gear was replaced by the normal Walschaert's gear of the four-cylinder engines. The footplating remained at its original height, so that *North Star*, which had been unique amongst 'Stars', now became a unique 'Castle'. In the partial renumbering of December 1912, which brought together engines of identical or similar type, *North Star* became No. 4000. It was withdrawn from service in May 1957.

CHAPTER 3

THE CELESTIAL 'STARS'

THE main attraction of the four-cylinder layout was that, by reducing the loads on axleboxes and motion bearings, it would enable the locomotive to run greater mileages between general repairs. It might therefore have been expected that a long period of trial running would have been necessary to produce evidence that the improvement in mileage would justify the additional cost of the four-cylinder express locomotive. The construction of a batch of ten 4—6—0s was authorised by the Locomotive Committee on 8 August 1906 at a cost of £3,700 each. Ten months only elapsed between the completion of *North Star* and the appearance of the first of the 4—6—0s—No. 4001 *Dog Star*. It is thus clear that Churchward had been impressed very quickly with the superior riding of the four-cylinder engine, and by its greater potentiality for future development as compared with the two-cylinder machine.

The most obvious change in the design of No. 4001 was the use of six coupled wheels. The verdict of the locomotive inspectors was that the two-cylinder 4—6—0s were more generally reliable in all weathers than the 'Atlantics', although the 'Atlantics' were freer running. At this distance in time it is a little difficult to appreciate why the *North Star* was ever built as a 4—4—2. Presumably the object was to make a closer comparison between its performance and that of the Frenchmen, and the 2-cylinder 'Atlantics'; but the decision to standardise upon 4—6—0s was evidently taken so soon after the completion of *North Star* as to raise doubts as to whether a comparison of 'Atlantics' of three kinds was the true reason.

The other important change in the design compared with *North Star* was in the valve gear, the scissors gear being replaced by Walschaert's. This was a notable step; Walschaert's gear between the frames has never been common in Britain, and in 1907 a well-laid-out Walschaert's gear was a novelty either inside or out. Like the scissors gear, the new gear was the work of W. H. Pearce. Following the pattern set by the development of the Churchward Stephenson gear, great care was taken in its design to ensure accurate compensation for the angularity of the connecting rods in a gear which gave, for its day, an exceptional valve travel.

The arrangement of the reversing gear linkage was similar to that used in No. 40, in that the reversing rod from the cab was connected to a reversing shaft extending across the locomotive. There was an individual auxiliary reversing shaft for each valve gear, connected by an auxiliary reversing rod and crank to the main reversing shaft. A short link was provided near each auxiliary reversing shaft by which the auxiliary reversing arm could be attached to a bracket on the engine frame if it was necessary to immobilise one cylinder. The auxiliary reversing shaft of the defective side was disconnected, leaving the other valve free to be operated by its own auxiliary reversing rod. This arrangement of the reversing gear made it a simple operation to put one side of the engine out of action in an emergency, but had the arrangement not been necessary in No. 40 for the scissors gear, a simpler arrangement might have been devised for the Walschaert's gear. The valves had a steam lap of $1\frac{5}{8}$ in., a lead of $\frac{1}{8}$ in., and a travel of $6\frac{7}{8}$ in. at the maximum cut-off of $76\frac{1}{2}$ per cent. A small but significant difference from No. 40 was an inspection hole in the framing opposite the inside slidebars. This gave a useful means of access to the slidebars and the front part of the valve gear, and mitigated the inaccessibility of the inside motion.

The exterior of No. 4001 was noticeably different from that of No. 40. The Churchward 'Atlantics' were ungainly engines; the closely-spaced driving wheels, combined with the large space under the

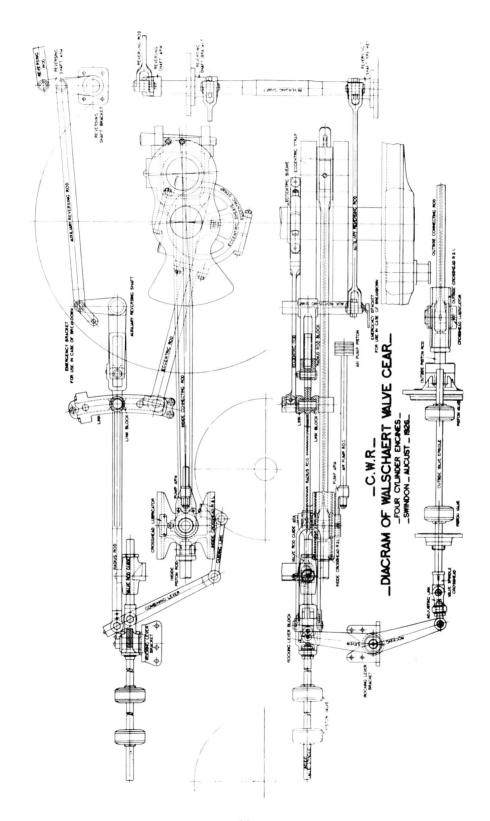

DIAGRAM OF WALSCHAERT VALVE GEAR

_C.W.R._

FOUR CYLINDER ENGINES

_SWINDON _ AUGUST _ 1926_

31

No. 4002 'Evening Star' as originally built in March 1907. The joggle in the main frame can be seen immediately behind the leading bogie wheel

firebox and cab, gave an impression that the boiler and chassis did not match. The additional driving wheels of the 4—6—0 dispelled that impression, and produced a much more pleasing blend of boiler with chassis. The rearward position of the outside cylinders of the four-cylinder engine seemed to make the improvement in the 4—6—0 more pronounced than in the two-cylinder design. The improvement apparent in No. 4001 was completed by the insertion of curved sections between the horizontal sections of the footplating, together with the lowering of the footplating under the cab. In its initial form the Churchward four-cylinder 4—6—0 attained what was, in the opinion of many people, its highest aesthetic level. The chimney was of smaller diameter and more graceful than that which was later adopted as standard, and the boiler was free from the fittings which later characterised it —top-feed, superheater fittings, and ejector.

The first batch of ten engines was built between February and May of 1907. They were numbered 4001-10, and were given the names of stars which had been carried by broad-gauge engines of 1839-41. The names were:

No.	Name
4001	*Dog Star*
4002	*Evening Star*
4003	*Lode Star*
4004	*Morning Star*
4005	*Polar Star*
4006	*Red Star*
4007	*Rising Star*
4008	*Royal Star*
4009	*Shooting Star*
4010	*Western Star*

Nos. 4001 and 4002 had a small but visible difference from the remainder of the class; whereas

No. 4008 'Royal Star' when running with front steps; the hindrance to access to the inside motion is apparent

the slidebars fitted to the later engines were of T-section those on 4001/2 were of I-section, that is, they appeared to have a slot cut in them. These slidebars were considered to be unsatisfactory. At a later date they were re-designed. The new pattern introduced the conspicuous tie-bar connecting the upper and lower bars, which had been seen first on the Frenchmen. It became a standard feature of all subsequent Swindon four-cylinder engines. Another visible difference which characterised 4002/8/9 for a time was the fitting of front steps, ahead of the outside cylinders. The last locomotive of the batch, No. 4101 *Western Star*, had a much more important variation—the fitting of a Cole superheater.

The first experiment with a superheater on the GWR had begun a year before the appearance of No. 4010 with the fitting of a Schmidt superheater to engine No. 2901, *Lady Superior*. The object of a superheater is to raise the temperature of the steam above that at which it has been formed in the boiler, without any further increase in pressure. The steam thus becomes 'dry', and when it enters the cylinder it can withstand appreciable loss of heat to the comparatively cold cylinder walls before condensation occurs. Condensation is accompanied by a great reduction in volume, a loss of pressure, and a consequent reduction in the useful work done by the steam. Churchward studied closely the developments in locomotive design in other countries, and he was attracted by any device which offered the possibility of a saving in fuel. The Schmidt superheater was a proven appliance, and it was natural that this should be tried first.

Subsequent history of superheating at Swindon provides a classic example of the way Churchward took an established principle, and then developed the details to suit his own requirements. There were some features of the Schmidt apparatus that did not appeal to him. Furthermore, the adoption of

it in its entirety was at that time generally governed by conditions involving the use of other patent Schmidt devices, such as the well-known 'wide' piston valve ring. Churchward was the last man to be constrained by any circumstances of that kind, and one can imagine that his development in the first place stemmed from a desire to avoid the Schmidt patents as much as anything else. From the maintenance viewpoint those elements which were attached to the rearmost part of the header could not be removed unless the elements in front of them were removed. The elements themselves were bent at the header end, so that internal cleaning was difficult. Churchward therefore turned to the Cole superheater, an American design, in which the elements were straight. A superheater of this type was fitted to No. 4010 when built in May 1907. It incorporated elements of a special and complicated design, but it was sufficiently successful for the first Swindon superheater to be developed from it.

It is convenient at this point to complete the story of superheating in the 'Stars', although it involves anticipating the account of the later engines of the class. No. 4011 appeared in March 1908 fitted with the Swindon No. 1 superheater, and the same pattern was fitted to *The Great Bear*. The elements of this superheater could be removed more readily than could those of the Schmidt design, but there were still complications in the joints by which they were made steamtight. The second Swindon superheater, No. 2, differed from No. 1 mainly in that the complicated elements were replaced by simple ones. It was fitted only to 'Saint' No. 2922 in October 1908. The third Swindon design appeared in No. 4021 in June 1909. Whilst retaining some of the features of the No. 1 and No. 2 designs, it was a more radical development than the earlier patterns. A notable characteristic was that the elements were of smaller diameter

No. 4006 'Red Star' as originally built with full-cone non-superheated boiler

No. 4010 'Western Star' as originally built, May 1907, with Cole superheater

C

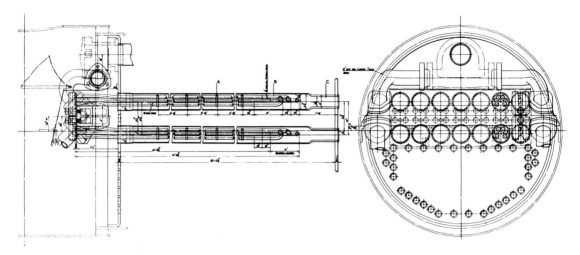

The standard Swindon No. 3 superheater

than in the earlier patterns, whilst the construction of the header was novel. Each flue tube contained a group of three pairs of elements (four pairs in boilers made between 1914 and 1919). The elements were expanded into a distribution box, or junction header, shaped like a hollow horseshoe, which was attached to the header by one stud and nut. The element group was released by the removal of this nut, and any group could be extracted independently. The weakness of the assembly was that a steamtight joint was maintained by one stud holding two flat surfaces together. Any steam which leaked from the joint blew across the ends of the tubes, with devastating effects upon the smokebox vacuum. In August 1909 the fitting of superheaters to the earlier 'Stars' began, and all engines of the class from No. 4031 of October 1910 were built with them. The conversion of the earlier engines was completed in May 1913.

The introduction of superheaters made it necessary to improve the lubrication of cylinders. The higher temperatures in the cylinders, and the absence of the lubricating action of particles of moisture, made it difficult to maintain adequate lubrication, and there was an increase in the wear of cylinder barrels. The problem of lubrication was greater in 1906 than in later years because less work had been put into the development of oils which could work at the temperature of superheated steam, and it is believed that Churchward's use of a lower superheat than was usual on other railways was influenced by the lack of suitable oils for use at higher temperatures. The additional wear of the cylinders was accentuated if the system of lubrication was such that the supply of oil was cut off

when the engine ran with steam shut off. The first Great Western superheated locomotives were fitted with mechanical lubricators but Churchward considered that a sight-feed lubricator emulsified the oil better than did a mechanical lubricator, and thus gave more uniform distribution of the oil over the walls of the steam chest and cylinder. Furthermore, the mechanical lubricator was an unnecessary complication, and took the control of lubrication out of the driver's hands.

An attempt was therefore made to devise a simpler arrangement by developing the sight-feed lubricator in the cab. With the adoption of the No. 3 superheater, with a lower temperature than in the Schmidt apparatus, a new system of hydrostatic lubrication was introduced. In this it was arranged that oil was supplied in atomised form to the steampipe between the superheater and the cylinders, the control of the steam supply to the lubricator being taken from the movement of the regulator handle. When the regulator was moved slightly from its closed position, a supply of oil, combined with a little steam, was fed to the cylinders. The regulator was put in this position when the engine was coasting, and a supply of oil was thus maintained to the cylinders, and sufficient pressure was maintained in the exhaust passages to discourage smokebox ashes from being sucked down the blastpipe.

In the early superheated engines both on the GWR and on other railways, dampers were fitted to cover the ends of the flues when steam was shut off. These were considered necessary to prevent the elements from overheating when they were not being cooled by steam passing through them. The

No. 4001 'Dog Star' after fitting with the de Glehn type bogie

dampers shut off the flow of gases through the flues. A common arrangement, and the one which was used on the GWR, was to have the dampers hinged, with a counterweight which normally held them shut. When the regulator was opened, steam was admitted to a small cylinder on the outside of the smokebox, and a piston thereby moved a lever to open the damper. The cylinder can be seen on the right-hand side of the smokebox of the early Great Western superheated engines. The first cylinders were kidney-shaped, but from 1910 a smaller and neater cylinder was introduced. Later it was found that the advantages to be derived from the use of dampers were not worth the additional expense, and between 1917 and 1924 they were removed. It may be mentioned that on other railways, using variants of the Schmidt superheater, the dampers were also discarded.

It has always been accepted that the Swindon superheater gives a lower degree of superheat than is obtained with the size of superheater used on most other British railways. There was ample evidence of this from Sir William Stanier's experiences on the LMSR and from the marked improvement in the performance of the 'Kings' when they were fitted with larger superheaters. It is therefore surprising to find that Churchward once denied that his superheaters gave a lower temperature. In January 1914, Sir Henry Fowler read a paper to the Institution of Civil Engineers on 'Superheating in Locomotives'. He had tried both Schmidt and Swindon superheaters in his No. 4 class 0—6—0s on the Midland Railway and had found that the Swindon apparatus gave 183 deg. of superheat (560 deg. Fah. steam temperature at 175 lb. per sq. in.),

whereas the Schmidt apparatus gave 250 deg. (620 deg. Fah. steam temperature at 160 lb. per sq. in.). Churchward said: 'The author must be labouring under some misapprehension. The position in which the pyrometer is placed—whether in the header or in the steamchest—makes a very considerable difference.'

After saying that he had not found pyrometers consistent over any series of tests, he added that from his own observation of the valves and pistons of other railways (that is, after running with superheated steam) he thought that the GWR superheat was higher than that commonly employed in England. After this evasive and inconclusive defence of his superheater, Churchward added that he had recorded steamchest temperatures of 550 deg. to 580 deg. at 225 lb. per sq. in., but this figure is higher than has been quoted by other people in contact with Swindon. In any case it was far lower than superheat temperatures regularly attained on the London & North Western Railway. Like Stirling's remarks on the appearance of Churchward's locomotives, Fowler's figures appear to have touched Churchward on the raw. But he then went on to say that it was incorrect to say that maximum superheat should be aimed at; anything could be got if desired. Any given engine required a certain degree of superheat for maximum economy and: 'Engines of modern design with small clearances showed less improvement by superheating than engines with longer and tortuous ports.'

Churchward said that the GWR had fitted superheaters for some years but 'he had not done much in the way of experiments'. In 12 months' working

35

in 1913, 625 engines with superheaters had saved 60,000 tons of coal. He considered it better to save coal now than to go on with experiments. As Churchward had made as many experiments in superheating as any engineer in the country, his disclaimer was modest. His total of superheated engines at that time exceeded that of all the other British railways combined. The superheaters had been fitted economically, for Churchward had sought approval for the expenditure of only £90 per boiler rebuilt with a superheater.

An attraction of the superheater which Churchward considered as important as the saving in coal was the saving in water. Superheated steam is much less dense than saturated steam, and a smaller weight of steam is therefore used in a superheated engine than in a saturated engine working at the same speed and at the same cut-off. This reduced the amount of water passing through the boiler, and reduced maintenance costs. The introduction of superheating on the GWR may be summarised by saying that Churchward had less to gain by this development than had other engineers, yet he tackled the problem more energetically and originally than his contemporaries, and was rewarded with a rapid and significant saving in coal, and a reduction in boiler repairs.

After this digression on superheating, the early history of the 4001-10 series may be completed. In 1909 the Cole superheater in 4010 was replaced by the Swindon pattern. For two periods (in 1911 and 1914/5) this engine carried a half-cone boiler, and five others of the series carried this type of boiler for a period. After a period of running by this series, the locomotive inspectors reported that the four-cylinder locomotives were 'a coach better' than the 'Saints' on 12 to 14-coach expresses at about 60 m.p.h. The boilers of the 'Stars' and 'Saints' were identical; despite the slight advantage of the Walschaert's gear at short cut-off, there can have been little difference in cylinder efficiency. The reported improvement must therefore have been due largely to an increase in mechanical efficiency, helped by the greater comfort of riding of the four-cylinder engines when working hard at speed. On a normal run, in which the evidence was based on visual and physical impressions, and not on quantitative measurements, the 'Saints' gave an impression of working harder than the 'Stars'. The characteristics of the valve gear made it necessary to limit them to a minimum cut-off of 22 per cent to prevent excessive knocking, whereas the 'Stars' could be, and were regularly, worked at 15 per cent. Against the locomotive inspectors' views it must be recorded that there exist a few logs of runs by 'Saints' on heavy West of England trains which equal the best work done by the 'Stars'; but this is not to say that the 'Stars' did not show a slight superiority in day-in, day-out running.

When the Churchward ten-wheeled engines were first introduced, the work which they were given was within the capacity of the existing 4—4—0s; but the combination of accelerated schedules, heavier traffic, and more commodious rolling stock soon made the larger engines necessary. The three-hour trains between Paddington and Exeter were an example of a service which was based upon the capacity of the larger engines; but even those trains

No. 4006 'Red Star', fitted with a half-cone boiler in October 1909; non-superheated, but with regulator lubricator feed. Large diameter chimney: de Glehn bogie

in their early days were made up to loads which were later considered light for a 4—6—0. Details are tabulated of a run by a non-superheated 'Star' on the 3.30 p.m. from Paddington in 1909. Although by this time loads of 400 tons were being worked through to Exeter on the three-hour trains this run is representative of the loadings for which the schedules were originally prepared.

The 3.30 p.m. train slipped one coach at Westbury and another at Taunton. The interest of this particular run lies in the delays which were encountered. After a fast start from Paddington, speed was up to 75 m.p.h. by Slough, but a signal check at Taplow caused a loss of 3 min. Its effects had been almost wiped out by Reading. At this time the turnout to the old Berks and Hants line had not been re-aligned, and a slack to 20 m.p.h. was in force. After this *Morning Star* ran well to Savernake, and without being pressed in the later stages of the climb, had 2½ min. in hand at that point. Unfortunately adverse signals approaching West-

bury made it necessary to stop to detach the slip coach. This caused a loss of 3½ min., which had been reduced to 1¾ min. by Castle Cary; but the combination of the cautious running which was still customary over the new line, and a permanent way slack at Curry Rivel Junction, made the train still 2 min. late at Cogload Junction. All seemed set for a good climb to Whiteball, but another signal check made a second stop necessary, to detach the Taunton slip portion. Despite a smart climb to Whiteball, another permanent way slack made the arrival at Exeter 6¾ min. late, though the net time was only 171½ min. In respect of the delay at Taunton it should be explained that until the rebuilding of the station in the 1930s there were only two running lines. If, as frequently happened in the holiday season, the down platform was occupied by another train, a non-stopping express would be diverted through the goods line to the east of the passenger station. This was sharply curved, and involved drastic reduction of speed at entry and exit of this by-pass.

A second table sets out details of three runs by saturated engines on the 11.50 a.m. from Paddington. These are from an extensive series recorded by A. V. Goodyear from 1909 to 1911. The train normally slipped portions at Westbury and Taunton. On the first run with *Royal Star* the load was 360 tons, which was normal at this period for the first part of the journey, but on this run there were no slip portions, so that after Westbury the load was above normal. The start was gentle, and speed did not reach 60 m.p.h. for the first 10 miles. Then there was a marked increase in effort, and for 16½ miles from Slough speed averaged 66 m.p.h. After the recovery from the Reading slack, speed was maintained mainly between 61 and 63 m.p.h. on the rising gradients to Bedwyn, and for 27 miles did not fall below 58. On the final climb to Savernake there was a fall from 62 to 52 m.p.h. Savernake was passed half a minute early, and a fast descent, with a maximum of 84 m.p.h., brought the train through Westbury 3 min. early. The driver then ran easily for the next 45 miles, but despite two slight permanent way slacks was still 3 min. ahead of time at Taunton. However, the train was turned through the loop at that station, requiring a slack to 10 m.p.h., and so lost its momentum for the climb to Whiteball. The recovery was vigorous, speed reaching 53 m.p.h. before the main part of the climb; the minimum of 37 was good for this load. Whiteball was passed 1 min. late, and after a maximum of 80 m.p.h. Exeter would have been reached on time had not the train been brought almost to a stand twice by signals.

3.30 p.m. PADDINGTON TO EXETER

Date: 1909

Engine: 4004 *Morning Star* (saturated)

Load: To Westbury, 287 tons tare, 305 tons full
To Taunton, 262 tons tare, 277 tons full
To Exeter, 237 tons tare, 250 tons full

Dist. Miles		Sch. Min.	Actual m. s.	Speeds m.p.h.
0·0	PADDINGTON .	0	0 00	
9·1	Southall . .	12	11 32	67
18·5	Slough . .	21	19 20	75
—			sigs.	30
24·2	Maidenhead .	26	26 20	45
34·0	*Milepost 34* .		36 07	69
36·0	READING .	38	38 10	20
44·8	Aldermaston .		48 17	64
53·1	NEWBURY .	57	55 50	66/63
58·5	Kintbury . .		60 53	68
61·5	Hungerford .		63 38	62
66·4	Bedwyn . .		68 13	66
70·1	Savernake . .	74	72 27	51
86·9	Lavington . .		86 47	73 (max.)
95·6	WESTBURY ∫ arr.	97	96 44	
—	⌊ dep.		98 26	
101·3	FROME . .	104	107 18	30/55
108·5	*Milepost 122¾* .	114	115 59	47/73
115·3	Castle Cary .	121	122 14	62
125·7	Somerton . .		131 32	69 (max.)
—			p.w.s.	
137·9	*Cogload Junction* .	144	146 04	68 (max.)
142·9	TAUNTON ∫ arr.	149	152 04	
—	⌊ dep.		153 12	
144·9	Norton Fitzwarren		156 52	46
150·0	Wellington . .		162 08	61
153·8	*Whiteball Box* .	161	166 42	41
158·8	Tiverton Junction		171 12	77
170·2	Stoke Canon .		180 54	
—			p.w.s.	30
173·7	EXETER . .	180	186 50	

Net time 171½ min.

11.50 a.m. PADDINGTON—EXETER

Run No.		1	2	3
Engine		4008	4008	4001
Load: tons, tare/full				
To Westbury		—/360	409/435	—/480
To Taunton		—/360	409/435	—/455
To Exeter		—/360	345/370	—/315
Weather		Fine	Strong S.W. wind	Slight W. wind, Wet

Dist. Miles		Sch. Min.	Actual m. s.	Actual m. s.	Actual m. s.
0·0	PADDINGTON	0	0 00	0 00	0 00
5·7	Ealing		8 58	8 59	9 45
9·1	Southall	11	12 28	12 27	13 32
15·0	*Milepost 15*			18 23	19 32
18·5	SLOUGH	20	21 32	21 38	22 45
				sigs.	
31·0	Twyford		32 57	34 15	34 35
36·0	READING	37	37 38	39 18	39 31
37·8	*Southcote Junction*		40 58	42 55	43 00
40·0	*Milepost 40*		43 21	45 28	45 35
53·1	NEWBURY	56	56 12	59 44	59 55
66·4	Bedwyn		69 08	73 57	74 45
70·1	Savernake	73½	73 04	78 30	79 19
81·1	Patney		82 41	89 04	89 58
95·0	*Milepost 95*		93 55	101 28	102 22
95·6	WESTBURY	97½	94 31	102 16	103 10
101·3	FROME		101 48	110 13	111 14
108·5	*Milepost 122¾*	113½	111 16	120 03	121 26
			p.w.s. 50 Bruton		
115·3	CASTLE CARY	120	117 18	126 00	127 45
			2 slight slacks	p.w.s. 30	p.w.s. 50 four times
137·9	*Cogload Junction*	144	139 45	148 32	152 00
			10 m.p.h. on to loop	p.w.s. 40	
142·9	TAUNTON	149	146 05	153 32	156 50
145·8	*Milepost 166*		151 19	156 39	159 55
150·0	Wellington		156 36	161 35	164 14
153·8	*Whiteball Box*	161	162 12	167 56	169 48
158·8	Tiverton Junction		167 10	172 54	174 39
171·8	*Milepost 192*		177 12	183 11	185 13
			sigs. 5 Cowley Br.		
173·7	EXETER	180	184 27	186 04	188 03

	1	2	3
Net time, min.:	174	182	185½
Minimum at Savernake, m.p.h.	52	41	41
Minimum at Brewham, m.p.h.	45	41	41
Minimum at Whiteball, m.p.h.	37	29	30
Maximum speed, m.p.h.	84	80	78½

On the second run, again with *Royal Star*, the load was 435 tons to Taunton, and in the face of a strong south-west wind the train did well to drop only 2 min. to Exeter. As in the first run, 60 m.p.h. was reached after 10 miles, and speed had risen to 64 when the train was checked by signals at Slough; the check cost 1¾ min. From Reading to Savernake speed ranged between 55 and 58 m.p.h., and fell to 41 at the summit, which was passed 5 min. late. The driver did not attempt to regain time before Westbury, and the maximum was only 70½ m.p.h. The minimum at Brewham was 41 m.p.h., and the train was then 6½ min. late. The descent from Brewham was more lively, speed reaching 78 before Castle Cary. Despite two permanent way slacks,

one to 30 and the other to 40 m.p.h., 2 min. had been recovered by Taunton. On the climb to Whiteball speed fell from 60 to 29 m.p.h., 2 min. being lost. The actual time to Exeter was 186 min. 4 sec. The combination of wind and older stock made the load equivalent to about 500 tons of modern stock in calm conditions, and the average power output was as high as was ever recorded with a saturated 'Star'.

The third run with engine No. 4001, *Dog Star*, was recorded at an August Bank Holiday weekend, when the train was made up to 15 vehicles, including two diners and nine heavy modern vehicles. The gross load from Paddington was 480 tons, but slips were shed at Westbury and Taunton, so that after Taunton the load was less than on the second run. The start was slower than in the previous runs, $2\frac{1}{2}$ min. being dropped on the optimistic 11 min. booking to Southall, instead of the more usual 1 min. Speed reached 60 m.p.h. at milepost 13, and 64 at Slough. From Slough to Reading the average was $63\frac{1}{2}$ m.p.h., and the time between these points was only 40 sec. longer than in the first run, but with 120 tons more of load. Between Reading and Bedwyn there was heavy rain, and the maximum speed was 56 m.p.h., falling to 41 at Savernake. Speed rose to $73\frac{1}{2}$ m.p.h. on the descent to Westbury, which was passed in 103 min. 10 sec., nearly $6\frac{3}{4}$ min. late, and the lateness had increased to 8 min. by milepost $122\frac{3}{4}$. The maximum after Frome was only 46 m.p.h., but to fall from 46 to 41 on Brewham bank with 455 tons was very good. Four permanent way slacks over the new line were observed scrupulously, but the timetable made allowance for easy running over this stretch, and no further time was lost to Taunton. The climb to Whiteball was below the standard of the first run in the table, speed being down to $34\frac{1}{2}$ m.p.h. before the tunnel, and averaging $30\frac{1}{2}$ through the tunnel. The actual time lost to Exeter was 8 min. 3 sec., but the net loss was $5\frac{1}{2}$ min.

From a study of runs 2 and 3 in this table it might be imagined that the losses in time indicated that the saturated 'Stars' were beyond their limit with loads of this magnitude. They were fine runs in themselves, but they were made in relatively early days of the class, and it is probable that neither the drivers nor the firemen had gained that experience that was necessary to extract the 'extra' needed to secure timekeeping in these conditions of exceptional loading. Nevertheless, from his long experience A. V. Goodyear was inclined to give the palm to the 'Saints' for heavy feats in non-superheater days. Apart from such outside observations Swindon opinion was unanimously in favour of the four-cylinder engines.

The expectation of longer mileages between general repairs was fulfilled. It was found that the 'Stars' could run from 120,000 to 130,000 miles, compared with 70,000 to 80,000 for the 'Saints'. This difference in mileage was not maintained in later years, when different criteria were adopted for deciding when an engine should have a general repair, and when the practice of intermediate repairs had become established. In these later days overhauls were determined by the general condition of the engine, and this led to the four-cylinder engines being shopped at lower mileages than could have been reached on the condition of the axleboxes alone; but they were in better condition at overhaul than were the two-cylinder engines.

No. 4006 'Red Star', approaching Chippenham with the Royal Train, conveying King Edward VII on a visit to Lord Lansdown, at Bowood

*No. 4003 'Lode Star' on down West of
England expresss near Southall*

*No. 4005 'Polar Star' during the interchange trials
with the LNWR in 1910, passing Kilburn*

In the 1950s the balance in favour of the four-cylinder engines would have been thought insufficient to justify the greater capital cost and the greater shed labour required. Before World War I the economics of locomotive operation were less stringent, and it was decided that four-cylinder engines would be built for heavy long-distance work. Two-cylinder engines would continue to be built for shorter-distance work where the advantages of the four-cylinder engines were less, and where the variable lead of the Stephenson valve gear gave more advantage at starting. In the event, construction of 'Saints' continued until 1913, after which all GWR express engines had four cylinders.

*'A' erecting shop, Swindon, showing left to right, engines 4022 (on the crane); a French
compound, 'City' No. 3708, 4035, and 2948*

4—6—0 No. 4003 'Lode Star' in later standard condition, and as now preserved in the Railway Museum, Swindon

CELESTIAL 'STARS'
Scintillating and Austere

4—6—0 No. 4010 'Western Star' as painted plain green with brass beadings to the splashers removed

CHAPTER 4

'STARS', CHIVALROUS AND ROYAL

TEN months after the appearance of No. 4010, in March 1908, the next batch of 'Stars' appeared, the 'Knights'. The first of these, No. 4011, *Knight of the Garter,* was, as mentioned in the account of the development of the Swindon superheater, the first engine to be fitted with a superheater of Swindon design. The batch introduced another change, and one which was destined to be adopted widely on British railways. The bogies so far fitted to the Churchward 4—6—0s had been of American pattern, in which the loads were applied to the axle-boxes by equalising bars. Two springs, parallel to the equalising bars, transmitted the load from the bogie frame to the bars, and the bogie was connected to the frame of the engine by swing links.

The swing links were troublesome, and various experiments were made to obtain more satisfactory wear from their pivots, and to reduce flange wear on the leading coupled wheels. The swing links allowed freedom of lateral movement at the front of the engine, but in doing so caused the leading coupled flanges to do a considerable part of the work of guiding the engine into curves.

The bogie used on the Frenchmen was of different construction, in that the weight of the engine was transmitted to the bogie through sliding flat surfaces. The lower surface was on the bogie frame, and the weight of the engine was applied to the upper surfaces by hemispherical cups, which allowed angular movement of the bogie relative to the engine frame. The bogie centre pin on the engine frame engaged a centre block on the bogie, but lateral movement of the block relative to the bogie frame could take place under the control of springs. Movement of the bogie relative to the engine frame applied a load through these springs

Engine No. 4016 'Knight of the Golden Fleece' as originally built, with non-superheated boiler, but having the de Glehn bogie from the outset

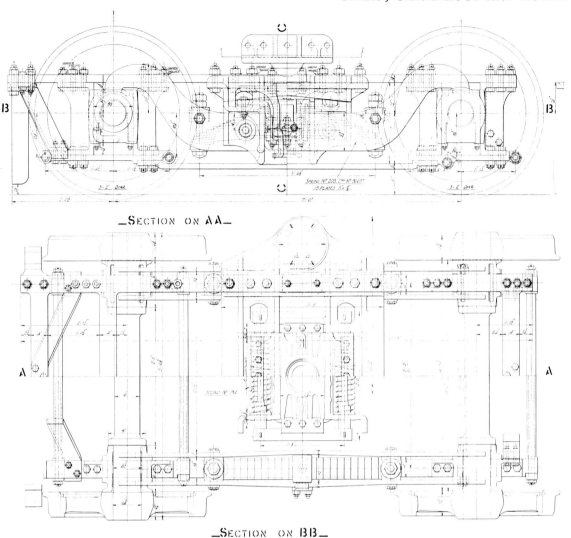

Section on AA

Section on BB

The de Glehn – Swindon bogie

which tended to lead the engine frame into the curve. Wear of the leading coupled wheel flanges would thus be reduced, at the expense of rather less increase in wear of the flanges of the bogie wheels and the trailing coupled or carrying wheels. A further benefit of the spring control was that it lessened the tendency for the front of the engine to develop lateral oscillations.

As Churchward gradually came to adopt practices brought over with the Frenchmen, he eventually tried the French type of bogie. The Swindon bogie was redesigned to incorporate the side control springs, and side bearers for transmitting the load. The equalising bar arrangement of wheel springing was retained. The modified bogie was soon accepted as an improvement on the old pattern, and was

applied to the earlier ten-wheeled engines as they came in for repairs. It became widely established on other railways, either with the equalising bar springing or with individual axlebox springs. Its adoption by Thompson on the LNER 'B1' 4—6—0 was probably the last example of the adoption of a Swindon feature of design by another railway.

In the Swindon development initially an existing bogie was modified, and after successful trials the 4011 series of 'Stars' was built with the new bogie. The side-bearers of the modified bogie are clearly visible in photographs. The same type of bogie was fitted to other classes also. The larger diameter chimney, which was to be the standard pattern on the 'Stars' for many years, also appeared on this batch. The diameter of the parallel portion was

43

No. 4011 'Knight of the Garter', as originally built in 1908, superheated

1 ft. $8\frac{7}{8}$ in., an increase of 2 in. on the earlier pattern. There were also slight variations in boiler dimensions. Nos. 4011-6/8 ran for a time with front footsteps.

THE 'KNIGHT' SERIES

No.	Name
4011	*Knight of the Garter*
4012	*Knight of the Thistle*
4013	*Knight of St. Patrick*
4014	*Knight of the Bath*
4015	*Knight of St. John*
4016	*Knight of the Golden Fleece*
4017	*Knight of the Black Eagle★*
4018	*Knight of the Grand Cross*
4019	*Knight Templar*
4020	*Knight Commander*

★ Renamed *Knight of Liege* in 1914

It is said that the grandeur of some of these names was not appreciated by all and sundry at Swindon, and some for a time had disrespectful nicknames. Engine No. 4014, for example, was known as 'Friday Night'!

Dynamometer car trials of a 'Star' were made in

No. 4015 'Knight of St. John', as modified with super-heater, top feed, and experimental lubricator fittings below the damper cylinder

April 1908 with No. 4013, *Knight of St. Patrick*. The locomotive developed a drawbar pull of 2.2 tons at 69 m.p.h., which was close to the figure of 2 tons at 70 m.p.h. which Churchward had taken as his target when developing the 'Saints'. The

12.5 p.m. EXETER TO PADDINGTON
Dynamometer Car test run on 28 April 1908
Engine: 4013 *Knight of St. Patrick*
Load: 368 tons tare, 390 tons full

Dist. Miles		Sch. min.	Actual m. s.	Speeds m.p.h.
0·0	EXETER . .	0	0 00	
3·5	Stoke Canon .		6 46	48
7·2	Silverton . .		10 58	57/56
12·6	Cullompton .		16 21	63
14·9	Tiverton Junction		18 40	56½/63
19·9	*Whiteball Box* .	25	23 57	47
23·7	Wellington . .		27 30	77½
—			sig.slight	
30·8	TAUNTON .	35	33 50	55½
35·8	Cogload Junction	40	38 55	62
42·7	*Curry Rivel Junc.*		46 05	59
46·8	*Milepost 127*			
	(*in tunnel*) .		50 21	50 (slip)
48·0	Somerton . .		51 46	
49·8	*Milepost 124* .		53 38	63
51·3	Charlton Mackrell		55 05	59
55·8	*Milepost 118* .		59 17	71
58·4	CASTLE CARY .	64	61 40	64
63·0	*Milepost 125* .		66 22	52
64·0	*Milepost 124* .		67 33	51
64·5	*Milepost 123½* .		68 10	47
65·0	*Milepost 123* .		68 50	44
65·25	*Milepost 123¾* .	73½	69 11	41
72·0	*Milepost 116* .		75 50	68
72·4	FROME . .		76 24	slack 27
77·0	*Milepost 111* .		83 14	63
78·1	WESTBURY .	87½	84 45	slack 32
86·8	Lavington . .		95 13	61
92·6	Patney . .		101 50	
97·7	*Milepost 76* .		107 25	60
			p.w.s.	
98·4	Pewsey . .		108 33	9
103·6	Savernake . .	114	118 36	41
112·2	Hungerford .		126 52	69/66½
115·2	Kintbury . .		129 29	71/66
120·6	NEWBURY .	130	134 10	70/67
124·1	Thatcham . .		137 16	70
127·0	Midgham . .		139 44	69/71
132·5	Theale . .		144 28	69
135·8	*Southcote Junction*		147 35	
136·7	*Milepost 37* .		149 08	slack 24
137·7	READING .	148	151 16	30
142·7	Twyford . .		157 56	58
149·5	Maidenhead .		164 15	68
155·2	SLOUGH .	166	169 15	69
157·5	Langley . .		171 16	68
160·5	West Drayton .		173 59	65½
164·6	SOUTHALL .	175	177 48	64½
168·0	Ealing Broadway .		180 52	66½
172·4	Westbourne Park .		185 18	
—			sigs.	
173·7	PADDINGTON	185	189 58	

Net time 183 min.
Allowances: 5½ min. lost at Pewsey
1½ min. lost at Royal Oak

An early view of the stationary testing plant, at Swindon, with engine No. 190

accompanying table shows the log of the test run on the 12.5 p.m. from Exeter to Paddington, 'The Torquay Diner', on 28 April 1908. The load of 390 tons full was heavy for the period, and an examination of the drawbar pull recorded at various points in the journey shows that the resistance to motion of the older stock made the equivalent of about 450 tons of modern stock. The running throughout was good, and no better performance was recorded by a non-superheated 'Star' on an up West of England train. A severe permanent way slack at Pewsey

caused a loss of $5\frac{1}{2}$ min., and signal checks at Royal Oak cost a further $1\frac{1}{2}$ min. Arrival at Paddington was 5 min. late, but the net time was 2 min. less than the schedule of 185 min. The interest in the run lies in the fact that it is the most complete record of the work of a non-superheated 'Star' which has survived.

RECORDED VALUES OF DRAWBAR PULL, ENGINE No. 4013

Location (near)	Speed m.p.h.	Cut-off per cent	Pull tons
Tiverton Junction .	63	25	2·8
Langport . . .	56	20	2·4
Keinton Mandeville .	69	20	2·1
Milepost $122\frac{3}{4}$ . .	41	25	4·3
Patney . . .	51	20	2·4

REGULATOR AND CUT-OFF CONDITIONS, ENGINE No. 4013

Location	Regulator position	Cut-off per cent
Milepost 192 to Whiteball .	Full	25
Whiteball to Curry Rivel Junc.	Part-open	$12\frac{1}{2}$
Curry Rivel Junc. to Bruton .	Full	20
Bruton to Milepost $122\frac{3}{4}$.	Full	25
Milepost $122\frac{3}{4}$ to Milepost $116\frac{1}{2}$	$\frac{1}{2}$	15
Recovering from Frome slack	Full	20
Milepost $94\frac{1}{2}$ to Milepost 76 .	Full	20
Recovering from Pewsey check	Full	35
Milepost $74\frac{1}{2}$ to Savernake .	Full	20
Savernake to Southcote Junc.	Part-open	15
Reading to Milepost $3\frac{3}{4}$.	Full	20

The Churchward dynamometer car as originally built

At this time the technique of driving the four-cylinder engines was not fully developed. The reverser was left in the same position for long periods, leading to uneven demands upon the boiler. Speed varied unnecessarily on some stretches and there were less vigorous accelerations and hill climbs than would have resulted had the cut-off been increased and decreased gradually. A further table shows the variations of regulator opening and cut-off, but there were some local variations not shown in this list, as some figures derived from this test include values of the drawbar pull at 11 per cent cut-off. Also tabulated are some values of drawbar pull recorded at various points. These figures are uncorrected for gradient and acceleration; an analysis of the drawbar characteristics of the engine based on corrected figures is included in the chapter on Test Results in Part 2. The coal consumption was about $3\frac{1}{2}$ lb. per drawbar horse-power hour. Had Churchward seen fit to publish this figure, it would have shaken his contemporaries as severely as did the figure published in 1924 for the tests of *Caldicot Castle*.

It is interesting to compare the running of No. 4013 with the performance of superheated engine No. 4011 on the run on the up 'Cornish Riviera Express' which is tabulated herewith. With almost

1.45 p.m. EXETER TO PADDINGTON
Engine: 4011 *Knight of the Garter*
Load: 360 tons tare, 380 tons full

Dist. Miles		Sch. Min.	Actual m. s.	Speeds m.p.h.
0·0	Exeter .	0	0 00	
3·5	Stoke Canon .		6 42	48
12·6	Cullompton .		17 05	56
14·9	Tiverton Junction .		19 44	$48\frac{1}{2}$
16·9	*Milepost 177*		21 55	$55\frac{1}{2}$
19·9	*Whiteball Box*	23	25 44	$39\frac{1}{2}$
23·7	Wellington .		29 13	82/78
28·8	Norton Fitzwarren .		32 54	90
30·8	TAUNTON .	$32\frac{1}{2}$	34 17	84
35·8	*Cogload Junction* .	$37\frac{1}{2}$	38 18	60 slack
42·7	*Curry Rivel Junc.* .		44 25	69
48·0	Somerton .		49 58	56
53·5	Keinton Mandeville		54 19	72
58·4	CASTLE CARY .	$61\frac{1}{2}$	59 20	65
61·8	Bruton .		63 02	50
65·2	*Milepost $122\frac{3}{4}$* .	$69\frac{1}{2}$	67 20	41
72·4	FROME .		74 32	30 slack
78·1	WESTBURY .	$83\frac{1}{2}$	82 00	27 slack
86·8	Lavington .		91 32	67
91·7	*Milepost 82*		96 39	52
98·4	Pewsey .		103 39	62
103·6	Savernake .		108 51	$57\frac{1}{2}$
107·3	Bedwyn .		112 05	75
—			sigs.	5
112·2	Hungerford .		117 20	
120·6	NEWBURY .	125	126 52	69
—			—	73 max.
137·7	READING .	143	143 28	30 slack
149·5	Maidenhead .	155	156 05	70
155·2	Slough .	$160\frac{1}{2}$	161 10	68
164·6	Southall .	$169\frac{1}{2}$	169 25	64
171·7	*Milepost 2* .		176 27	
			sig. stop	
173·7	PADDINGTON .	180	182 45	

Net time $176\frac{1}{2}$ min.

A detail of the rear-end of No. 4016 showing the first modified form of slide-bars

Engine No. 4022 'King William' as originally built, non-superheated

the same load as No. 4013, the superheated engine made very similar times over much of the journey. The start of No. 4011's run was slower, and despite the incentive of a late start of 7 min., nearly 3 min. was dropped to Whiteball. Then came a display of high speed so sudden as to suggest that the driver had left his controls unchanged from the positions used in climbing to Whiteball. After checking the speed from 82 to 78 m.p.h. at Wellington, he opened out again to reach the unusual maximum—for that time—of 90 m.p.h. at Norton Fitzwarren, and speed remained high until the slack at Cogload Junction. By Castle Cary the train was 2 min. within booked running time, and remained so until a bad signal check at Hungerford. Again time was recovered but a final signal stop before Paddington caused a total loss on running time of $2\frac{3}{4}$ min. The test run of No. 4013 was one of the best efforts recorded by a non-superheated 'Star', and it is therefore interesting to see a superheated engine making a very similar run in ordinary service at the same period.

In 1909 there appeared the third series of 'Stars', named after Kings of England. The first of the batch, No. 4021, *King Edward*, has already been

THE 'KING' SERIES

No.	Name
4021	*King Edward*
4022	*King William*
4023	*King George*
4024	*King James*
4025	*King Charles*
4026	*King Richard*
4027	*King Henry*
4028	*King John*
4029	*King Stephen*
4030	*King Harold*

mentioned as the first engine to be fitted with the Swindon No. 3 superheater. The remaining engines of the batch had saturated boilers with, as commonly happened in this period, slight variations in dimensions. Even these nine boilers were not identical. There was a small but significant change in the shape of the casing over the inside cylinders, the sides of which were given concave curvature. The effect was to make the casing less obtrusive, and to blend it more into the generally tapered front of the engine. This feature continued through the remainder of the 'Stars' and was also seen in the earlier 'Castles'. The names of this series were as shown in the previous column.

Whilst this batch was appearing, *The Engineer* published a series of articles on 'British Locomotive Practice of Today'. The articles invoked a long correspondence, including some letters from one correspondent which were highly critical of the GWR. It was pointed out that numerous types of ten-wheeled passenger engines had been built, which, to the writer, seemed to have made no difference to the 'revenue earning capacity of the locomotive'. The writer quoted from the half-yearly returns which railways made to the Board of Trade. These showed that on the GWR the expenditure on locomotive renewals and repairs for the half year ending in December 1908 were £175 per locomotive, which was quite the highest of any railway. For the Lancashire & Yorkshire the figure was £100, and other railways ranged up to £157, which applied to the Great Eastern and to the North Eastern. The total figure of locomotive expenditure for the GWR had increased half-year by half-year. The appearance of one particularly critical letter in a reputable technical journal could not escape the notice of the Directors of the GWR, and Churchward was asked to explain how it was

Engine No. 4021 'King Edward' decorated for hauling the funeral train of King Edward VII, carrying the standard GWR Royal Train headlamps, and with the side shield draped in purple

that the London & North Western could build three 4—6—0 locomotives for the cost of two of his. Churchward is said to have replied, rather tartly across the Board table: 'Because one of mine could pull two of their b—— things backwards!'

Although this incident had no bearing on future locomotive policy on the GWR, it is generally known to have been the inspiration of a locomotive exchange which was made with the London & North Western in 1910. Bowen-Cooke had arranged exchanges with other railways to assist him in formulating his ideas on future passenger engines, but there is evidence that the exchange of non-superheater 4—6—0 locomotives with the GWR was proposed by Churchward. As an exchange it was an uneven test, for there can have been little expectation that an 'Experiment' could equal the work of a 'Star'. That Bowen-Cooke was more interested in the work of the 'Star' on the London & North Western than in the work of his own Company's engine on the GWR is borne out by the fact that it was left to Camden shed to select the engine, and they were so little apprised of the importance of the trials that they sent the engine which they could most easily spare, that is, the one in the most run-down condition. As a result, whereas No. 4005 *Polar Star* went to the London & North Western in the pink of condition, No. 1471 *Worcestershire* was in a condition below that of an 'Experiment' at its best. *Worcestershire* found the work allotted to it on the GWR beyond its capacity, chiefly through water difficulties, and lost time badly. The circumstances so far as the LNWR engines were concerned are discussed fully in the Locomotive Monograph dealing with *The Precursor Family*. By contrast, *Polar Star* showed complete mastery

	L.N.W.R. 12.10 p.m. EUSTON—CREWE Engine: GWR 4-6-0 No. 4005 *Polar Star* Driver: J. Springthorpe (Old Oak Common) Load 388 tons tare, 410 tons full			
Dist. Miles		Sch. min.	Actual m. s.	Av. Speeds m.p.h.
0·0	EUSTON . .	0	0 00	
1·3	Chalk Farm .		3 35	
2·4	Loudoun Road .		5 20	
5·4	WILLESDEN Jn. .	9	9 15	46·0
11·4	Harrow . .		16 35	49·2
13·3	Pinner . .		19 05	45·6
17·5	WATFORD JN. .	23	24 10	49·5
21·0	King's Langley .		27 55	56·0
28·0	Berkhamsted .		35 35	54·8
31·7	Tring . .	40	39 40	54·4
46·7	BLETCHLEY .	55	54 20	61·5
52·4	Wolverton . .		59 35	65·2
59·9	Roade . .	69	67 40	55·7
62·8	BLISWORTH .		71 05	50·9
—			p.w.s.	
69·7	Weedon . .		79 20	50·2
75·3	Welton . .		86 25	47·5
82·5	RUGBY . .	93	94 55	51·6
88·0	Brinklow . .		101 45	48·4
91·4	Shilton . .		105 15	56·5
93·5	Bulkington . .		107 45	52·8
97·1	NUNEATON .	109	111 15	61·7
102·3	Atherstone .		115 55	66·8
106·5	Polesworth .		119 35	68·7
110·0	TAMWORTH .	122	122 40	68·0
116·3	Lichfield . .		128 30	64·8
121·0	Armitage . .		133 45	53·7
—			sigs.	
124·3	Rugeley . .	137	138 40	40·3
—			sigs.	
127·2	Colwich . .		145 15	26·4
133·6	STAFFORD .	147	155 15	38·4
138·9	Norton Bridge .	154	161 40	49·5
143·4	Standon Bridge .		166 50	52·4
147·6	Whitmore . .		171 35	53·0
150·1	Madeley . .		174 25	53·0
153·3	Betley Road .		177 25	64·0
158·0	CREWE . .	175	183 25	

over the work given to it on the North Western.

The exchange workings were between 15 and 27 August. In the first week *Polar Star* worked the 12.10 p.m. from Euston, allowed 175 min. for a non-stop run to Crewe, on Monday, Tuesday, and Wednesday. The load was 11 cars, including two twelve-wheeled dining cars, a gross load of about 370 tons. The engine returned each day on the 5.2 p.m. from Crewe, allowed 188 min. to Euston, including a stop of 5 min. at Rugby and one of 2 min. at Willesden. Thursday was shed day, and on Friday and Saturday the engine worked the 10 a.m. down Glasgow and Edinburgh express, and the 4.7 p.m. up from Crewe.

In the second week *Polar Star* worked the 10 a.m. down on Monday and Tuesday, had a shed day on Wednesday, and worked the 12.10 p.m. down on Thursday, Friday, and Saturday. The 'Experiment' *Herefordshire* worked the opposite turns each week.

A run was logged by Cecil J. Allen on the 5.2 p.m. up from Crewe, with a moderate load of 330 tons on which *Polar Star* kept time with ease, running the 75.5 miles from Crewe to Rugby in 84½ min. start to stop, and continuing over the 77.1 miles to Willesden Junction in 84 min. 25 sec.—an aggregate gain of 2 min. on schedule. But a fully authenticated record exists of a run on the 12.10 p.m. down which shows the GWR engine in a less favourable light. The log of this run is tabulated herewith, and it would seem that the driver was definitely 'coal-dodging' rather than trying to run the train to time. The checks were severe, it is true; but little attempt was made to regain the lost time, and the arrival at Crewe was 8½ min. late. The net time was certainly inside the scheduled allowance, but the driving lacked any particular enterprise and the running, particularly after the signal checks, was well below the standards established very shortly afterwards by the 'George the Fifth' class 4—4—0s over that section of line. The coal consumption of *Polar Star* was appreciably lower than that of the 'Experiment' class 4—6—0 *Herefordshire* against which it was tested.

For Churchward the exchange was a complete vindication; for Bowen-Cooke it was a spur to better things. For the GWR management the interchange with the London & North Western in August 1910 was very opportune, for in October of that year the direct route to Birmingham came into use, and two-hour trains were introduced in direct competition with the North Western. As the GWR had the more difficult route, the superiority of its engines was reassuring, even though the loads were at first so light that 4—4—0 engines could time the trains.

The fourth series of 'Stars' appeared in October

Royal Train on the Shrewsbury and Hereford Joint Line, hauled by engine No. 4033 'Queen Victoria'

49

Interior of Churchward's historic dynamometer car, as originally built

1910, Nos. 4031-40, named after Queens of England. They were fitted with No. 3 superheaters when built, but the boilers had the customary slight variations in dimensions from the previous series. For the interchange trials with the London & North Western, the tender of No. 4005 had its side fenders lengthened, and this change was incorporated as standard from engine No. 4031 onwards.

THE 'QUEEN' SERIES

4031	*Queen Mary*
4032	*Queen Alexandra*
4033	*Queen Victoria*
4034	*Queen Adelaide*
4035	*Queen Charlotte*
4036	*Queen Elizabeth*
4037	*Queen Philippa*
4038	*Queen Berengaria*
4039	*Queen Matilda*
4040	*Queen Boadicea*

These names were a much more satisfying lot than

the 'Kings', for with all of them there was no mistaking which Royal Lady was intended. With the 'King', only the last three admitted of no ambiguity, though of course in the year 1909 *King Edward* would naturally have been associated with the reigning monarch, rather than with any of the six preceding Edwards, and after his death No. 4023 *King George* would obviously be similarly associated with King George V.

One of this series, No. 4039, *Queen Matilda*, was given a dynamometer-car trial on the 11 a.m. from Paddington to Bristol on 1 November 1911. The load was heavy for this train, 13 coaches weighing 400 tons full as far as Bath, and 12 coaches weighing 370 tons full after the shedding of the Bath slip. A log of the run is tabulated herewith, and the details include the dynamometer-car records of the conditions at which the engine was worked, and the drawbar pull at various locations. It is evident that the cut-off was changed from time to time to give readings at various combinations of speed and cut-off. For example, at milepost $40\frac{1}{2}$, with the train nearly 5 min. late, the cut-off was reduced from 23 per cent to 11 per cent. The readings shown are of interest in that speed variations were small for much of the journey, and the gradients easy, so that in many places the actual values of drawbar pull would differ little from the equivalent values at constant speed on the level.

The changes of cut-off for test purposes contributed to a loss of 2 min. on schedule, after allowing for two signal checks. Had the cut-off been sustained at 20 per cent as far as Wantage Road, this loss would probably have been avoided. Unfortunately no figures of coal consumption for this test have survived, for it would have been interesting to have seen the outcome of the working at short cut-off for much of the distance.

11 a.m. PADDINGTON—BRISTOL
Dynamometer Car Test Run on 1 November 1911
Engine: 4039 *Queen Matilda*
Load: To Bath, 13 cars, 378 tons empty, 400 tons full
To Bristol, 12 cars, 351 tons empty, 370 tons full

Dist. Miles		Sch. Min.	Actual m. s.	Speed m.p.h.	Reg. opening	Cut-off %	Drawbar pull, tons
0·0	PADDINGTON	0	0 00				
			sigs.				
1·3	Westbourne Park		3 42	23½			
2·5	*Milepost 2½*		6 12	37	Full	22	2·9
5·7	Ealing Broadway		10 49	49	”	22	2·6
7·4	Hanwell		12 43	51	”	20	2·2
9·1	Southall	11	14 42	53	”	20	2·2
13·2	West Drayton		19 10	59	”	17½	1·85
16·2	Langley		22 14	60½	”	17½	
18·5	SLOUGH	20	24 24	62	”	15	1·6
—	Taplow			57½	”	20	2·1
24·2	Maidenhead		30 16	59	”	20	
31·0	Twyford		37 05	60	”	20	2·2
34·0	*Milepost 34*		40 03	61	”	19	1·9
36·0	READING	37	41 58	63½	”	19	1·9
38·7	Tilehurst		44 29	64	”	23	2·25
40·5	*Milepost 40½*		46 13	64½	”	11	1·2
44·8	Goring		50 30	57	”	16	1·8
47·0	*Milepost 47*		52 49	58	”	20	2·2
48·5	Cholsey		54 22	59	”	24	2·4
51·5	*Milepost 51½*		57 22	61	”	24	2·4
53·1	DIDCOT	53½	58 56	63	”	19	
56·5	Steventon		62 15	60½	”	19	2·0
61·5	*Milepost 61½*			58	”	20	
63·9	Challow		69 48	57	”	22	
71·5	Shrivenham		77 36	61	”	23	
76·0	*Milepost 76*		81 57	61	”	23	2·2
			sigs.		Shut		
77·3	SWINDON	77	83 40	41	Full	30	3·3
78·0	*Milepost 78*			48½	”	25	
80·0	*Milepost 80*		86 57	56	”	19	2·0
82·9	Wootton Bassett		89 53	63	”	19	1·9
83·3	*Milepost 83¼*			63	”	16	1·7
87·7	Dauntsey		94 07	76	”	16	1·4
90·0	*Milepost 90*		95 57	74	”	12	1·0
94·0	CHIPPENHAM	93½	99 24	62	”	17½	1·85
96·1	*Thingley Junc.*		101 22	58	”	20	
98·3	Corsham		103 50	57	”	20	2·1
99·0	*Milepost 99*				¼	20	
101·9	Box		107 07	76	¼	20	
102·5	*Milepost 102½*			75	½	20	
104·6	Bathampton		109 17	73	½	20	1·45
105·8	*Milepost 105¾*			69½	Shut	38	
106·9	BATH	107	111 55	36½	”		
107·0	*Milepost 107*				Full	28	3·0
109·0	*Milepost 109*		114 16	55	”	24	
113·8	Keynsham		118 56	67	”	24	1·85
116·7	St. Anne's Park		121 34	66	Shut	42	
118·4	BRISTOL (Temple Meads)	120	124 15				

Net time 122 min.

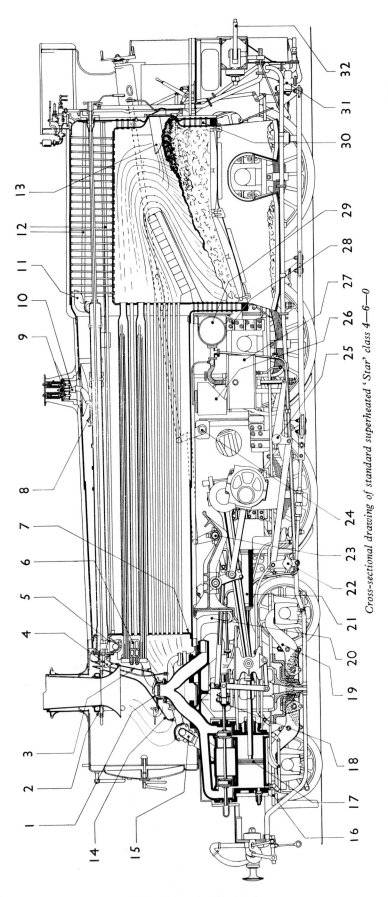

Cross-sectional drawing of standard superheated 'Star' class 4–6–0

KEY:
1. Jumper-top blast-pipe
2. Blower-ring
3. Spark-plate
4. Distributor for cylinder-oil
5. Regulator valve
6. Superheater header
7. Front tube-plate
8. Tray for feed-water
9. Safety valves
10. Delivery nozzle for feed water
11. Steam-collecting mouth
12. Longitudinal boiler stays
13. Fire-hole deflector-plate
14. Pipe discharging oil into steam passing to inside cylinder
15. Steam-pipe to inside cylinder
16. Top member of bogie frame
17. Piston
18. Rocking lever connecting inside and outside valve-spindles
19. Equalizing beam for bogie axle-loading
20. Steam-pipe to outside cylinder
21. Vacuum pump
22. Brake shaft
23. Reversing shaft
24. Intermediate reversing shaft
25. Intermediate brake-shaft
26. Sand-box
27. Brake cylinder
28. Horncheek
29. Vacuum brake reservoir
30. Fire-box water-space
31. Injector
32. Drawbar between engine and tender

As has been mentioned, Churchward's intention was to build 'Stars' for long non-stop runs and 'Saints' for runs with a number of intermediate stops. This policy continued until 1913, further batches of 'Saints' being built in 1907, 1911, and 1912. In 1913 a further batch of ten 'Saints' was ordered, but before the order was executed it was decided that in future only 'Stars' would be built. As a result, five 'Saints' only were built to this order, and the remainder of the batch appeared as 'Stars', Nos. 4041-5. This was the smallest batch of four-cylinder engines ordered at any time at Swindon. They were named after the five sons of King George V.

The 'Princes' incorporated the last major development in the Churchward boilers: top-feed. In the discussion on Churchward's paper on boilers, a speaker had suggested that the deleterious effect of introducing cold-feed water into a boiler could be mitigated by feeding the water into the steam space. Churchward replied that he was working on that question, and that he intended to pursue the plan until he had some success with it. Five years passed before the standard Swindon top-feed was perfected. Prior to its introduction the feed into the standard boilers was normally delivered at the bottom of the barrel immediately behind the smokebox. There was a hood which directed the water along the bottom of the barrel, where it promoted the general circulation. The release of air which had been trapped in the feed water led to pitting and corrosion of the barrel near the feed box.

The advantage of top feed is that the water is heated by contact with the steam before it makes contact with the metal of the boiler, and any entrapped air is released into the steam space. The air is then carried away with the steam. Deposits in the water, some of which result from water treatment, are left partly on the trays of the top-feed apparatus which can readily be removed for cleaning.

Top-feed had been tried in France in 1890, but had made no headway, and it seems that, although like many of Churchward's ideas it was not entirely original, the Swindon application was the first to be successful. The feed was delivered through clack boxes at the side of the safety valve on to sloping trays, which broke the feed into a fine spray and delivered it forwards over a wide area. The shape and slope of the trays was established by experiments in which a metered water supply was fed over trays standing in the yard at Swindon. After its adoption as standard in 1911, top-feed was soon fitted to all the Churchward boilers.

No. 4041 had cylinders 15 in. diameter, whereby

Nameplate of No. 4017, as altered in 1914

the nominal tractive effort was raised from 25,090 lb. to 27,800 lb. The main justification for this increase was the greater volume of steam which could be produced from the superheated boilers. The increase was not so great as might appear at first glance, as the cylinders of the earlier engines of the class had already been bored out at successive overhauls. A total increase in diameter of about $\frac{9}{16}$ in. was permissible on this type of cylinder. Cylinders of the 'Star' pattern but with a diameter when new of 15 in. had already been fitted to *The Great Bear*. The increase in diameter was considered successful and in due course all the 'Stars' had their cylinders increased to at least this size. The cylinders made new at that size would, in the course of time, increase beyond 15 in.

The continued growth of long-distance passenger traffic on the GWR, aided by successive improvements to the main lines, maintained a need for additional express engines, and in 1914 a further 15 'Stars' were built—Nos. 4045-60, named after Princesses. Externally they differed from the previous batch in having fluted coupling rods, this being one of the experiments with alloy steel rods previously mentioned. Some years later these rods were replaced by the normal pattern. On this batch also appeared the four-cone ejector.

Nameplate of No. 4056, the last 'Star' to remain in service

THE GWR STARS, CASTLES & KINGS

The standard GWR vacuum brake apparatus had incorporated a handle which served as an application valve, and which controlled also the single ejector cone. The vacuum was maintained during running by a vacuum pump driven from a crosshead, and the ejector was used to release the brakes after an application, and to hold them off when the train was standing. The increasing length of passenger trains made an enlargement of the ejector necessary, and a new ejector was therefore designed with four separate cones combined in one casing. The ejector was placed outside the firebox, with an exhaust pipe running along the boiler to the smokebox. In the earlier four-cone ejectors the steam to all four cones was controlled from one stop valve, but later two valves were fitted, one of which controlled one cone and the other the remaining three. The single cone could be used for maintaining the vacuum whilst the train was standing, and three or four cones could be used to release the brakes quickly. These ejectors were sometimes known as the 'three-one' pattern. The application of the brake was controlled by a separate handle. All the 'Stars' had been fitted with four-cone ejectors by 1919, and this feature was the last main development in the 'Stars', although many minor changes were made over the years. With the completion of the 'Princesses', construction of passenger engines ceased until 1922. The names of these 20 engines were:

THE 'PRINCE' AND 'PRINCESS' SERIES

No.	Name	No.	Name
4041	*Prince of Wales*	4051	*Princess Helena*
4042	*Prince Albert*	4052	*Princess Beatrice*
4043	*Prince Henry*	4053	*Princess Alexandra*
4044	*Prince George*	4054	*Princess Charlotte*
4045	*Prince John*	4055	*Princess Sophia*
4046	*Princess Mary*	4056	*Princess Margaret*
4047	*Princess Louise*	4057	*Princess Elizabeth*
4048	*Princess Victoria*	4058	*Princess Augusta*
4049	*Princess Maud*	4059	*Princess Patricia*
4050	*Princess Alice*	4060	*Princess Eugenie*

An exceptionally interesting photograph showing No. 4017 at the time it bore the original name of 'Knight of the Black Eagle'

CHAPTER 5

EARLY WORK OF THE 'STARS'

THE 'Stars' were built to work trains which made long non-stop runs, and were therefore used primarily on the West of England services in their early days. In due course the two-cylinder engines were gradually displaced from these workings, and for some time dominated the Bristol and Birmingham services. When the series from 4041 to 4060 were built, 'Stars' became more numerous on Bristol and Birmingham trains, but on the Birmingham line in particular there were few workings before World War I which taxed a 'Star' to its limit.

On the West of England services loads continued to grow, but the capacity of the 'Stars' also increased, partly by the increase in cylinder diameter in the later engines, and partly because the enginemen improved their techniques of handling the

engines. Firemen perfected the 'Haycock' fire, with a deep bed of coal on the horizontal section at the rear of the grate. Welsh coal gave excellent results with this method of firing, and there developed a tradition of rock-steady steaming, with the needle of the pressure gauge apparently fixed just below the blowing-off point. On other lines some engines might run for long periods with the boiler pressure well below the blowing-off point, the full pressure being used only for hill climbing or other extra efforts, but on the GWR a feather of steam from the safety valves became a sign that the engine was steaming normally. If the pressure fell by 20 lb. per sq. in. below the blowing-off point, the engine was considered to be steaming badly.

An important feature that assisted in the maintenance of 'rock-steady' steaming conditions was the

Up Birmingham and North express near Knowle; engine No. 4023 'King George'

continued use of Ramsbottom-type safety valves. The 'pop' type of valve was never used on GWR engines. With Ramsbottom valves the pressure could be kept at 'sizzling point', without full blowing off. There was no 'in-between' stage with 'pop' valves and full blowing off usually resulted in a drop of 5 or 10 lb. per sq. in. before the valves closed.

The ability to hold pressure near to blowing-off point for long periods depended not only on skilful firing but also upon the driver maintaining a fairly constant steam rate to the cylinders. On the long, gentle gradients of the Brunel routes this was easy, but on routes with rapidly-changing gradients frequent adjustments of the reverser were required. Over the years drivers developed the habit of making the necessary adjustments to keep the steam rate as near as possible steady, and some intermediate passing times were regularly disobeyed because they made uneven demands upon the boiler. In later years, when the testing of engines at constant steaming rates was perfected, it was shown that the most important contribution to working an engine economically was a steam rate which remained as nearly constant as the gradients and speed restrictions allowed. Many GWR drivers had, by their own instinct and experience, long since arrived at very nearly the ideal conditions. The haycock fire was developed to suit the properties of Welsh coal, which burns most effectively on a thick and very hot firebed; but variations of the technique

THE DOWN 'CORNISH RIVIERA EXPRESS'

Run No.	1			2	
Date	Summer 1914			1916	
Engine	4045			4018	
Engine name	*Prince John*			*Knight of the Grand Cross*	
Load: cars, tons, tare/full					
To Westbury	13 441/470			14 457/490	
To Taunton	13 441/470			11 373/400	
To Exeter	13 441/470			9 301/320	

Dist. Miles		Sch. Min.	Actual m. s.	Speed m.p.h.	Actual m. s.	Speed m.p.h.
0·0	PADDINGTON	0	0 00		0 00	
9·1	SOUTHALL		13 39		12 49	
16·2	Langley				19 53	64
					severe sig.	
18·5	SLOUGH	20	22 38	67 max.	22 41	
24·2	Maidenhead				30 32	
31·0	Twyford				37 24	64
35·0	*Milepost 35*		37 35			
36·0	READING	37	38 40		42 17	
44·8	Aldermaston				52 29	58
53·1	NEWBURY	56	57 41		61 21	
61·5	Hungerford				70 28	53/58
70·1	Savernake	73½	76 23	42½	80 20	44
81·1	Patney				90 38	71/66
82·0	*Milepost 82*		87 05			
91·4	Edington				98 42	83
94·0	*Milepost 94*		96 30	80½ max.		
95·6	WESTBURY	97½	98 17	slack	102 39	slack
101·3	FROME			slack	110 32	slack
106·6	Witham				117 26	
108·5	*Milepost 122¾*		116 23	39½		
115·3	CASTLE CARY	120	122 17	79½	125 42	80 max.
125·7	Somerton				134 17	
137·9	*Cogload Junction*	144	141 10		144 29	78 max.
142·9	TAUNTON	149	145 38	63·4†	149 14	
150·0	Wellington		153 03	51·0†		
150·8	*Milepost 171*		154 01	51·0†	157 33	
151·8	*Milepost 172*		155 26	42·5†	158 50	46·7†
152·8	*Milepost 173*		157 15	32·8†	160 19	40·5†
153·8	*Whiteball Box*		159 31	26·5†	161 54	37
158·8	Tiverton Junction				166 33	76 max.
166·5	Silverton				172 52	
173·7	EXETER	179*	177 41		179 29 slip	arrival

* 180 minutes on run No. 2   Net time 175¼ min.
†Average over full mile.

Cornish Riviera Express leaving Paddington, engine No. 4042 'Prince Albert'

proved equally effective with the hard coals from Staffordshire and North Wales which were supplied to the northern sheds of the GWR.

The growth of the West of England traffic was due largely to the popularity of the holiday resorts, and exceptional peaks of traffic at holiday periods were therefore inevitable. From about 1910 onwards train-loads of 500 tons were found at these periods. In the early years of World War I no further increases were made in train services, but the traffic continued to grow, and very heavy trains became more common. There were no general decelerations until January 1917, and the 'Stars' proved their ability to work the heaviest trains to pre-war schedules. Not all the heavy trains kept time, but sufficient records exist to show that the engines could reach Exeter in three hours with trains of up to 470 tons, although some of the intermediate times would not be observed with such a load. Five years earlier it seemed that 400 tons was the limit for timekeeping on these services.

The accompanying table shows two examples of heavy loads on the down 'Cornish Riviera Express'. Run No. 1 was unusual in that the full load of 470 tons was taken through to Exeter, and it is probably the finest down run recorded in the pre-war period. In the early days of the 3-hour bookings to Exeter, the passing times allowed for cautious running over the Somerton cut-off line where the earthworks were still consolidating. Subsequent alterations to the timetable never made the demands upon the locomotive even throughout the journey from Paddington to Exeter, and drivers could normally count on recovering some lost time between Castle Cary and Taunton. The driver of *Prince John* was thus able to drop nearly 3 min. in the first 70 miles to Savernake, in which there is little respite other than the Reading slack, and after passing milepost $122\frac{3}{4}$ $2\frac{1}{4}$ min. late, to be nearly $3\frac{1}{2}$ min. early at Taunton, without attaining any unusually high speeds. The allowance of 24 min. for the 22.6 miles from Castle Cary to Cogload Junction was cut to 18 min. 53 sec., an average of 71.8 m.p.h. Speed was well maintained on the approaches to Wellington, suggesting that cut-off was being advanced progressively, and the train thus had sufficient momentum to cover the final mile from milepost 173 to Whiteball box at an average of 26.5 m.p.h. without excessive demands upon the engine. Time was dropped on the climb, but the driver had judged his running well, and he was through Exeter in $1\frac{1}{4}$ min. less than the allowance of 179 min.

On the second run in the table, made in 1916, coaches were slipped at Westbury and Taunton, as was normal for the 'Limited'. For a train of 490 tons the start was vigorous, with a time of 12 min. 49 sec. to Southall. Speed rose to 64 m.p.h. at Langley, but there was a bad signal check at Dolphin Junction, Slough. This cost at least 4 min. but the driver was not discouraged, and on the gentle rise to Twyford he worked up to 64 m.p.h. again. The train was $5\frac{1}{4}$ min. late through Reading, and a further $1\frac{1}{2}$ min. were dropped to Savernake, despite a fine climb from Bedwyn, with a minimum

West of England express near Twyford, engine No. 4024 'King James'

Bristol express near Twyford: engine No. 4021 'King Edward'

of 44 m.p.h. On the falling gradients to Westbury time was soon recovered; a maximum of 83 m.p.h. was reached near Lavington, and the Westbury slip was detached less than 5 min. late. Even with the load reduced to 400 tons, the allowance of $22\frac{1}{2}$ min. for the 19.7 miles from Westbury to Castle Cary was not easy, including as it did the recovery from the slacks to 30 m.p.h. at Westbury and Frome, and the climb to milepost $122\frac{3}{4}$. On this stretch $\frac{1}{2}$ min. was dropped, but the recorder did not note the details of the climb. Between Castle Cary and Taunton the remaining lateness was wiped out. With the load reduced to 320 tons, there was no difficulty in reaching Exeter on time. For the passenger travelling to Exeter or beyond this was an excellently judged performance, but against this it must be noted that the Westbury passengers reached their destination 5 min. late, due nevertheless mainly to the signal check near Slough.

Many excellent runs must have escaped the attention of recorders, and the only record of them was in the guard's journal. Fortunately, on the publicity-minded GWR the details from the guards' journals of a number of notable runs were published from time to time, and the run tabulated herewith was revealed in this way. On 10 June 1916 the down 'Limited' loaded to 15 coaches from Paddington, and as the train was crammed with passengers the gross load must have been at least 535 tons. This was reduced by slipping at Westbury, Taunton and Exeter to about 435, 340 and 265 tons. Even if a variation of a minute either way is allowed in the guard's passing times, the performance remains outstanding. Four minutes were dropped to Reading, and a permanent-way slack between Reading and Newbury contributed to a further loss of $3\frac{1}{2}$ min. to Savernake; the Westbury

slip was detached $6\frac{1}{2}$ min. late. The running from Castle Cary to Taunton was slower than on the two previous runs described, but time recovery continued right to Exeter, a minute being recovered between Taunton and Whiteball and another minute by Exeter. The train was finally recorded as one minute early at Plymouth.

THE DOWN 'CORNISH RIVIERA EXPRESS'
Date: 10 June 1916
Engine: 4018 *Knight of the Grand Cross*
Load: To Westbury 15 cars, 494 tons tare, 535 tons full
To Taunton 12 cars, 402 tons tare, 435 tons full
To Exeter 9 cars, 314 tons tare, 340 tons full
To Plymouth 7 cars, 244 tons tare, 265 tons full

Dist. Miles		Sch. Min.	Actual Min.	Average speed m.p.h.
0·0	PADDINGTON .	0	0	
18·5	SLOUGH . .	20	$23\frac{1}{2}$	47·3
36·0	READING .	37	41	60·0
			p.w.s.	
53·1	NEWBURY .	56	62	48·8
70·1	Savernake . .	$73\frac{1}{2}$	81	53·7
95·6	WESTBURY .	$97\frac{1}{2}$	104	66·6
115·3	CASTLE CARY .	120	127	51·4
137·9	*Cogload Junction* .	144	$146\frac{1}{2}$	69·5
142·9	TAUNTON .	149	151	66·7
153·8	*Whiteball Box* .	$161\frac{1}{2}$	$162\frac{1}{2}$	56·9
173·7	EXETER . .	180	180	68·3
193·9	NEWTON ABB.	203	$202\frac{1}{2}$	53·8
202·5	Totnes . .	$215\frac{1}{2}$	$214\frac{1}{2}$	43·0
209·4	Brent . .	225	$227\frac{1}{2}$	31·9
225·7	PLYMOUTH .	247	246	52·9

The only run in the up direction with loading comparable to the down runs just described was recorded by Cecil J. Allen in the summer of 1913. The 3.27 p.m. from Exeter to Paddington loaded to 14 coaches, weighing 490 tons full, and with this load No. 4030 made a moderate run to Taunton, dropping $5\frac{1}{2}$ min., of which 3 min. could be debited to a bridge repair slack. At Taunton a further coach was added, so that the total load increased to 520 tons. The delays which resulted from the crush of passengers, and from the addition of the extra coaches both at Exeter and Taunton, made the train half an hour late from Taunton, and inevitably signal checks were encountered. Nevertheless the driver made a determined effort, and without the checks might just have kept the booked time of 154 min. for the 142.9 miles to Paddington. On the level beyond Athelney a speed of $63\frac{1}{2}$ m.p.h.

Down West of England express near Acton, engine No. 4035 'Queen Charlotte'

4.11 p.m. TAUNTON TO PADDINGTON
Date: 1913
Engine: 4030 *King Harold*
Load: 15 cars, 473 tons tare, 520 tons full

Dist. Miles		Sch. Min.	Actual m. s.		Speed m.p.h.
0·0	TAUNTON .	0	0	00	
5·0	*Cogload Junction* .		7	55	51/63½
17·2	Somerton .		21	05	48½
27·6	CASTLE CARY .		32	20	61½
34·4	*Milepost 122¾* .		41	40	30½/68
41·6	FROME . .		49	20	slack 67
47·3	WESTBURY .		56	20	slack 60
56·0	Lavington .		66	25	45 on 1 in 222
61·8	Patney . .		73	45	59
67·6	Pewsey . .		80	20	
72·8	Savernake .		86	25	48
	Bedwyn . .				71½
81·4	Hungerford .		94	15	74
89·8	NEWBURY .		101	30	
—	Thatcham .				70½
—	Aldermaston .				68
101·7	Theale . .		111	55	67
	Reading West .				long check
106·9	READING . .		119	20	severe check
111·9	Twyford . .		125	35	58
118·8	Maidenhead .		132	10	62½
	Taplow . .				64
124·4	SLOUGH . .		137	30	67
133·8	SOUTHALL .		146	35	62½
138·6	Acton . .		151	30	eased
142·9	PADDINGTON .	154	160	20	

Net time: 154 min.

was reached and sustained, and the fall from $61\frac{1}{2}$ m.p.h. at Castle Cary to $30\frac{1}{2}$ at milepost $122\frac{3}{4}$ was good with this load. But an even better effort was made from Westbury to Savernake. On the level before Lavington speed rose to 60, and on the 1 in 222 to Patney it fell to a steady 45 m.p.h., requiring about 1,200 drawbar horsepower. There was a recovery to 59 before Pewsey, and the minimum at Savernake was 48 m.p.h. The average speed over the $16\frac{3}{4}$ miles of uphill running from Lavington to Savernake was 50.3 m.p.h. This is one of the most

notable uphill efforts recorded by a 'Star' in pre-war years.

Between Savernake and Newbury speed ranged between 71 and 74 m.p.h., falling gradually to 68 to Theale, but with the train so much behind time it was not surprising that checks were encountered at Reading, costing about $2\frac{1}{2}$ min. After Reading there was a gradual recovery to 68 m.p.h. at Slough, and it was not until after Southall that the engine was eased. Final checks outside Paddington made the overall time 160 min. 20 sec., but the net time was about equal to the booking of 154 min.

In assessing the merits of the runs described in this chapter so far it must be noted that the trains were composed almost entirely of modern stock, whereas the trains hauled by saturated engines in the runs described in Chapter 3 consisted largely of older coaches, with a higher resistance per ton. Furthermore, a full assessment of a run requires a knowledge of the wind conditions, and these are not available in detail for the period up to and including the runs described in this chapter. On the assumption of a slight westerly wind, the runs by superheated engines in this chapter required a slightly smaller average horsepower than run No. 2 on page 38, which was noted to have been made against a strong south-west wind, and in which the train included some older stock.

Down express passing Old Oak Common engine No. 4026 'King Richard'

There are insufficient records of runs by 'Saints' on very heavy trains for a comparison to be made with the 'Stars', but A. V. Goodyear analysed a number of runs which he made between 1909 and 1913 to compare the uphill work of the two classes. An analysis of 18 up runs showed that for six trains hauled by 'Saints' the average time from milepost 88 to Savernake was 19 min. 40 sec., with an average load of 369 tons. For 12 trains hauled by 'Stars' the average time was 19 min. 32 sec. with an average load of 338 tons. This showed a slight advantage to the 'Saints'. The engines included saturated and superheated members of both classes. The best time was made by No. 4041, with 295 tons. The time over the 17.7 miles from milepost 88 to Savernake was 16 min. 51 sec., giving an average speed of 63.3 m.p.h. The initial speed on this stretch was 69, after six miles of 1 in 222 it fell to 59, and at Savernake was $59\frac{1}{2}$ m.p.h. The best performance by a saturated engine equalled this in merit, when allowance is made for the greater load. Goodyear was on the footplate of No. 4013 on 29 July 1909 with Driver Springthorpe, who drove *Polar Star* on the London & North Western, and whose work appears again in Chapter 6. The train was the 12.5 p.m. from Exeter with a load of 310 tons. The time for the climb was 17 min. 3 sec., giving an average of 61.6 m.p.h. Speed was $66\frac{1}{2}$ m.p.h. at milepost 88, fell to 55 on the 1 in 222, and rose to 63 at the summit.

The heaviest load worked by a 'Star' in this series was 455 tons behind No. 4002, by that time superheated. The time for the climb was 21 min. 40 sec., speed falling from 60 to 42 on the 1 in 222, and recovering to 48 m.p.h. at the summit. A similar comparison of 15 ascents from Exeter to Whiteball showed that eight 'Saints' took an average of 25 min. 41 sec. with 384 tons, and seven 'Stars' took an average of 25 min. 53 sec. with an average load of 360 tons.

A more detailed comparison of saturated engines of the 'Saint' and 'Star' classes is shown in the accompanying table. This shows the detailed times for two down runs between Frome and milepost $122\frac{3}{4}$. On the first run 'Saint' No. 2903 *Lady of Lyons* was hauling 360 tons, and on the second No. 4008 *Royal Star* had 350 tons. This second run is shown in full in column 1 on page 38. The times shown are from a point at Frome (evidently not the middle of the station, as the times to milepost 117 are insufficient). On both runs the trains had slowed to about 30 m.p.h. to observe the slack through the station. The 'Saint' made the more rapid recovery from the slack and the more rapid ascent. The average horsepower required between

Engine No. 4015 'Knight of St. John', as originally built in March 1908, standing in Paddington station

mileposts 117 and $122\frac{3}{4}$ was about 890 for No. 2903 and 760 for No. 4008. Too much importance should not be attached to these isolated runs, but as an experienced recorder had picked them out for detailed comparison he probably considered them representative of the two classes. They support the general impression which was formed by many observers of the superiority of the 'Saints' at starting and at hill climbing at moderate speeds.

By 1914 the 'Stars' were appearing on some of the Bristol 2-hour workings, and the accompanying table shows three runs on these trains. These were all behind superheated engines. On the first run No. 4005 encountered a signal check near the start, and was $2\frac{1}{2}$ min. down on schedule by Southall. The passing time of 11 min. to Southall

COMPARISON OF THE UPHILL WORK OF 'SAINT' AND 'STAR' CLASS LOCOMOTIVES ON THE CLIMB FROM FROME TO MILEPOST $122\frac{3}{4}$

The times shown are from an unspecified point in Frome station, which was passed at about 30 m.p.h. on both runs. The milepost distances are from Paddington via Chippenham. The average gradient is 1 in 310.

| Engine | | 2903 | | 4008 | |
| Load, tons | | 360 | | 350 | |
Location	m. s.		Speed m.p.h.	m. s.	Speed m.p.h.
FROME	0 00			0 00	
Milepost 117	1 59		$48\frac{1}{2}$	2 09	43
Milepost 118	3 10		50	3 27	46
Milepost 118½	3 43		$54\frac{1}{2}$	4 06	46
Milepost 119	4 16		$54\frac{1}{2}$	4 43	$48\frac{1}{2}$
Milepost 119½	4 49		$54\frac{1}{2}$	5 21	$47\frac{1}{2}$
Milepost 120	5 23		53	5 58	$48\frac{1}{2}$
Milepost 120½	5 55		56	6 35	$48\frac{1}{2}$
Milepost 121½	7 00		55	7 50	48
Milepost 122	7 32		56	8 28	$47\frac{1}{2}$
Milepost 122½	8 05		$54\frac{1}{2}$	9 08	45
Milepost 122¾	8 23		50	9 28	45

PADDINGTON TO BATH

Run No.			1		2		3
Date			1916		1915		1914
Train			11.5		11.5		11.0
Engine No.			4005		4019		4017
Engine Name			*Polar Star*		*Knight Templar*		*Knight of the Black Eagle*
Load: cars, tons, tare/full			11 358/380		13 398/420		— /505

Dist. Miles		Sch. Min.	Actual m. s.	Average Speed m.p.h.	Actual m. s.	Speed m.p.h.	Actual m. s.
0·0	PADDINGTON	0	0 00		0 00		0 00
—	Westbourne Park		sigs.				
—	Ealing				p.w.s.		
9·1	SOUTHALL	11	13 30		14 05		13 30
18·5	SLOUGH	20	22 24	63·4	23 15	69	23 00
24·2	Maidenhead		27 34	66·3			
31·0	Twyford		33 40	66·8			
36·0	READING	37	38 10	66·7	39 05	69	40 15
44·8	Goring		45 43	70·0	46 50	69	
53·1	DIDCOT	53½	53 00	68·3	54 20	64	57 00
60·4	Wantage Road		59 38	66·0	61 05	64/62½	
66·5	Uffington		65 22	63·7	66 55	64	
71·5	Shrivenham		70 06	64·5			
77·3	SWINDON	77	75 30	63·3	76 50	65	80 45
82·9	Wootton Bassett		80 46	63·9	82 05	66	
87·7	Dauntsey		84 45	72·1	86 15	76	
					sigs.		
94·0	CHIPPENHAM	93	89 41	76·5			95 15
98·3	Corsham		93 41	64·5			
101·9	Box		97 04	63·9			
102·0	*Milepost 102*						
104·6	Bathampton		99 29	67·0			105 00
106·9	BATH	105	101 53	57·5	108 15		107 45*

Maximum and minimum
speeds, run No. 1:
Uffington 63 m.p.h.
Dauntsey 82 ,,
Corsham 61 ,,
Box 69 ,,

* Arrival of slip portion,
schedule 107 min.

made an undue demand upon an engine at the beginning of a long run, before the fire was fully burned through, and it was normal to drop time on this section in the knowledge that it could be recovered later. Despite this check even time was attained by Didcot, and over the 53.1 miles from Maidenhead to Swindon the average was 66.5 m.p.h. The steady speed over the easier gradients to Didcot, followed by a gradual fall to Swindon, showed that the steaming rate remained steady during this period. By Swindon the train was 1½ min. early, and despite easier running from there onwards, the gain had increased to 3 min. by Bath. The overall time to Bristol was 116 min. 35 sec.

The second run, with a load of 420 tons, was only slightly slower, until spoiled by signal checks from Chippenham onwards. From Slough to Swindon the time was only 19 sec. slower than in the previous run, and the variation in speed was between 62½ and 69 m.p.h. The train evidently included some older coaches, so that the resistance would be slightly greater than the increase in weight alone would suggest.

The third run was made with a load of 505 tons, but the recorder did not note the composition, nor, unfortunately, did he record more than the barest details of the run. There is, however, sufficient evidence to show that it was a notable performance. The time of 40 min. 15 sec. to Reading was an improvement on the times recorded earlier in this chapter for West of England trains (which would, however, have slowed in anticipation of the slack for Reading West Junction). The average speed from Slough to Didcot was 61.2 m.p.h., which was good, but even better was the maintenance of the same average from Didcot to Swindon. The 97.7 miles from Southall to Bath were covered in 94¼ min., which was 1¾ min. under a scheduled time which had been laid down for loads of 100 tons less than on this run.

Engine No. 4004, 'Morning Star', as fitted with the forward-chimney smokebox in 1927. This photograph was taken at the same time as that on page 121, at Old Oak Common

On another run by the 11 a.m. down express, No. 4028 had a load of 530 tons. In the early stages the work was as good as that of No. 4017, the times to Southall and Slough being 13 min. 25 sec. and 23 min. 15 sec. Between Slough and Reading speed varied between 56 and 58 m.p.h. and reached a maximum of 60 at Tilehurst. From Slough onwards the times were greater than for No. 4017, and by Swindon the difference between the runs was 4 min. 10 sec. (84 min. 55 sec. from Paddington by No. 4028). On this day the train was booked to call at Bath, and as this would increase the steam consumption in the long gap between Goring troughs and Fox's Wood troughs, the driver was anxious to conserve water, and this was reflected in the easier running after Swindon. The time to the Bath stop was 115 min. 5 sec.

Records of up runs by 'Stars' on Bristol trains do not show any efforts comparable with those given above for down runs, but one run is interesting in pointing the way to the later schedule of the 'Bristolian'. A run by No. 4020 with 230 tons on the 12 noon from Bristol is tabulated. As far as Swindon the train observed the pre-1939 schedule of the 'Bristolian'. The load was the same as that of the 'Bristolian' in its early days, and the passing times as far as Didcot differ by no more than 9 sec. from those recorded on a typical unchecked 'Bristolian' run with the same load. After Swindon the running was less vigorous, although the speed of 75 m.p.h. at Wantage Road was unusual for the

period. Signal checks were encountered approaching Reading, and after a recovery to 72 m.p.h. at

	12 noon BRISTOL TO PADDINGTON			
	Date: 1911			
	Engine: 4020 *Knight Commander*			
	Load: 230 tons full			
Dist. Miles		Sch. Min.	Actual m. s.	Speed m.p.h.
0·0	BRISTOL . .	0	0 00	
4·8	Filton Junction .		8 45	
13·0	Chipping Sodbury		18 00	
17·6	Badminton . .		22 30	62 before tunnel
27·9	Little Somerford .		31 00	83
34·7	Wootton Bassett .		36 55	
40·3	SWINDON .		42 40	
51·1	Uffington . .		52 20	
57·2	Wantage Road .		57 30	75
64·5	DIDCOT . .		63 45	
72·9	Goring . .		71 00	
—			sigs. Reading West Junction	
81·6	READING .		79 30	
—	Taplow . .			72—eased
93·4	Maidenhead .		90 50	
99·1	SLOUGH .		95 45	
108·5	SOUTHALL .		103 45	
			sigs. Acton	
116·3	Westbourne Park .		114 00	sigs.
			sig. Royal Oak	
117·6	PADDINGTON .	120	117 30	

Net time 113 minutes.
Average speed, Chipping Sodbury to Badminton 61 m.p.h.
Average speed, Swindon to Didcot 69 m.p.h.

11.5 a.m. PADDINGTON TO BIRMINGHAM

Run No.				1		2	
Date				August 1915		pre-1914	
Engine				4048		4023	
Engine name				*Princess Victoria*		*King George*	
Load: cars, tons, tare/full							
To Leamington				12 348/370		14 /435	
To Birmingham				10 297/315		12 /375	

Dist. Miles		Sch. Min.	Actual m. s.	Speed m.p.h.	Actual m. s.	Speed m.p.h.
0·0	PADDINGTON	0	0 00		0 00	
3·3	*Old Oak Common West*	7	6 10	35	6 18	
7·8	Greenford	(11)	11 28	59	12 15	
10·3	*Northolt Junction*	15½	14 05	60		
14·1	*Milepost 3¾*				19 12	
14·8	Denham		18 30	60		
21·1	*Milepost 10¾*				28 00	45
21·7	Beaconsfield		26 15	51½	28 55	
26·5	HIGH WYCOMBE	32	slight sig.			
		(30)	31 20	35	33 55	slack
28·8	West Wycombe				37 12	
31·5	Saunderton		37 50	47		
33·0	*Milepost 22¾*			45	43 54	37
34·7	PRINCES RISBOROUGH	42	41 30	62	46 00	
		(40)				
40·1	Haddenham		45 40	82		
44·1	*Ashendon Junction*	(50)	48 12	slack	54 03	slack
50·4	Blackthorn		54 30	73		
51·6	*Milepost 7½*				61 13	
53·4	BICESTER	(60)	57 10	65	63 05	
57·1	*Milepost 13*				67 41	46
57·2	Ardley		61 14	51½		
62·4	*Aynho Junction*	69	66 25	60	73 15	
67·5	BANBURY	74	71 30	63½	78 25	
73·4	*Milepost 92*				84 52	
76·3	Fenny Compton		80 52	55/70½		
81·2	Southam Road		85 15	69/72½		
87·3	LEAMINGTON	93	90 50	40	98 05	
89·2	Warwick		93 00			
93·5	Hatton		99 58			35
100·2	Knowle		106 55		sigs.	
103·6	Solihull		110 25			
107·4	Tyseley		114 02			
				sig. 50		
109·5	Bordesley		116 50			
				p.w.s. 35		
110·6	BIRMINGHAM	120	119 05			

Net time 117½ min.

The schedule times in brackets apply to run No. 2, where different from run No. 1.

Taplow the engine was eased. Further signal checks from Acton onwards made the total time 117 min. 30 sec. but the net time, based on the standard of running displayed, was about 113 min. Had the energy of the early stages been maintained, a net time of 105 min. would have been possible, and 110 min. could have been attained easily.

Loads on the Birmingham 2-hour trains were at first light, and of many runs recorded on these trains by A. V. Goodyear, few had loads in excess of 300 tons south of Banbury. These loads were well within the capacity of the 'Stars' and 'Saints',

but interest in the running of up trains was heightened by the extensive improvements which were made to track layouts and stations in the Birmingham area in the years before 1914. Up trains often had the incentive of late starts caused by delays in the Birmingham area, whereas down trains booked to call at Leamington could not prepare for these delays by gaining time in the early stages of a run.

Two runs are tabulated relating to the 11.5 a.m. from Paddington. This train slipped coaches at Leamington, and the driver could therefore attempt

Up Torquay and Kingswear express on the sea wall near Teignmouth:
engine No. 4060 'Princess Eugenie'

to gain some time to allow for the slacks near Birmingham. On the first run No. 4048 was driven by Bill Brooks of Wolverhampton, one of the best enginemen of his day on this route. The load was 12 coaches, weighing 370 tons gross, and reduced to 10 coaches at Leamington. There was a steady gain of time all the way. The run was made in August 1915, and the passing times are those which applied at that date. The additional figures in brackets show where the booked times in force before 1914 (which apply to run No. 2) differ from those in force in 1915. It will be seen that the times to High Wycombe and Princes Risborough had each been eased by 2 min., and the times made by No. 4048 show the wisdom of this change. On a run on which the driver was clearly making a continual effort to gain time, he failed to observe the old passing times, although he was well within the new ones. Of the GWR routes from London, the Birmingham road is the least amenable to uniform steaming. If a driver had time in hand, it would pay him not to force his engine on the principal gradients, as each of them was followed by a downhill stretch on which high speeds were possible. On this run the minima at the summits were not abnormally high, but there was fast run-

ning on the easier stretches. A fast start gave a gain of $1\frac{1}{2}$ min. to Northolt Junction, but this had been reduced to 40 sec. by High Wycombe as a result of a slight check approaching that station. Exact time was kept from High Wycombe to Princes Risborough, with a minimum of 45 m.p.h. at Saunderton. Fast running to Bicester, and a good climb to Ardley, brought the train $2\frac{1}{2}$ min. ahead of schedule, and this gain was maintained until reduced by a signal check to 50 m.p.h. near Bordesley, and a permanent-way slack to 35 m.p.h. after that station. Snow Hill was reached 1 min. early, and the net time was $117\frac{1}{2}$ min.

The second run was made with two additional coaches, giving a gross load of 435 tons from Paddington. With this load timekeeping proved impossible, and the impression is given that 400 tons was about the limit for timekeeping in all weathers. On this run there was a side wind, and it is just possible that without it time might have been kept. The minima at the various summits compare favourably with the previous run. Lateness reached a maximum of 6 min. at Princes Risborough and had been reduced to 3 min. at Bicester, the average from Princes Risborough to Bicester being 65.6 m.p.h. Signals were encountered so severely from Knowle onwards that the recorder did not note the remainder of the times.

The last table shows a run on the 2.5 p.m. 2-hour train from Birmingham to Paddington. This train attached a coach at Leamington and slipped others at Banbury. On 29 May 1914 it had 13 coaches from Birmingham, a gross load of 370 tons, increased to 400 tons by the addition of a coach at Leamington, and reduced to 300 tons by the slipping of four coaches at Banbury. Severe signal checks had delayed the train between Hatton and Leamington, so Driver Moore had every encouragement to gain time. On the 1 in 187 past Fosse Road a steady speed of 44 m.p.h. was maintained, increasing to 58 in the dip before Fenny Compton, and falling only to 54 m.p.h. at the summit beyond that station. Speed reached 73 m.p.h. below Cropredy, and the time of 24 min. 16 sec. to Banbury was good with this load. A further rise to 78 m.p.h. by King's Sutton gave useful momentum for the climb to Ardley, on which the minimum was 53 m.p.h. The average from Bicester to Princes Risborough was 68½ m.p.h., with a maximum of 80. A further fast sprint from Beaconsfield gave a maximum of 82 m.p.h., and the train made even time by Northolt. Despite signal checks at Royal Oak, including a stop for ¼ min., the train gained 28 sec. on the schedule of 91 min. from Leamington, but the net time was only 88½ min. for 87.3 miles.

At this stage a pause can be made to reflect upon the results achieved so far, in the great development work on the four-cylinder simple engines of Swindon design, pioneered by Churchward. The close of the year 1916 rang down the curtain upon the first phase of high-speed express running. The development of the design had taken seven years, in moving from the 'Atlantic' No. 40 to the first of the 15 in. engines, No. 4041. Runs like those of *Prince John* and *Knight of the Grand Cross* on the down Limited showed clearly the potentialities of

these engines; but the loadings were exceptional, and everyday demands were not so severe. No 'Star' had yet produced a dynamometer-car record of power output to equal, let alone surpass the maximum achieved up to that time at Crewe. But the quality was there, and what was more, the design was capable of very considerable enlargement. Four lean years were nevertheless to follow before the 'Stars' began really to sparkle once again.

2.34 p.m. LEAMINGTON TO PADDINGTON
Date: 29/5/14
Engine: 4036 *Queen Elizabeth*
Load: cars, tons, tare/full To Leamington 13 349/370
To Banbury 14 378/400
To Paddington 10 276/300
Driver: Moore
Weather: Wet

Dist. Miles		Sch. Min.	Actual m. s.	Speed m.p.h.
0·0	LEAMINGTON	0	0 00	
—				44 steady
6·1	Southam Road .		10 15	48/58
11·0	Fenny Compton		15 56	54
16·2	Cropredy . .		21 20	71
19·8	BANBURY		24 16	73/78
24·9	*Aynho Junction* .		28 25	
30·1	Ardley . .		33 30	53 min.
33·9	BICESTER .		36 48	80
36·9	Blackthorn .		39 02	
39·9	Brill . . .		41 25	70
43·2	*Ashendon Junction*		44 25	60 slack
47·2	Haddenham .		48 11	68/60
52·6	PRINCES RISBOROUGH		53 12	62
55·1	*Milepost 22* .		55 53	52
58·5	West Wycombe .		59 12	
60·8	HIGH WYCOMBE		61 55	slack
65·6	Beaconsfield .		67 28	56
69·9	Gerrards Cross .		71 18	77
72·5	Denham . .		73 15	82
77·0	*Northolt Junction* .		76 40	78
79·5	Greenford . .		78 38	78
84·0	*Old Oak Common West Junction* .		83 10	
—	Royal Oak . .		signal stop	¼ min.
87·3	PADDINGTON .	91	90 32	

Net time 88½ min.

Up Torquay express, running on the relief line at Twyford East:
engine No. 4019 'Knight Templar'

E

CHAPTER 6

AUSTERITY AND RESURGENCE

THE first two years of the war brought little change in locomotive practice or train working on the GWR. There were less extra trains at peak periods, with consequent overloading of regular trains, but the 'Stars' had already shown their ability to work trains of 450-500 tons on existing schedules. From January 1917 austerity set in; restaurant cars were withdrawn and schedules eased. At Swindon there were signs of austerity also. Copper caps on chimneys were painted over, safety-valve bonnets were painted green, and all lining was omitted. In 1915 Swindon had adopted a sandy shade of khaki for the upper parts of engines, but this was replaced in 1917 with unvarnished green. The brass beading was removed from the edges of splashers of the 'Stars', never to be replaced except on engines which were rebuilt as 'Castles'. New chimneys were made with steel caps. There was a plan to fit all engines with plain cast-iron chimneys, but these never appeared on the 'Stars'. Instead, in common

A wartime holiday express leaving Paddington, for Falmouth and Newquay: engine No. 4060 'Princess Eugenie'

Engine No. 4061 'Glastonbury Abbey' as built at Swindon, 1922

with other ten-wheeled passenger engines, they were fitted for a time with smaller chimneys reminiscent of the Dean type.

In 1919 a tapered cast-iron chimney was introduced for use on all types except some small tank engines, and these were duly fitted to 20 'Stars' in the period 1919-24.★ With the introduction of the 'Castles', the fitting of copper caps to chimneys was renewed, and in due course all the 'Stars' again received chimneys of this type.

In 1920, No. 4060 appeared with an experimental smokebox, with the chimney further forward than usual. The aim of this experiment was to get a more uniform distribution of draught over the tubes, but it produced no apparent difference. The boiler was removed from 4060 in 1923, and appeared on 4043 in 1925 and on 4004 in 1927, after which it disappeared. A further sign of austerity introduced during World War I and continued afterwards was the use of snap-head rivets, of which the head is visible, in place of countersunk rivets, which cannot be seen when properly painted. Snap-head rivets are stronger and cheaper, and can be removed much more easily. They were used on smokeboxes, cabs, and tenders, where previously countersunk rivets had been used.

On 1 January 1922, Mr. Churchward was succeeded as Chief Mechanical Engineer by C. B. Collett, who had been Deputy CME since 1919. The title of the office had been changed from Locomotive Carriage and Wagon Superintendent in 1916. Unlike the arrival of a new C.M.E. on some railways, Collett's succession made little change in locomotive practice on the GWR and Churchward can have had nothing but satisfaction at seeing his work continued so ably by his successor.

At the time of Churchward's retirement there

★Nos. 4000/1/8/10/3/7/8/21/2/4/8/35/8/44/7/51/4/5/ 7/60

were already on order twelve more 'Stars', Nos. 4061-72. These appeared between May 1922 and February 1923. Although they were ordered under the same 'Lot' number, there was a gap of six months between the second and third engines of the batch. Externally they showed all the signs of post-war austerity—cast-iron chimneys, no beading or lining, and snap-head rivets. Internally they had a small change in that the crank axles had the webs extended on the opposite side of the crank to form balance weights for the rotating parts of that axle. The crank pins were of heat-treated steel, and it was soon found that the heat treatment did not penetrate to the centre of the crank pin. The crank pins were therefore drilled hollow to give better penetration of the heat treatment. The series were named after Abbeys as follows:

THE 'ABBEY' SERIES

No.	Name
4061	*Glastonbury Abbey*
4062	*Malmesbury Abbey*
4063	*Bath Abbey*
4064	*Reading Abbey*
4065	*Evesham Abbey*
4066	*Malvern Abbey*
4067	*Tintern Abbey*
4068	*Llanthony Abbey*
4069	*Margam Abbey*★
4070	*Neath Abbey*
4071	*Cleeve Abbey*
4072	*Tresco Abbey*

★ Renamed *Westminster Abbey* in 1923

Nos. 4061/2/7-72 had I-section coupling rods. Lining-out of 'Stars' began again in 1923. Nos. 4021 and 4038 retained cast-iron chimneys for a time after receiving lining, but otherwise copper-capped chimneys were restored with the new livery.

A scene near the end of the austerity period: engine No. 4018 'Knight of the Grand Cross' in plain green, but with most of the coaches in chocolate and cream

The GWR had for long prided itself in its braking system, and a characteristic of all the Churchward locomotives was the fitting of brakes to the bogie wheels. This contributed to the high figure of 70 per cent of the total weight available for braking. The vacuum brake cylinder for the bogie was originally 11 in. in diameter, but this was later increased to 13 in. to allow of a redesign of the brake levers. With the smaller cylinders the leverage was so great that very little wear of the blocks was needed to bring the brake piston to the end of its travel. With the larger cylinders, a smaller leverage sufficed, and more wear could be allowed before adjustments to the brake rigging were needed. Despite this improvement, bogie brakes

remained a doubtful asset, causing more trouble than they were worth. Churchward, however, would not agree to their removal, but shortly after Collett's succession their use was discontinued. Tests were made with and without the bogie brake in use, and no perceptible difference in braking was found. From November 1923 they were gradually removed from all engines. Small footsteps were then fitted to the bogie frames to assist drivers in oiling the inside motion.

Nos. 4000/3/6 were reported as fitted with automatic train control in 1908 when the system was installed on the main line between Reading and Slough. From 1923 the apparatus was fitted generally to the class.

Engine No. 4063 'Bath Abbey', as built

Engine No. 4070 'Neath Abbey' on Birmingham express at Kensal Green

Boiler changes were made between the various classes carrying the No. 1 standard boiler, and this resulted in 'half-cone' boilers appearing on a total of 24 'Stars' at various times between 1909 and 1921. These boilers had originally been fitted to 'Saints', but were in due course modernised with superheaters and top-feed. All the 'Stars' were built with 'long-cone' boilers. From 1925 to 1927, with pre-war lining restored, and all boiler and other modifications incorporated, the appearance of the class was fairly uniform, but in 1927 further external modifications began to appear. During this period the fitting of whistle shields began. These were inclined plates between the whistle and the cab to discourage steam from the whistle from drifting across the cab windows. In 1927 variations of tender also began to appear, and boilers with the more modern short safety valve bonnets were fitted. These bonnets were first required when one of the Frenchmen was fitted with a Great Western boiler, and they were also used on *The Great Bear* and the 47XX 2—8—0s. After the first 'Castles' had been fitted with them, they came into general use. There were two variants, one being intermediate in height between the original and final forms.

Experience with the 'Castles' soon showed that the cost of maintenance was less than that of 'Stars' employed on similar work (the difference was later estimated at one penny per mile). The reason for this was that on the heaviest work the 'Star' boilers were steamed very hard, whereas the 'Castle' boilers were less extended at the same steam rate. The 'Castle' boilers therefore suffered less wear than those of the 'Stars'. It was therefore decided to rebuild a number of 'Stars' into 'Castles', and in 1925-6 four engines which were in need of new cylinders were converted. The work was financed out of the annual allocation for repairs, and Lot numbers were not therefore issued, nor did the conversions appear in the list of withdrawals from, or additions to, stock. The rate of rebuilding was determined partly by the rate at which 'Castle' boilers became available, and few of them could be spared. By 1927, with sufficient 'Castles' and 'Kings' now available to cover the heaviest duties, there was less case for the conversions.

The first renaming of a 'Star' was made necessary by the outbreak of World War I in August 1914. No. 4017 had been *Knight of the Black Eagle*, but it was renamed *Knight of Liège*. The accent on the 'e' of Liège was later altered from grave to acute, and this apparent correction led, according to *Locomotives of the GWR*, to 'a great deal of unexpected and rather erudite correspondence, with the resultant conclusion that whereas the grave

No. 4026 'King Richard', on down 2-hour Bristol express, near Old Oak Common

accent is correct in French, the acute accent is correct in Belgium for certain words of Flemish origin with a different shade of pronunciation'. The accent remained acute. Fortunately subsequent re-namings of 'Stars' were not attended by such complications. In 1927, when the 'King' class appeared, Nos. 4021-30 were renamed after monarchs, in the form *The British Monarch*. A few months later the names were again altered by the omission of 'The' (*Italian Monarch* was renamed later than the others and missed the intermediate stage). There were a few other changes of name, which will be listed in the tables in Part 2.

From the time of the deceleration of the main-line trains in 1917 until 1921 there was little of note in GWR locomotive performance. On occasional runs in which time was recovered there was some vestige of pre-war standards, but those standards had been so high that nothing short of the restoration of pre-war schedules could revive them. This revival came sooner than many people had

No. 4054 'Princess Charlotte' on the Birkenhead – Bournemouth express (LSWR stock)

expected. Marked accelerations were planned for the summer services of 1921, but these had to be postponed for two months because of labour troubles in the coal industry. Despite this setback further accelerations followed in October 1921, when full pre-war speeds were restored on the principal main-line services of the GWR. It was soon clear that Swindon had done its work well, for the deterioration in the condition of the engines during the war had been made good, and the 'Stars' were ready to perform even better work than before 1917. This was timely, for it was soon apparent that loads of 500 tons were to become more common on West of England trains.

Cecil J. Allen travelled from Paddington to Penzance and back on the 'Cornish Riviera Express' soon after the restoration of the old schedule. On the down journey, J. Springthorpe was driving No. 4003, *Lode Star*, with loads of 406/425 tons to Westbury, 341/355 tons to Taunton, 282/295 tons to Exeter, and 249/260 tons to Plymouth. Four permanent-way slacks were in force, and a rather slow recovery from one of them caused the engine to lose 1 min. 50 sec. to Westbury. From there Springthorpe made a determined recovery, and by Plymouth had gained $12\frac{1}{2}$ min. in actual running time, and $16\frac{3}{4}$ min. net. Deducting the loss by the engine before Westbury left a clear gain to the engine of 15 min. From Brewham to Exeter the average speed was 68.9 m.p.h., and 113.2 miles from Brewham to Plympton were covered in 111 min. 50 sec.

The accompanying table shows three runs on down West of England expresses, the first two on the 'Cornish Riviera Express' and the third on the 12 noon from Paddington. On the first run, No. 4018 with 460 tons made a good start, dropping only $1\frac{1}{2}$ min. on the optimistic allowance of 11 min. to Southall. Speed reached 61 m.p.h., but then came the first of four signal checks. This reduced speed to 42 m.p.h., but there was a recovery to 68 by Twyford. The second check came at Reading and the third approaching Patney. Up the Kennet Valley speed ranged between 57 and 60 m.p.h., and the minimum at Savernake was 45 m.p.h. After the Patney check there was a quick recovery to 74 m.p.h., and despite the checks the train passed Westbury only $2\frac{1}{4}$ min. late. With the load reduced to 385 tons there was now some fast running. The fall from $51\frac{1}{2}$ to $47\frac{1}{2}$ on the climb to milepost $122\frac{3}{4}$ was good, and the allowance of 28 min. from Castle Cary to Taunton was cut to $23\frac{1}{2}$ min., with a maximum of 74 m.p.h. A signal check to 45 after Taunton hindered the climb to Whiteball. There was a permanent-way slack near the summit, but

this had little effect as speed had already fallen almost to the required 30 m.p.h. Exeter was passed a minute early in $174\frac{1}{2}$ min. net.

On the second run No. 4020 had a load of 485 tons from Paddington, and dropped $2\frac{3}{4}$ min. to Reading, partly because of a slow start. A permanent-way slack at Southcote Junction spurred Driver Cresswell to greater efforts, and the allowance of $41\frac{1}{2}$ min. from Newbury to Westbury was cut to 40 min. 12 sec., with an unusual maximum of $85\frac{1}{2}$ m.p.h. at Lavington. Despite a further permanent-way slack between Westbury and Frome, recovery of time continued, and the train was almost on time at Cogload Junction. Unfortunately Cogload troughs were under repair, and in addition to the permanent-way slack for this work, a stop was needed at Taunton for water. This cost fully 8 min., and a brisk run brought the train to Exeter $7\frac{3}{4}$ min. late, but in a net time of 176 min. Beyond Exeter, with the load reduced to 260 tons, there was more fast running; the allowance of 68 min. for the last 52 miles of the journey was cut to $59\frac{1}{4}$ min., and the train reached Plymouth a minute early.

The third run was made on the last Friday before the introduction of the summer service in 1925. The full load of thirteen 70-foot coaches was taken through to Exeter. This run may be compared with the one shown on page 56, in which a load of 470 tons was taken through to Exeter on an unchecked run. The difficulties which developed in run No. 3 of the accompanying table make the performance even more meritorious. In the early stages the run was normal for the load, 2 min. being dropped to Reading. A permanent-way slack at Kintbury was followed by a signal stop at Hungerford. A vigorous start from Hungerford brought speed to 48 m.p.h. at Bedwyn, and it fell only to 41 at the summit, where the train was $10\frac{3}{4}$ min. late. After Westbury the run was of greater interest, as the load was above normal for this part of the route. Another hard acceleration gave a maximum of 55 m.p.h. between Westbury and Frome, and the fall from $50\frac{1}{2}$ to $44\frac{1}{2}$ m.p.h. on Brewham bank was very good.

The allowance of $22\frac{1}{2}$ min. from Westbury to Castle Cary was tight, including as it did the climb to Brewham, for which little momentum could be attained. To observe this allowance with 500 tons of train was notable. Fast running from Castle Cary to Taunton recovered a further minute, despite a permanent-way slack at Keinton Mandeville. With this load the driver would have been fully justified in stopping at Taunton for a banker, but given a clear road through Taunton he proceeded without

PADDINGTON TO EXETER

Run No.			1		2		3	
Train			10.30 a.m.		10.30 a.m.		12 noon	
Date			—		—		7/25	
Engine			4018		4020		4042	
Engine name			*Knight of the Grand Cross*		*Knight Commander*		*Prince Albert*	
Load: cars, tons, tare/full								
To Westbury			— 429/460		— 459/485		13 469/500	
To Taunton			— 359/385		— 387/410		13 469/500	
To Exeter			— 359/385		— 324/345		13 469/500	
Driver			—		Cresswell		Perry	

Dist. Miles		Sch. Min.	Actual m. s.	Speed m.p.h.	Actual m. s.	Speed m.p.h.	Actual m. s.	Speed m.p.h.
0·0	PADDINGTON	0	0 00		0 00		0 00	
1·3	Westbourne Park		3 04		3 22		3 05	
5·7	Ealing		9 02		9 53	51½	9 20	50
9·1	Southall	11	12 38	61	13 51	56	13 10	55
			sig.	42				
18·5	SLOUGH	20	22 30	56	22 58	66½	22 25	65
24·2	Maidenhead		28 18	65	28 15	65	27 45	63½
31·0	Twyford		34 35	68	34 30	64	34 15	61½
36·0	READING	37	38 55	slack	39 43	slack	39 05	slack 45
			sig.	20	p.w.s.			
37·9	*Southcote Junction*		41 54		43 47		41 40	
46·7	Midgham		51 51	59	54 02	56	51 00	59
53·1	NEWBURY	56	58 17	60	60 38	58	57 50	56
							p.w.s.	
61·5	Hungerford		66 44	57	69 30	53	69 00	signal
							70 05	stop
66·4	Bedwyn		71 46	57½	74 50	58	79 15	48
70·1	Savernake	73½	76 05	45	79 06	43	84 15	41
75·3	Pewsey		81 18	65½			89 45	69/64½
			sig.					
81·1	Patney			45	89 28		94 55	68
86·9	Lavington		92 10	74	93 51	85½	99 40	80½
91·4	Edington		95 55	70½	97 09		103 10	74
95·6	WESTBURY	97½	99 50	slack 30	100 50	slack 30	107 00	slack 30
				54½	p.w.s.			55
101·3	FROME		106 48	slack 30	108 07	slack 30	114 00	slack 30
			Blatchbridge	51½		50½		50½
108·5	*Milepost 122¾*		115 53	47½/72½	117 22	47½	123 15	44½/75
115·3	CASTLE CARY	120	121 30	65/74	123 28		129 25	69
							p.w.s.	
125·7	Somerton		130 22		132 23		140 30	
137·9	*Cogload Junction*	143	141 15	slack 55	143 21		151 55	60/62½
				65	p.w.s.			
142·9	TAUNTON	148	146 00	60	151 16	water	156 50	55½/57½
			sig.	45	154 06	stop		
150·0	Wellington		153 42	46	163 48	50½	164 55	47½
			p.w.s.					
153·8	*Whiteball Box*		160 08	30	169 41	32	171 45	25½
158·8	Tiverton Junction		165 15	73½	174 28		176 55	74
170·2	Stoke Canon		174 48	72	183 45		186 05	76½
173·7	EXETER	179	177 55	pass	186 44	pass	190 10	stop
	Net time, min.:		174½		176		180	

assistance. Speed was only 55½ m.p.h. at that station, so that it required complete confidence in his engine for the driver to tackle the climb of 11 miles with a train so much in excess of what the regulations required. The last quarter of a mile before Whiteball tunnel was covered at 30 m.p.h.

to the accompaniment of a truly thunderous exhaust as I vividly recall, having timed the run. In the last mile speed fell to 25½ m.p.h., and the engine then made the fastest time on any of the three runs from Tiverton Junction to Stoke Canon. The net time was just the three hours allowed to

*No. 4034 'Queen Adelaide' on up Cornish Riviera
Express near Reading*

Exeter. From the Hungerford stop to Exeter the net time was 117½ min., giving an average speed of 57 m.p.h., which with this load was outstanding, even by 'Star' standards. It is also notable that the run was made two years after the introduction of the 'Castles', when the driver might reasonably have felt that he was entitled to have one of the larger engines for such an assignment.

The working of up trains at this period is well illustrated by the run of the 6.28 p.m. from Taunton to Paddington which is shown in a second table; this also I clocked personally. The further addition of three coaches at Taunton to a 13-coach train brought the total load to 550 tons, reduced to 515 tons at Newbury by the slipping of a coach. This is the heaviest load behind a 'Star' of which records have remained, and the work was of the highest standard. A signal stop shortly after leaving Taunton would have discouraged many drivers, but not Walter Springthorpe, a son of James Springthorpe, who drove *Polar Star* on the London & North Western in 1910. At the first timing point, Cogload Junction, the train was 6 min. down on

*No. 4016 'Knight of the Golden Fleece',
in plain green livery*

6.28 p.m. TAUNTON TO PADDINGTON

Date: July 1925
Engine: 4026 *King Richard*
Load: To Newbury   16 cars, 514 tons tare, 550 tons full
To Paddington   15 cars, 480 tons tare, 515 tons full
Driver: W. Springthorpe (Old Oak Common)
Weather: Hot and still

Dist. Miles		Sch. Min.	Actual m. s.	Speeds m.p.h.
0·0	TAUNTON .	0	0 00	
—			sig. stop	
2·4	*Creech Junction* .		7 40	
5·0	*Cogload Junction* .	6	11 00	50
8·0	Athelney .		14 15	58½
11·9	*Curry Rivel Junc.* .		18 15	61
15·0	Long Sutton .		21 40	50
17·2	Somerton .		24 15	48
				58½
20·5	Charlton Mackerell .		27 45	55
22·7	Keinton Mandeville .		30 05	60
25·5	Alford Halt. .		32 45	64½
27·6	CASTLE CARY .	30	34 45	58½
31·1	Bruton .		38 35	45
34·4	*Milepost 122¾* .		44 40	24
36·3	Witham .		47 05	66
41·6	Frome .		52 30	slack
—	*Fairwood Troughs* .	.		62½
47·3	WESTBURY .	53	59 40	slack
51·5	Edington .		65 00	53
56·0	Lavington .		69 35	61½
—	*Milepost 82* .			48
61·8	Patney .		76 20	
67·6	Pewsey .		82 35	60
72·8	Savernake .		88 10	53
76·5	Bedwyn .	82	91 50	66
81·4	Hungerford .		96 00	72½
84·4	Kintbury .		98 30	75
89·8	NEWBURY (Slip Coach) .	94	102 55	74
93·3	Thatcham .		105 50	72½
96·2	Midgham .		108 15	72
98·1	Aldermaston .		109 50	72
101·7	Theale .		112 50	72
105·0	*Southcote Junction* .		115 55	
106·9	READING .	112	118 20	40
108·8	*Sonning Box* .		120 45	50
111·9	Twyford .	117	124 15	57
118·7	Maidenhead .	124	130 45	65
121·9	Burnham Beeches .		133 40	68
124·4	SLOUGH .	130	135 50	69½
126·7	Langley .		137 50	68
129·7	West Drayton .		140 30	67
133·8	SOUTHALL .	140	144 25	62½
137·2	Ealing .		147 35	64½
138·6	Acton .		148 55	
—			sig.	
141·6	Westbourne Park .		154 40	
—			sigs.	
142·9	PADDINGTON. .	152	158 00	

Net time, 152 min.

booked running time. A further 5 min. was dropped on the uphill stretches, but on the downhill and level sections 6½ min. were recovered, so that by Southall the engine had made a net gain of 1½ min. from Cogload. But for signal checks in the later stages of the run the recovery would have been greater. The net time just equalled the booked

The Torbay Express near Twyford: engine No. 4070 'Neath Abbey', fully lined out and with large chimney

time of 152 min. The most notable uphill work was from Lavington to Savernake. The speed of 61½ m.p.h. on the level at Lavington was good with a load of 550 tons, and the 1 in 222 to Patney brought it down only to 48. There was a good recovery to 60 m.p.h. at Pewsey, and Savernake was passed at 53. After Savernake there was no restraint. A speed of 72 to 75 m.p.h. down the Kennet Valley was followed by a steady acceleration from the Reading slack, culminating in the surprising maximum, with this load, of 69½ m.p.h. at Slough. This run, like the third one in the table on page 71, was made two years after the introduction of the 'Castles', and would have been a highly creditable performance for a 'Castle'. Indeed less than a fortnight later one of the new engines, with nearly 100 tons *less* load, barely kept time on this same train.

On another journey of the down 'Limited',

recorded only in the guard's journal, No. 4042 had loads, on the four sections of the journey, of 525, 450, 385 and 310 tons full, and was at no point in the journey more than 2½ min. behind booked passing time. The journey ended 3 min. early at Plymouth. With lighter loads there was some fast running on the 'Limited'. On an up run No. 4008, with 370 tons, converted a lateness of nearly 8 min. at Savernake into an arrival at Paddington 2 min. early, covering 70.1 miles in 61 min. 16 sec.; 36.0 miles from Reading to Paddington occupied 32 min. 43 sec. On another run No. 4060, also with 370 tons, having been stopped by signals at Reading, passed Southall at 71½ m.p.h., and ran from Ealing to milepost 4 at 75 m.p.h. These runs are a great tribute not only to the engines and those who maintained them, but also to the enginemen, who made such determined efforts to keep time with loads with which they could justifiably have

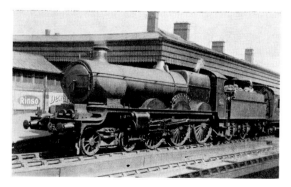

No. 4031 'Queen Mary' at Shrewsbury

French compound No. 104 in final condition with standard No. 1 boiler, at Oxford September 1927

dropped several minutes. It must not, however, be inferred that all heavy loads were handled with such competence by the 'Stars', for it is only fair to note that observers did from time to time express disappointment at the running of West of England trains. But this disappointment came only from the knowledge of what had been achieved on runs such as those described above.

The Paddington to Birmingham expresses were almost certainly documented more thoroughly than any other British services in the inter-war years. The considerable collection of logs by A. V. Goodyear and his friends were sufficient to give an excellent picture of the work of the 'Stars', 'Castles' and 'Kings', but it was overshadowed by the massive contribution of G. P. Antrobus, who logged

1,412 runs on the 6.10 p.m. from Paddington alone, mostly behind 'Kings'. As has been mentioned several times above, the Birmingham trains rarely taxed the 'Stars' before World War I; but after the restoration of the 2-hour schedules in 1921 the traffic grew rapidly, and within ten years the workings fully justified the use of 'Kings'.

Although a single journey on a Birmingham train was only half the length of the West of England workings to Plymouth, the task of the enginemen was no easier. There was less opportunity for the recovery of lost time, and the combination of more frequent changes of gradient and numerous speed restrictions made an intimate knowledge of the road essential if no time was to be lost. The majority of the trains on the service were worked by Stafford

6.10 p.m. PADDINGTON TO BIRMINGHAM

Run No.		1	2	3	
Date		1928	4/10/24	1925	
Engine No.		4071	4050	4067	
Engine name		*Cleeve Abbey*	*Princess Alice*	*Tintern Abbey*	
Load: cars, tons, tare/full					
To Bicester		— 353/385	13 396/425	11 340/365	
To Banbury		— 353/385	12 367/390	10 313/335	
To Leamington		— 353/385	11 334/355	9 285/305	
Driver		—	W. Brooks	J. Williams	
Weather		fine	calm	—	

Dist. Miles		Sch. Min.	Actual m. s.	Actual m. s.	Actual m. s.	Speed m.p.h.
0·0	PADDINGTON	0	0 00	0 00	0 00	
3·3	*Old Oak West Junction*		6 05	6 08	6 45	slack 25
					p.w.s.	
7·8	Greenford		11 40	11 33	15 00	30
			p.w.s.		sig.	
10·3	Northolt	15½	14 40	14 10	19 35	
14·8	Denham		19 30	18 32	24 50	61½
17·4	Gerrards Cross		22 25	21 15	27 30	
21·7	Beaconsfield		27 20	25 58	31 50	58½/79
26·5	HIGH WYCOMBE	32	32 05	31 00	36 05	slack 35
31·5	Saunderton		38 30	37 10	42 30	55
34·7	PRINCES RISBOROUGH	41	42 10	40 48	45 40	74
40·1	Haddenham		46 20	45 15	49 30	90
44·1	*Ashendon Junction*	49	49 25	48 39	52 25	slack
47·4	Brill		52 45	52 05	55 25	64
50·4	Blackthorn		55 15	54 38	57 50	80½
53·4	BICESTER	58	57 50	57 10	61 10	
57·2	Ardley		61 55	60 58	6 45	48½
62·4	*Aynho Junction*	67	66 50	65 49	11 40	slack 62
67·5	BANBURY	72	71 45	70 32	17 20	
71·1	Cropredy		75 10	73 55	5 40	
			p.w.s.	sig.		
76·3	Fenny Compton		80 40	80 22	10 30	
81·2	Southam Road		85 05	84 51	14 10	82/92
				sig.		
87·3	LEAMINGTON	91	90 30	91 38	19 40	
Net times, minutes:			89½	89½	83	
Average speeds:						
Gerrards Cross—Beaconsfield			52·5	54·8	59·6	
Haddenham—Ashendon Junction			77·8	70·7	82·3	

Road engines and men, and the engines normally made a return trip between Wolverhampton and Paddington without re-coaling; this limited the coal consumption to about 50 lb. per mile. Under normal conditions of loading and of weather this was ample, but when loads were heavy or the wind adverse there was little to spare.

A further table shows the logs of three runs on the 6.10 p.m. from Paddington. On each run the net time from Paddington to Leamington was less than the allowance of 91 min. The runs were timed by myself, A. V. Goodyear and Cecil J. Allen respectively.

Run No. 1 was recorded at a holiday period, when the train was divided, and the full load of 385 tons was taken through to Birmingham. After a permanent-way slack near Greenford, speed recovered to 61½ m.p.h. at Denham, and fell to 50 at Gerrards Cross. After a minimum of 44 m.p.h. at Saunderton there was some fast running, with speeds of 85 m.p.h. at Haddenham, 75 at Blackthorn, 51 at Ardley, and 69 before Aynho. Despite a further permanent-way slack between Cropredy and Fenny Compton the arrival at Leamington was ½ min. early.

On the second run No. 4050 was driven by W. Brooks, and slip portions were detached at Bicester and Banbury. The load from Paddington was 13 cars totalling 425 tons, reduced by one coach each at Bicester and Banbury. The climb to Beaconsfield was excellent, with an average of 54.8 m.p.h. from Gerrards Cross to Beaconsfield. Downhill speeds were not unusually high, but with a load of 390 tons the climb to Ardley was also very good, the average speed over the last 4 miles being 60 m.p.h. Signals before Leamington made the arrival ½ min. late, but the net time was 89½ min. On another run with No. 4034 on 14 coaches weighing 440 tons full, reduced to 410 and 350 tons at Bicester and Banbury, Driver A. Taylor made a net time of 89 min., but his average speeds on the uphill stretches were lower than in the run just described—48.7

No. 4025, when named 'Italian Monarch', at Shrewsbury

m.p.h. from Gerrards Cross to Beaconsfield and 55.0 on Bicester bank. The improvement on run No. 2 of the table came from higher downhill speeds.

Run No. 3 was probably the fastest ever recorded on this route with a train of more than 300 tons; the loads on the three sections were 365, 335 and 305 tons. No slip coaches had been provided in the rake, and stops were therefore needed at Bicester and Banbury. The engine was No. 4067 and the driver J. Williams. A very severe permanent-way slack at Greenford, and a signal check later, gave additional incentive, and Williams responded fully. Up the 1 in 175-264 gradients to Beaconsfield speed was between 58½ and 59 m.p.h., and there followed a quick acceleration to 79 before High Wycombe. Slacks were observed scrupulously, and from a speed of 50 m.p.h. at West Wycombe there was a gradual recovery to 55 at Saunderton summit, a fine ascent. This was followed by a very fast descent at Ashendon Junction, with an average of 84.4 m.p.h. from Princes Risborough to Ashendon, and a maximum of 90. After the Banbury stop even faster running followed, even time being made between Banbury and Leamington, including the climb to Fenny Compton. The distance of 10.2 miles from Fenny Compton to milepost 105 was covered in 7 min. 20 sec. at an average of 83.5 m.p.h., and the exciting maximum speed of 92 m.p.h. was reached and sustained for three-quarters of a mile. This equalled the highest speed recorded by a 'Star'. Allowing 4¾ min. for the Greenford and Northolt checks, 5¼ min. for the stop at Bicester and 5 min. for Banbury, gives an equivalent non-stop run of 83 min. 10 sec. for the 87.3 miles from Paddington to Leamington, a remarkable achievement with these loads.

The runs quoted above were all of great merit, but with the heavier trains timekeeping was not always possible. A. V. Goodyear commented that on the evidence of about 50 down runs by 'Stars' with loads of 330 to 427 tons, mainly on the 6.10

No. 4026, when named 'The Japanese Monarch'

p.m. from Paddington, he had found that time was usually kept to Leamington with tare loads up to 360 or 370 tons. Beyond that load the main influence on timekeeping was the quality of the coal. Beyond Leamington the 6.10 p.m. down was allowed 36 min. for the remaining 23.3 miles to Birmingham, but this part of the schedule was difficult to maintain with loads in excess of the official maximum of 320 tons. No. 4067, on the run described above, cut this time to 24 min. 20 sec. with a fall from 57 to 49½ m.p.h. on Hatton bank, and a maximum of 76½ m.p.h. at Tyseley, but this was as exceptional as the earlier part of the run.

In 1924, Cecil J. Allen published details of a series of four runs on the down Birmingham 2-hour trains with loads which ranged between 190 and 290 tons to Bicester, and between 190 and 235 tons from Leamington to Birmingham. The minimum station-to-station times of these runs combined to give an equivalent non-stop run to Birmingham in 105 min. 55 sec., showing a generous recovery margin on the prevailing schedules. The growth of train loads ruled out any possibility of an acceleration below the 2-hour timing. Even the introduction of larger engines, combined with the incentive of a cut to 1 hour 55 min. of the principal trains from Euston to Birmingham, never persuaded the GWR to improve upon the 2-hour schedule.

Up running on the Birmingham line was equally good. The up 2-hour trains were the only trains in the country at this period which commonly reached speeds of 80 m.p.h. at four separate locations on one journey—on Hatton bank, and near Cropredy, Bicester and Denham. The fastest snippet recorded by a 'Star' on an up train was timed by C. Mannison on 29 August 1925. No. 4029, *King Stephen*, driven by Thomas, with a 7-coach train weighing 225 tons on the 9 a.m. from Birmingham,

3.28 p.m. LEAMINGTON TO PADDINGTON
Date: 29/8/25
Engine: 4063 *Bath Abbey*
Load: 14 cars, 418 tons tare, 445 tons full
Driver: Field (Old Oak Common)
Weather: Fine and calm

Dist. Miles		Sch. Min.	Actual m. s.	Speed m.p.h.
0·0	LEAMINGTON	0	0 00	
1·1	*Milepost 105*		3 04	
4·1	*Milepost 102*		7 00	48½
6·1	Southam Road		9 38	46½
11·0	Fenny Compton		14 52	60
13·1	*Milepost 93*		16 53	57½
16·2	Cropredy		19 49	70
18·6	*Banbury Junction*		21 57	70½
19·8	BANBURY	24	23 49	
3·5	Kings Sutton		5 49	55½
5·1	*Aynho Junction*	6	7 22	62
10·3	Ardley		13 07	52
14·1	BICESTER		16 19	75
17·1	Blackthorn		18 32	83½
20·1	Brill		20 52	70
				66½/70½
23·4	*Ashendon Junction*	23	23 53	slack 55
27·4	Haddenham		27 29	70
32·8	PRINCES RISBOROUGH	33	32 28	61
36·0	Saunderton		35 48	50½
38·7	West Wycombe		38 14	68
41·0	HIGH W'COMBE	42	40 41	slack 45
—	*Tylers Green*			58½
45·8	Beaconsfield		46 00	56
50·1	Gerrards Cross		49 54	71
52·7	Denham		51 52	84
55·4	Ruislip		53 51	80
57·2	Northolt Junction	58	55 13	78½
59·7	Greenford	60	57 04	84½
62·9	Park Royal		59 30	73½
64·2	Old Oak Common West Junction	65	61 02	
66·2	Westbourne Park		64 10 sig.	
—				
67·5	PADDINGTON	70	67 24	

Oxford and Worcester Express passing Reading West Junction; engine No. 4066 'Malvern Abbey'

covered the 17.2 miles from Beaconsfield to Park Royal in 12 min. 30 sec. at an average speed of 82.7 m.p.h., with a maximum of 92 m.p.h. at Denham, and a further maximum of 90 at Greenford.

As with the down trains, the loads of up trains gradually increased, and interest centres mainly on the runs by heavy trains. Of many runs recorded by A. V. Goodyear and his friends, the one shown in the table on this page stands out above all others. This run was also recorded by C. Manison on 29 August 1925. The second part of the 3 p.m. from Birmingham loaded to 14 coaches, weighing 445 tons full, and was hauled by No. 4063, *Bath Abbey*. This train was worked by Old Oak men, and the driver on this occasion was Field. Delays

Cornish Riviera Express leaving Paddington, engine No. 4050 'Princess Alice'

were encountered soon after leaving Snow Hill, but from Leamington the run was unchecked until the approaches to Paddington. The start from Leamington set the standard for the remainder of the run, with an acceleration to $48\frac{1}{2}$ m.p.h., followed by a fall only to $46\frac{1}{2}$ m.p.h. on the 1 in 187 gradient after Fosse Road. A quick recovery to 59 m.p.h. after Southam Road and a minimum of $57\frac{1}{2}$ m.p.h. after Fenny Compton completed an excellent climb. Speed reached $70\frac{1}{2}$ m.p.h. at Cropredy, and after a slow run into Banbury the stop was made in 23 min. 49 sec. for the distance of 19.8 miles. After

Banbury the acceleration was again good for such a load, although time was dropped as far as Ashendon Junction. *Bath Abbey* reached 62 m.p.h. at Aynho Junction, and fell to 52 at Ardley. After a maximum of $83\frac{1}{2}$ m.p.h. at Blackthorn, the Ashendon Junction slack was observed carefully. On gradients which are on the average slightly unfavourable, speed recovered from 55 at Ashendon to 70 m.p.h. at Haddenham, and another excellent climb brought the train over Saunderton summit at a minimum of $50\frac{1}{2}$ m.p.h. A smart acceleration from the High Wycombe slack was followed by a fast descent from

3.54 p.m. BANBURY TO PADDINGTON

Engine No.	Name			Load tons tare	Actual time		Net time	Max. speed
					m.	s.	min.	m.p.h.
4065	Evesham Abbey	.	.	323	68	52	$68\frac{3}{4}$	82
4023	King George	.	.	358	70	17	$69\frac{3}{4}$	87
4058	Princess Augusta	.	.	363	69	46	$69\frac{1}{4}$	82
4033	Queen Victoria	.	.	362	72	00	69	81
4030	King Harold	.	.	377	70	10	$69\frac{1}{2}$	$85\frac{1}{2}$
4067	Tintern Abbey	.	.	409	74	16	$68\frac{3}{4}$	$86\frac{1}{2}$
4045	Prince John	.	.	453	75	17	$72\frac{1}{2}$	79

Engine No. 4040 'Queen Boadicea,' with
outside steam pipes

Engine No. 4043 'Prince Henry, with large
4000 gallon tender

Beaconsfield, with an average of 80.3 m.p.h. from Gerrards Cross to Park Royal, and maxima of 84 m.p.h. at Denham and 84½ at Greenford. Despite a loss of about ½ min. by a check outside Paddington, the terminus was reached in less than even time— 67 min. 24 sec. for 67.5 miles. This was in every way a magnificent performance.

A table, p.77, shows a summary of seven other runs on the 3.54 p.m. from Banbury to Paddington. Only on one of these, when No. 4045 had a load of 453 tons tare, and about 500 tons full, was the net time greater than the allowance of 70 min.

The post-war running so far described was made by trains which were working to schedules which had been originally introduced before the war. The first post-war accelerations of note came in 1923, when the 2.30 p.m. from Cheltenham to Paddington was accelerated to cover the 77.3 miles from Swindon to Paddington in 75 min. The average speed of 61.8 m.p.h. was the first advance on the North Eastern Railway's old-established booking of 43 min. for the 44.1 miles from Darlington to York, and the distinction thus conferred on the train was emphasised by its receiving the nickname 'Cheltenham Flyer'. At first it was worked by 'Saints', but soon the 'Star' class took over, and the

3.45 p.m. SWINDON TO PADDINGTON, 'THE CHELTENHAM FLYER'

Run No.			1		2			3	
Engine No.			4059		4017			4072	
Engine name			*Princess Patricia*		*Knight of Liege*			*Tresco Abbey*	
Load: cars, tons, empty/full			7 212/235		8 239/260			8 251/265	
Dist. Miles		Sch. Min.	Actual m. s.	Average speed m.p.h.	Actual m. s.	Average speed m.p.h.	Sch. Min.	Actual m. s.	Speed m.p.h.
0·0	SWINDON	0	0 00		0 00		0	0 00	
5·8	Shrivenham		7 15					7 06	
10·8	Uffington		11 12	76·2	11 27			11 07	
13·4	Challow		13 12	79·6				13 09	
16·9	Wantage Road		15 50	79·7	16 16	76·7		15 47	
20·8	Steventon		18 40	82·3	19 02	84·0	19	18 40	83½
24·2	DIDCOT	24	21 12	80·7	21 23	86·8	22	21 13	sig. *70
28·8	Cholsey		24 45	78·9	24 45	83·1		24 58	76½
32·5	Goring		27 38	77·3	27 26	83·0		27 58	72½
35·8	Pangbourne		30 10	76·2	29 49	80·9		30 36	
38·6	Tilehurst		32 28	75·7				32 52	
41·3	READING	40	34 35	75·3	33 56	81·7	36½	34 54	79
46·3	Twyford		38 45	71·3	37 45	78·0		38 49	75
53·1	Maidenhead	50½	44 20	73·0	42 45	81·3		43 54	82
58·8	SLOUGH	55½	49 15	70·7			51	48 09	
64·1	West Drayton		53 35	72·3				52 08	
68·2	SOUTHALL	64	57 05	71·2			59	55 25	
71·6	Ealing		59 52	71·0	56 51	78·8		58 00 sigs.	80†
76·0	Westbourne Park		63 40	70·2				61 59	
77·3	PADDINGTON	75	66 12				70	64 24	

Net time 63½ min.
*Foxhall Jc.
†Acton

train remained the preserve of four-cylinder engines until it lost its distinction once and for all in the 1939 wartime decelerations.

Successive accelerations eventually brought the time from Swindon to Paddington down to 65 min., and the early days of the 65-minute booking brought the most spectacular displays of high speed running which had ever been seen in Britain. By that time the 'Castles' were responsible for the working and, apart from one run by No. 4072 when the schedule was 70 min., there are no records of the train being worked by a 'Star' after the schedule was cut below 75 min. However, some performances of the 'Stars' when the schedule was 75 min. show that these engines were quite capable of observing the 65-minute schedule with 8 coaches, which was the most that the 'Castles' were required to do except at holiday times. Two notable runs by 'Stars' on this train are tabulated. The second of these was included in a summary of 27 runs on the train recorded by J. P. Pearson, which was published in *The Railway Magazine* in December 1924 by Cecil J. Allen. The summary showed the minimum times between each successive pair of stations

on any of the 27 runs, and gave a cumulative time for the whole journey of 60 min. 55 sec. Although most of the best times were made by 'Castles', No. 4072, *Tresco Abbey,* had the best time from Ealing to Acton, but more strikingly No. 4017, *Knight of Liége,* had the best times over five of the 25 sections of the journey, and had the longest continuous stretch at an average of 80 m.p.h. of any of the runs. The distance of 60.8 miles from Uffington to Ealing was covered in 45 min. 14 sec. at an average of 80.7 m.p.h. Unfortunately the full details of this run were not published, and column No. 2 of the table shows as much of the log as was recorded. This was the fastest sustained running recorded by a 'Star', and was comparable with contemporary 'Castle' running. With a clear run into the terminus Paddington could have been reached in 63 min.

Run No. 1 in the table shows a performance of No. 4059 in more detail. With a coach less than No. 4017, No. 4059 made a better start, and continued to gain as far as Wantage Road; but thereafter its level of speed fell. Even so, time was gained progressively, and the total time of 66 min. 12 sec. was 9 min. less than schedule.

Up Worcester and Hereford express entering Evesham:
engine No. 4066 'Malvern Abbey'

CHAPTER 7

'THE GREAT BEAR'

STRICTLY speaking, this huge 'Pacific' engine does not fall within the scope of this monograph; but it was so closely associated with the 'Star' class in its machinery, and could, both in design and name be considered a development of them that it is certainly appropriate to include it. Eventually, of course, in its conversion to a 4—6—0 it became a member of the 'Castle' class. Nevertheless to all who have studied the work of Churchward in any detail the reasons behind the building of this engine have always been a matter of conjecture. One thing can now be said for certain; the conception was entirely due to Churchward, and not to outside influences that pressed the project upon him. In his classic paper, 'Large Locomotive Boilers', to which reference has already been made, he opened with these significant words: 'The modern locomotive problem is principally a question of boiler.' In that paper he illustrated, in drawings beautifully executed by F. W. Hawksworth, the relative proportions of many British, French and American locomotive boilers, and the latter included several examples of wide fireboxes.

At that time Churchward was very attracted to American practice, and had already included some of its features in his standard Swindon designs;

and although he had not adopted compounding as a standard on the GWR his interest in current French practice remained strong. The later French compound 'Atlantics' imported were of Paris-Orleans design, and it so happened that the first European 'Pacific' was also put to work on that line. His interest in the development of large boilers, together with current events in both America and France, without much doubt inspired the idea of a Swindon 'Pacific'. The suggestion of a 'super' locomotive was accepted by the Board and on 30 January 1907 a sum of £4,400 was voted for the construction of it, while a subsequent vote of £860 was made to cover additional expenditure on the project. Churchward had already shown himself one of the most far-sighted of British locomotive engineers, and such was the upward surge in traffic resulting from the enterprising new services put into operation since 1906 that he foresaw the time when his 4-cylinder 4—6—0s would be extended to their limit. It was not his nature to allow himself to be overtaken by circumstances, and the building of the 'Pacific' was a step toward the provision of still greater power.

It is remarkable that he should have turned to the 'Pacific' type as early as the year 1907. In this

'The Great Bear', as originally built

A front view of 'The Great Bear'

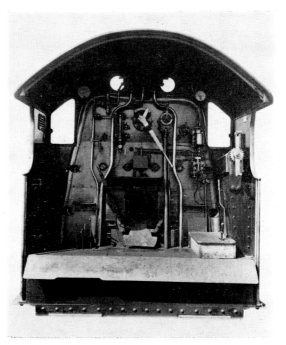

Cab layout, showing reverser extended back, as on early 'Stars'

he was followed by Gresley 15 years later, and Stanier on the LMSR in 1933. The senior draughtsman responsible for the boiler design was W. L. Watson, and at his drawing-board Churchward spent much time. The American boilers with wide fireboxes illustrated in his paper to the Institution of Mechanical Engineers were mostly designed for using low-grade coals and had grate areas varying between 44 up to no less than 72 sq. ft., even at that time in history. Churchward himself was mindful of some of the disadvantages of using a very large grate, because in that same paper he wrote: 'The wide firebox evidently requires a higher standard of skill in the fireman, for unless the grate is kept well and evenly covered, there is a tendency to have an excess of air, reducing efficiency and increasing tube trouble.' On *The Great Bear* he used a grate area of 41.9 sq. ft. This was a very big step forward from the 27 sq. ft. of the standard No. 1 boiler, and in practice it took a good deal of getting used to.

Before considering the boiler in detail reference must be made to the 'engine'. The front end lay-out was the same as that of the 'Stars', but with the cylinders increased to the maximum diameter permissible using the standard GWR tyre width of $5\frac{3}{4}$ in. This was wider than usual on other British railways, and a narrowing of this to the more customary $5\frac{1}{4}$ in. would have permitted larger cylinders

to be used, and still give adequate clearance for the rear bogie wheels. But Churchward would not consider changing the existing GWR standard tyre width, and the cylinders were made to 15 in. diameter. The drawing on page 82 shows a longitudinal section at the front end, and illustrates the layout of the smokebox, blastpipe and superheater. A further drawing relates to the trailing end. Unlike the trailing truck, an existing piece is used here.

So we come to the boiler. None of the American wide-firebox boilers which Churchward had studied so carefully had combustion chambers extending forward into the boiler barrel, as became common in later years. But that practice involved some very intricate press-work, and flanging of the firebox front and tubeplate, and at that time in the development of high-pressure boilers at Swindon it was enough to perfect a firebox with a relatively simple shape. Having decided that point, and at the same time maintaining the same dimensional relations as on the 'Star' for the smokebox tubeplate in relation to the cylinders, the length of the boiler barrel was determined by the wheel spacing. On *The Great Bear* the spacing between the centre and the rear pair of driving wheels was made 7 ft., as with the leading pair and centre pair. But even with this slight reduction the boiler barrel came out at 23 ft. By comparison with British 'Pacifics' of much later years this dimension could be criticised as exces-

F

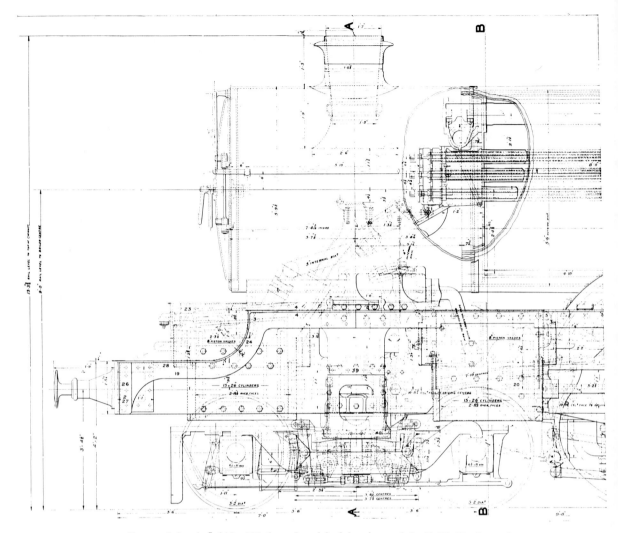

Front end drawing of No. 111, from the original drawing made by F. W. Hawksworth

sive, but it was the subject of very careful consideration in the design stage, and the tube size was increased from 2 in. diameter on the 'Stars' to $2\frac{1}{2}$ in. In his paper of 1906 to the Institution of Mechanical Engineers, Churchward said:

'The ratio of diameter to length of the tube undoubtedly has a most important bearing upon the steaming qualities of the boiler and upon the efficiency of the heat absorption. This is more particularly noticeable when the boilers are being worked to the limit of their capacity. If 2 in. tubes, say, are employed in barrels 11 to 12 feet long, when the boiler is being forced the length is not sufficient to absorb the heat from the amount of gases that a 2-inch tube will pass, and overheating and waste result.'

While the ratio of diameter to length of tube was less on *The Great Bear* than on the 'Stars', the reputation that the engine earned at first for being an indifferent steamer was almost certainly due to the difficulty firemen experienced in feeding a grate that was so unlike those already in use on the Great Western Railway. This has occurred time and again with new locomotive designs, when engineers from the drawing office have had to ride the locomotives for weeks on end, fire themselves, and find by hard experience the correct technique to use. One has known firemen almost break their hearts, and their backs (!), shovelling for dear life, when a much simpler and less fatiguing method would have produced far better results. This was certainly the case on the first Stanier 'Pacifics' on the LMSR, the

Rear end of No. 111, showing the firebox arrangement, and the radial guides for the trailing axle mounting

'The Great Bear' in No. 1 platform Paddington

boiler proportions of which have many points of similarity to those of *The Great Bear*. In later years the engine steamed well. I came to know some of the men who worked regularly on her, and they had nothing but praise for her general working, and beautiful riding.

Like the Gresley 'Pacifics', however, good riding was not obtained from the start. The springing of the trailing truck was subject to some modification. The engine had the characteristic short cab, though at first a move to provide more top shelter was made by extending the roof rearwards beyond the side-sheets. It is extraordinary how enginemen of the 'old school' seemed to rebel against any attempt to close them in on the footplate. On 'The Bear', a fireman unused to having a roof above the fall-plate managed to get a fire-iron so jammed between that roof and the floor that three men were needed to

'The Great Bear' on the 6.30 p.m. Plymouth express at Paddington

dislodge it. After, the roof was cut back somewhat. The tender was something of a curiosity. In capacity it was no larger than the rather small 6-wheeled standard type at first attached to the 'Stars', carrying 3,500 gallons of water and 6 tons of coal. It was nevertheless built as an 8-wheeler, to match more appropriately the impressive appearance of the engine. It was adapted, after construction had already begun, and to the end of its days it carried a patch covering the hole where the water scoop would have been on a 6-wheeler. The bogies were of standard locomotive type but with shorter wheelbase.

The water pick-up was in the middle, and a questionable feature was the siting of the manhole for filling in the dome covering the top end of the duct from the water-scoop. This did not last long. One day someone either forgot to fasten the manhole cover, or did not fasten it down securely, and at the first water troughs the strong upward rush of water burst it open, and surged with such force over the back of the tender as to burst open the gangway door of the leading coach, and flood that coach throughout to a depth of some 18 in.!

The engine had its first trial trip on 4 February 1908. As with many large engines of new design there were minor clearance troubles. When 'The Bear' went to Paddington for the first time the leading step, opposite the smokebox, scraped a platform, and was later removed. At the time of its construction the civil engineer would not accept the engine on any route except between Paddington and Bristol, because of its axle-loading. But while this would have given adequate scope for the development of the design to perfection, in the haulage of heavy loads at high speed over a level track that could be very trying in adverse weather conditions, it so happened that the engine took the road at the time of the celebrated feud between many senior officers of the GWR, led by Churchward, and the General Manager, Sir James Inglis. A new organisational 'tree' of responsibility had been proposed by Inglis, and was being strenuously resisted. Churchward had to walk warily so far as track loading was concerned, and so it came about that the full capacity of the engine was never really determined.

How far development work would ultimately have been carried out on the engine it is not possible to say. The 1913 modifications had scarcely begun to show their effect when war broke out, and any further experimenting with a prototype locomotive had inevitably to stop. Nevertheless, although there had never seemed to be any occasion for proving the full capacity of the engine, either

A later view of No. 111, after fitting of top-feed apparatus

on a special dynamometer-car test, or in regular service, in many ways, both officially and by railway enthusiasts, it continued to be regarded as the 'flag-ship' of the fleet, and it occupied the principal position in published material and internal documents. In 1919, when the GWR published its shilling booklet, containing the names, numbers, types and classes of its locomotives, while all other classes were illustrated by no more than a broadside official photograph 'The Bear' had in addition a weight diagram, and she was the only engine of the entire stud for which full details of the heating surfaces, boiler and firebox dimensions, and even steam and exhaust port sizes, were quoted.

In her earlier days 'The Bear' had worked on the Bristol expresses, and a regular turn was the down evening dining-car train, non-stop to Bath. After the war, however, still stationed at Old Oak Common, she was in a link of four engines which included the first 5 ft. 8 in. 2—8—0 No. 4700 and two 4—6—0s. This was before the '47XX' class

had grown beyond the pioneer engine, and No. 4700 was in some ways an isolated engine, as much as *The Great Bear* was. It was during the years 1919 to 1923 that the engine became most familiar to travellers and to the limited number of railway enthusiasts then existing. Although working, as always, on the Paddington-Bristol route it was, however, not used on the fastest and hardest trains. There were, from the autumn of 1921, four expresses running non-stop between Paddington and Bristol in the even two hours. Three of these, the 11.45 a.m. and 5.15 p.m. up, and the 1.15 p.m. down, were Bristol turns, and were thus worked by 'Saint' class engines. The remaining train was the 11.15 a.m. down, worked by Old Oak and Laira sheds on alternate days as part of a double home duty between Paddington and Plymouth. *The Great Bear* worked on such unexciting duties as the 10.45 a.m. down, and it was on this train that it became frequently photographed in those years.

A very interesting record of the engine's work,

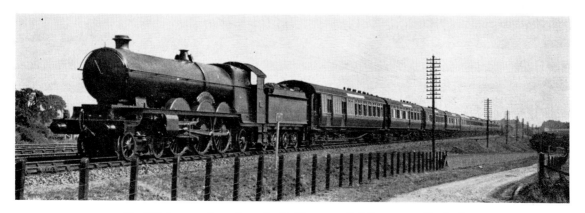

No. 111, in austerity style on the 10.45 a.m. ex Paddington near Twyford

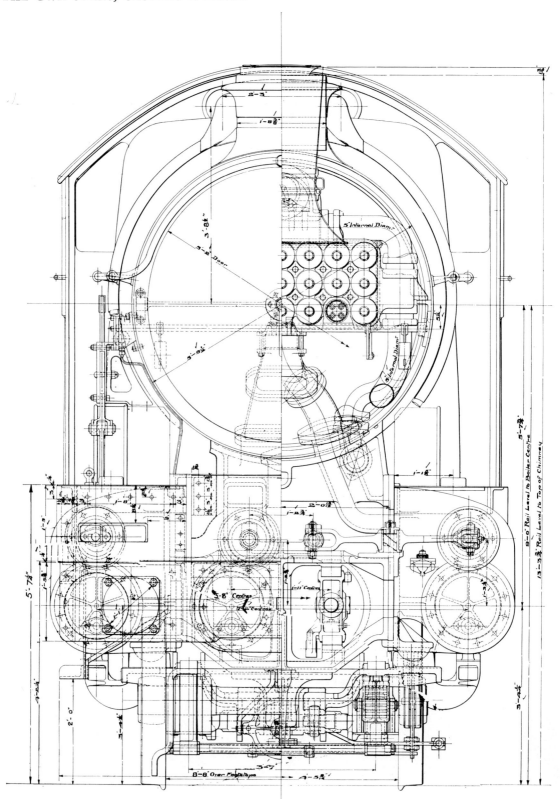

Front end cross-section of No. 111, showing the engine as fitted with top feed

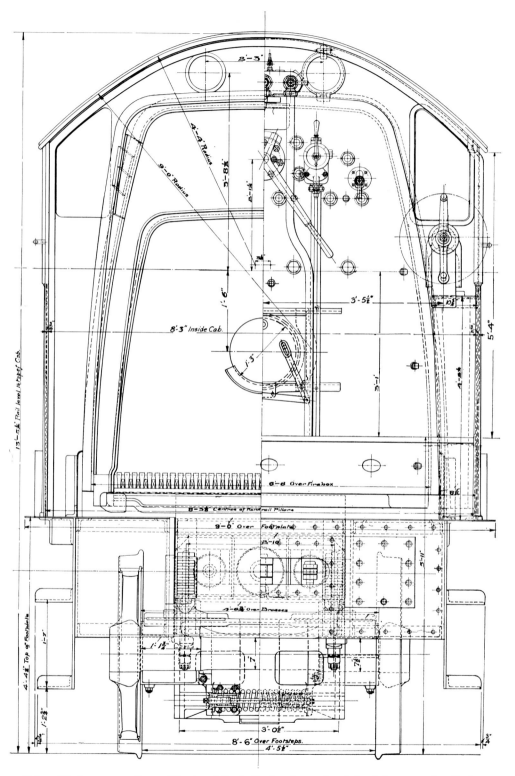

Cab and firebox cross-sections. The dotted line indicating the turning circle of the reverser handle shows why it was necessary to mount it so far back

'The Great Bear' on the 10.45 a.m. down passing Twyford East Box

which relates to the 6.40 p.m. from Paddington to Bath on 5 February 1913, has been put at our disposal by Mr. E. L. Bell, and is detailed in the accompanying log. The load of 310 tons was not heavy; but the engine started briskly from Paddington, and after a leisurely acceleration after Ealing ran well until the slight check nearing Reading hindered progress. The recovery was good, with speeds ranging round 66-68 m.p.h. on to Didcot. But there was a sudden falling off afterwards, presumably because the train was by then well on time. The average speeds after Wootton Bassett indicate a maximum of over 70 m.p.h. on Dauntsey bank, and despite very easy running after Chippenham the train would have been comfortably on time at Bath—112-minute schedule—but for the final check.

Over the years several modifications were made to *The Great Bear*. It was in shops from June to December 1913, when the Swindon No. 1 superheater was replaced by the No. 3 pattern. The superheating surface was reduced from 545 sq. ft. to 506 sq. ft. This was a special form of No. 3 superheater with four pairs of elements in each flue. In about 1920 the normal pattern of No. 3 superheater, with three pairs of elements per flue, was fitted, making the superheating surface 399 sq. ft. Each of the superheater modifications made a slight increase in the free area through the tubes, and thus made some small improvement to the steaming. At this same period a cast-iron chimney, four-cone injector, and a steel cab roof were fitted.

6.40 p.m. PADDINGTON—BATH

Load: 310 tons (less 25 tons slipped at Chippenham)
Engine: 4—6—2 No. 111 *The Great Bear*

Dist. Miles			Actual m. s.	Av. Speed m.p.h.
0·0	PADDINGTON	.	0 00	
1·3	Westbourne Park	.	3 28	
5·7	Ealing	. . .	9 25	44·3
9·1	Southall	.	12 59	57·2
13·2	West Drayton	.	17 14	57·8
16·2	Langley	. .	20 09	61·8
18·5	SLOUGH	.	22 17	64·3
22·5	Taplow	. .	26 06	63·0
24·2	Maidenhead	.	27 48	60·0
31·0	Twyford	. .	34 22	62·2
			sigs.	
36·0	READING	.	40 22	50·0
38·8	Tilehurst	.	43 07	58·8
41·5	Pangbourne	.	46 01	
44·8	Goring	. .	49 03	65·2
48·5	Cholsey	. .	52 26	66·5
53·1	DIDCOT	.	56 42	64·8
56·5	Steventon	. .	60 05	60·3
60·4	Wantage Road	.	64 07	58·8
63·9	Challow	. .	67 48	57·1
66·5	Uffington	.	70 42	53·8
71·5	Shrivenham	.	76 09	55·0
77·3	SWINDON	.	82 12	57·5
82·9	Wootton Bassett	.	87 33	62·8
87·7	Dauntsey	.	91 46	68·3
94·0	CHIPPENHAM	.	97 15	69·0
98·3	Corsham	. .	101 57	54·9
101·9	Box	. . .	105 45	56·8
—			sigs.	
106·9	BATH	. .	113 38	

Cost of checks: Reading 1½ min.
Bathampton 2 min.
Net time: 110 min.

A broadside view of No. 111 in her final condition (at Old Oak Common)

Modifications were also made to the springing, and a number of adjustments were made to the weight distribution. In 1916 the total adhesive weight was given as 61 tons 6 cwt, and Ahrons quoted 61 tons 7 cwt, the distribution between axles being different in the two cases.

In his own last years of office, from the end of the war till December 1921, Churchward apparently took no further steps to develop the 'Pacific', and instead sought to increase the steaming capacity of his larger tender engines by the fitting of larger boilers to the 'Saints', 'Stars' and 28XX 2—8—0s. This proposal was coupled with the design of the 47XX 2—8—0. A drawing dated May 1919 showed the estimated weights for these types fitted with a larger boiler; but the Civil Engineer could not accept the increase in axle load of the 4—6—0s. In the event, the 47XX was the only one of these types to receive the larger boiler, and the first of that type ran for some time with a No. 1 boiler. Although officially allowed only between Paddington and Bristol, it is recorded that the 'Pacific' made at least one appearance each at Newton Abbot and Wolverhampton.

After Churchward's retirement at the end of 1921, his successor resumed work on the design of a larger passenger engine, and found that by careful design a worthwhile increase in size could be attained in a 4—6—0 which met the requirements of the Civil Engineer. The introduction of this class, the 'Castle', in 1923 was the occasion for a big publicity campaign, proclaiming the 'Castle' as the most powerful passenger engine in Britain (based on a dubious criterion of tractive effort). *The Great Bear* then ceased to have any publicity value; indeed it became an embarrassment in the

A striking view of the great engine inside Old Oak Common shed

Engine No. 111 rebuilt as a 'Castle' and named 'Viscount Churchill': the 8-wheeled tender attached

presence of the 'Castles'. In 1924 it required heavy repairs, and it was therefore dismantled, work beginning on 7 January 1924. Parts of the engine were used in the production of a 'Castle' carrying the same number but a different name. Despite the removal of the need of *The Great Bear* for publicity purposes, there is said to have been indignation in some quarters at Paddington when news was received of its decease, and Churchward is known to have been very upset.

Under the 1919 scheme, No. 111 was classified as 'Special Red', indicated by a black plus sign on a red disc. The total mileage of the engine as a 'Pacific' was 527,272. The bogie tender, No. 1755, survived the 'Pacific' by twelve years. Between 1924 and 1936 it ran behind the following engines, in order: 'Counties' 3804/2/16, 'Saints' 2914/6/2, 'Stars' 4045/22. It was then condemned, but is believed to have been used as a water carrier for some time afterwards. There is no doubt Churchward had a deep affection for the engine, as one could have for a child on which much care and attention had been lavished in early youth, but who had not come up to expectations. Affection or not, even Churchward came to regard the engine more as a 'white elephant' rather than 'a great bear', and when he heard of the construction of the first Gresley 'Pacific' for the Great Northern he remarked jocularly: 'What did that young man want to *build* it for? We could have sold him ours!'

The first 4-cylinder 4—6—0, No. 4001 'Dog Star', in plain green, with small chimney, as fitted to the 'Abbeys'

'STARS' IN AUSTERITY

No. 4064 'Reading Abbey' as originally built, in full austerity style

CHAPTER 8

THE 'CASTLES'

IN the previous chapter it was mentioned that Churchward had a scheme in 1919 for fitting larger boilers to the 'Stars' and 'Saints', a proposal which was vetoed by the Civil Engineer on account of weight. The restoration of pre-war speeds on the GWR main lines in 1921, together with the continued increase in traffic to the West Country resorts, made the need for a larger passenger engine even greater in 1922 than it had seemed in 1919. Little increase in weight beyond the 'Star' could be accepted without reduction of route availability. Collett therefore compromised by making the greatest increase in boiler size which was possible consistent with retaining the full 'Red' route classification. This resulted in a boiler which was significantly better than the No. 1 boiler, but was lighter than the No. 7 boiler proposed in 1919.

In basic dimensions the 'Castle' showed remarkably little difference from the 'Star' other than in the boiler. The wheelbase of the engine was the same, but 1 ft. was added to the rear of the frame. This helped to accommodate a longer firebox, but it also allowed the fitting of a larger cab. By reducing tyres and clearances, it was found possible to increase the cylinder diameter to 16 in. As the same size of valve was used as in the 'Star', the valve and port size in relation to cylinder diameter was less favourable than in the 'Stars'. The design of the cylinders was so similar to that of the 'Star' that the initial drawing for issue to the works was made by altering in red certain dimensions on a copy of the cylinder drawing of the 'Star'. The pattern for the inside cylinders had a loose section which provided the smokebox saddle, and could be changed to allow the manufacture of cylinders for both 'Star' and 'Castle' boilers. There was a minor change in the valve setting in that the lead was $\frac{3}{16}$ in., in place of $\frac{1}{8}$ in. in the 'Stars'. The layout of the motion and chassis was almost identical with the 'Stars'. Changes in the dimensions of the motion parts were made, where necessary, by alterations to a 'Star' drawing.

In the boiler, the main increase was an addition of 1 ft. to the length of the firebox, making it 10 ft. To give a further increase to the grate area the water space above the foundation ring was

Engine No. 4073 'Caerphilly Castle' as originally built—in photographic grey

C. B. Collett, Chief Mechanical Engineer 1922–1941

reduced below the normal Churchward figure of $3\frac{1}{2}$ in. to 3 in. The grate area was thus 30.3 sq. ft. This was an increase of 12 per cent on the 'Stars', which closely matched the increase of 14 per cent in the nominal tractive effort. The barrel was 3 in. greater in diameter throughout than in the No. 1 boiler, but 3 in. less than in the No. 7. The back of the firebox was sloped slightly outwards, so that the increase in length was less at the top than at the bottom. The back of the firebox in the No. 1 boiler was vertical. The general proportions of the boiler followed normal Churchward lines, except for the reduction in the water space.

Outwardly the changes in the locomotive were more spectacular than the internal changes. The outside steam pipes were an innovation for the GWR. This change brought several benefits. The joints of the steam pipes for the outside cylinder were removed from an inaccessible position at the rear of the smokebox to the outside. The 'Star' steam pipes emerged from the bottom of the rear of the smokebox, and then turned through two right angles to reach the cylinders. Their removal from this position not only made a useful clearance in the congested space between the frames, but also removed an obstruction from the lower smoke tubes, which had previously made access to those tubes difficult. The new pattern of steam pipe was more flexible than the old one, and was therefore less affected by those movements of the cylinders on the frames, and flexing of the frames themselves, which were euphemistically described as 'breathing'.

The other notable change from Churchward

practice was the longer cab, with side windows. It is said that Churchward's apparent lack of interest in the comfort of his enginemen stemmed from complaints which were made about the side-window cab of the 4—4—0 *Earl Cawdor*. Whether that is true or not, it is a fact that Churchward's cabs were meagre, even by the standards of the early twentieth century. There were no seats, and there was rarely a position in which the enginemen could stand comfortably, whilst the combination of high footplate and low tender made them very exposed. Some men, however, say that older cabs were less draughty than the later ones, although more exposed to side and following winds. The Frenchmen had introduced a more commodious cab to the GWR, but it was not until the 47XX 2—8—0 of 1919 that any attempt was made to improve the lot of the enginemen (and then not a very successful one). It remained for Collett to produce a cab of which it could at least be said that it was no worse than was being fitted on two of the other three groups. The roof was extended over the fall plate, giving much better shelter, and the cut-out of the side plates made it possible for the enginemen to lean out without losing all protection from the roof. Cab seats were fitted, but these were not upholstered. Even forty years later many drivers found it more comfortable to stand in a GWR cab. The first engine had an inclined gutter on the cab roof, but this was soon removed.

The appearance of the 'Castle', with its higher boiler, larger cab, and outside steampipes, was automatically more impressive than that of the 'Star', but the effect was clinched by the restoration of the embellishments which had characterised Swindon engines in pre-war days—copper-capped chimney, brass beading on the splashers, and fully-lined livery. The only weakness in the effect was

No. 4082 'Windsor Castle', hauling the LNWR Royal Train

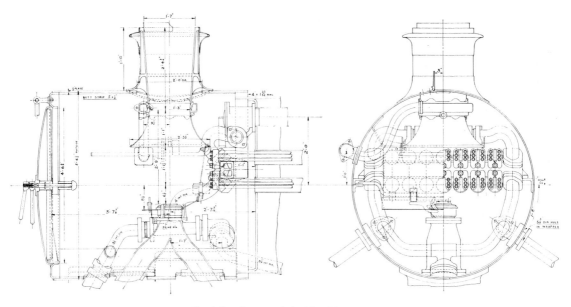

Smokebox layout of the 'Castle' 4—6—0

the continuation of the small 3,500-gallon tender. The increase of 12-14 per cent in potential output was achieved for an increase of 6 per cent in the weight. This permitted a total increase of 5 tons 9 cwt on the coupled wheels. For this small increase in weight, a significant improvement was made in the most outstanding British type of the pre-war period; adherence to existing standards made manufacture simple and cheap, and the engine was able to go straight into main-line service.

The tractive effort of the 'Stars' had been unsurpassed in British passenger engines until the introduction of the Hughes four-cylinder 4—6—0 in 1921; but from 1922 there had also been the Gresley and Raven 'Pacifics' to surpass them. The 'Castles' restored the lead to the GWR, and this was seized upon by the Publicity Department. A book was published under the name of the first locomotive—*Caerphilly Castle*—in which the engine was described as a 'super-locomotive' and the 'most powerful passenger train engine in the Kingdom'. The validity of this claim, based upon nominal tractive effort, was dubious, but it emerged two years later, in the locomotive exchanges with the London & North Eastern, that the claim had been nearer the mark than the authors could have supposed in 1923. The first edition was of 10,000 copies of the book, but within a month a further 30,000 copies were required. This was publicity on a grand scale, and the large crowds at the end of the old No. 1 platform at Paddington showed its effectiveness.

The names of the first ten of these engines were:

No.	Name
4073	*Caerphilly Castle*
4074	*Caldicot Castle*
4075	*Cardiff Castle*
4076	*Carmarthen Castle*
4077	*Chepstow Castle*
4078	*Pembroke Castle*
4079	*Pendennis Castle*
4080	*Powderham Castle*
4081	*Warwick Castle*
4082	*Windsor Castle*

No. 4073, *Caerphilly Castle*, appeared in August 1923, and was followed, between December 1923 and April 1924, by nine more. The first six were named after Welsh castles, but the series ended with *Windsor Castle*. The publicity which had attended the introduction of the class was further developed with this last engine. On 28 April 1924, Their Majesties King George V and Queen Mary visited Swindon works. The Royal Train was worked by *Windsor Castle*; at the end of the visit, on the return journey from the works yard to the station, the King and Queen rode on the engine, and the King drove. Brass plates were later fitted to the cab sides bearing the remarkable inscription set out on the following page. From that time, for many years, *Windsor Castle* became the recognised GWR Royal engine.

All concerned had cause to thank Collett for providing a more roomy cab; a gathering of this size on a 'Star' would have been too matey for a Royal party.

G   R

This engine
No. 4082 "Windsor Castle" was built at
Swindon in April 1924
and was driven from the works to the
station by
His Majesty King George V
accompanied by Queen Mary
on the occasion of the visit by their
Majesties
to the Great Western Railway Works at
Swindon on April 28th 1924
With Their Majesties on the footplate
were

Viscount Churchill	Chairman
Sir Felix Pole	General Manager
Mr. C. B. Collett	Chief Mechanical Engineer
Locomotive Inspector	G. H. Flewellyn
Engine Driver	E. R. B. Rowe
Fireman	A. W. Cook

In March 1924, No. 4074, *Caldicot Castle*, was given a thorough series of tests between Swindon and Plymouth. The test trains were made up to the maximum tonnage allowed to an unassisted engine over each section of the line. These limits were as follows:

Down line:

Swindon to Taunton	485 tons
Taunton to Newton Abbot	390 tons
Newton Abbot to Plymouth	288 tons

Up line:

Plymouth to Newton Abbot	288 tons
Newton Abbot to Swindon	485 tons

The logs of the three down journeys, as between Swindon and Taunton, are tabulated herewith. Weather conditions varied between the runs, the effect of west winds being very apparent on the exposed stretch of line over the marshes south of Bridgwater. Before Badminton the passing times were fairly uniform, and a further table shows the variations in cut-off which contributed to this uniformity.

No high speeds were attempted down to Stoke Gifford, and it was beyond Pylle Hill Junction that the running became energetic again. On each run 25 per cent cut-off was used as far as the summit at Flax Bourton, and on the first run this cut-off was maintained to Uphill. On the dead level between Yatton and Puxton speed was between $73\frac{1}{2}$ and 75 m.p.h., with a drawbar pull of 2.3 to 2.4 tons and full boiler pressure. At Uphill cut-off was reduced to 22 per cent, and speed fell away gradually to 62 m.p.h. south of Bridgwater.

On the second run cut-off was reduced to 21 per cent at Flax Bourton, and speed fell to $62\frac{1}{2}$ m.p.h. at Uphill, but it then varied by no more than 2 m.p.h. over the next 18 miles. On the third run conditions were more favourable, and a cut-off of 20 per cent from Flax Bourton gave a steady speed of 68 for 14 miles from Brent Knoll. The effect of the wind was also marked on the return trips; on 15 March a drawbar pull of 2.25 tons sufficed for a speed of 64 on the level, but on 20 March 2.75 tons was needed for 56 m.p.h.

The handling of the engine on the climb to Whiteball was interesting. Cut-off was fixed at 30 per cent once the train was under way from Taunton, and was left in this position to the summit. By this date it was more usual for cut-off to be advanced progressively on a climb such as this. A further table shows the log of one of the runs between Taunton and Exeter.

Although these were full-dress trials, the per-

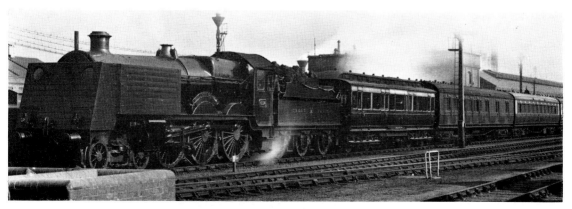

Engine No. 4074 'Caldicot Castle', with dynamometer car, ready for the 1924 trial runs

DYNAMOMETER CAR TRIALS—MARCH 1924

Engine: 4074 *Caldicot Castle*

Load: 14 cars + dynamometer car, 484 tons tare

| Run No. | | 1 | | 2 | | 3 | |
| Date | | March 14 | | March 19 | | March 25 | |
Dist. Miles		Actual m. s.	Speed m.p.h.	Actual m. s.	Speed m.p.h.	Actual m. s.	Speed m.p.h.
0·0	*Milepost 78*	0 00		0 00		0 00	
2·0	*Milepost 80*	5 55		5 06		4 55	
		check		check			
4·9	Wootton Bassett	9 43		9 20		8 36	
9·0	*Milepost 87*	15 12		13 53		12 56	
11·0	*Milepost 89*	17 07	63½	15 47	65	14 43	69
16·0	*Milepost 94*	22 15	52	20 57	53	19 37	53
18·0	*Milepost 96*	24 34	51½	23 16	50½	21 54	52
20·0	*Milepost 98*	26 55	51½	25 36	51½	24 14	50½
21·0	*Milepost 99*	28 07	50	26 46	51½	25 24	51½
22·0	Badminton	29 19	50	27 56	51½	26 36	50
		check		check		check	
26·6	Chipping Sodbury	34 12		33 00		31 24	
31·9	Winterbourne	40 51	65	39 19	66	37 48	66
34·8	Filton Junction	44 46		43 18		41 35	
38·0	Stapleton Road	50 26		49 06		47 08	
				sigs.			
40·3	*Pylle Hill Junction*	55 14		55 43		52 49	
41·6	*Milepost 120*	58 11		57 43		54 53	
44·6	*Milepost 123*	62 18	45	61 51	44	58 51	45
45·9	Flax Bourton	63 51		63 26		60 09	
50·6	*Milepost 129*	68 00	75	67 44	71	64 37	73
55·2	Puxton	72 05	73½	72 04	68	68 47	72
59·6	*Milepost 138*	75 23		75 37		72 12	
60·2	Uphill	75 57	70½	76 14	66½	72 48	69
64·1	Brent Knoll	79 23	65½	79 47	66½	76 13	68
66·9	HIGHBRIDGE	81 57	63	82 17	64½	78 39	68
70·7	Dunball	85 35	62	85 49	65½	82 02	68
73·2	BRIDGWATER	87 55	63	88 03	65½	84 12	68
77·6	*Milepost 156*	92 05	62	92 04	65½	88 05	68
						sigs.	
79·6	*Milepost 158*	94 12	55½	93 59	61	90 03	
81·6	*Milepost 160*	96 14	60	95 53	64½	sigs.	
83·6	*Milepost 162*	98 15		97 46		sig.	
84·7	TAUNTON	100 30		100 15		stop	
	Average speeds: Milepost 129 to 138	73·2		68·5		71·3	
	Mileposts 138 to 156	64·7		65·7		68·0	

formance of the engine was in accordance with everyday running. This was demonstrated very clearly by a run that I recorded myself with the same engine in 1953 on the 8.55 a.m. from Paddington, with 14 coaches loading to 495 tons. The train experienced a check at Wootton Bassett similar to the first two test runs, and the cut-off was set at 25 per cent for the climb to Badminton, as on 14 March 1924. Between Hullavington and Badminton the difference in speeds between the 1924 and 1953 runs was no more than 1 m.p.h.

In 1924 there was held in London the First World Power Conference. A number of papers was read on railway electrification, and the only one on steam locomotives was by Collett on 'Testing of Locomotives on the Great Western Railway'. The paper gave an account of testing methods on the GWR—itself the most detailed account of that part of Swindon's work which had yet been published—but later in the paper came the great surprise. Churchward's reticence about details of performance went by the board, for there appeared the results of a series of tests made with No. 4074, *Caldicot Castle*. The figures were more detailed than had ever before been published about a British locomotive, and they included one which shook many British locomotive engineers—the coal per unit of work done. As mentioned in Chapter 4, the figure obtained from tests of a saturated 'Star' was 3½ lb. per drawbar horsepower hour. By 1923

DYNAMOMETER CAR TEST RUN, MARCH 1924
Engine: 4074 *Caldicot Castle*
Load: Dynamometer car+11 cars, 385 tons tare
Driver: Rowe

Location	Actual m. s.	Av. speed m.p.h.	Cut-off %	Reg. opening
Milepost 163¼ (Taunton yard) . . .	0 00		45	Full
,, 163¾			35	,,
,, 164	1 57		35	,,
,, 164½			30	,,
,, 165	3 23	41·9	,,	,,
,, 166	4 34	50·6	,,	,,
,, 167	5 42	52·9	,,	,,
,, 168	6 51	52·2	,,	,,
,, 169	7 59	52·9	,,	,,
,, 170	9 08	52·2	,,	,,
,, 171	10 15	53·7	,,	,,
,, 172	11 29	48·6	,,	,,
,, 173	13 00	39·6	,,	,,
,, 174 (Whiteball)	14 48	33·3	18	⅛
,, 177	18 03	55·4	,,	,,
,, 179 (Tiverton Junction) . . .	19 42	72·7	,,	,,
,, 180	20 34	69·2	,,	,,
,, 182	22 13	72·7	,,	,,
,, 185	24 45	71·0	,,	,,
,, 187	26 27	70·6	,,	Full
,, 189	28 03	75·0	,,	,,
,, 191	29 40	74·3	,,	⅛
,, 192	31 29	73·5	,,	Shut
,, 193½	32 08	54·6	,,	,,
EXETER (193·9 miles) . . .	32 50		25	Full
Milepost 194 . . . . PASS	32 59	35·3	,,	,,

there were few British locomotives off the GWR which could better 4 lb., and many famous types were using 4½ to 6 lb. The figure for No. 4074 was 2.83 lb. To make this figure a true basis for comparing engines burning different grades of coal, allowance must be made for the heat content, or calorific value, of the coal. For Northern hard coals the figure equivalent to this would be about 3.0 lb., but no allowance for calorific value could make this other than a remarkable result. More than one engineer came to the conclusion that it just could not be true; E. S. Cox has told how this opinion was reached at Horwich after a detailed comparison had been made of the 'Castle' and of the Hughes 4—6—0 to see if any difference in design could be found which would account for the difference between the 2.83 lb. of the 'Castle' and the 5 lb. of the Lancashire & Yorkshire engine.

In fairness it should be said that, although this figure came from the average of several trials, in later years, when the standard of testing at Swindon had been raised still higher, more confirmation of figures between road and plant tests would have been demanded before a published claim was made. At this time the testing plant at Swindon could not absorb the power of a large locomotive so road tests were the only means of obtaining the information.

The years 1924 and 1925 provided further opportunities for the publicity value of the 'Castles' to be exploited. In those years there was staged the Empire Exhibition at Wembley the greatest exhibition seen in Britain. In the Palace of Engineering were displayed, end to end, No. 4073 *Caerphilly Castle* and London & North Eastern No. 4472 *Flying Scotsman*. Both engines glistened in the highest finish which their respective works could achieve, the brass beading and copper chimney cap of the 'Castle' being matched by the fittings of the 'Pacific' which were made from an alloy devised at Doncaster to look more like gold than normal brass. To the casual observer there can have been little doubt about the capacities of the engines. With its extra wheels, higher boiler and vast firebox, the 'Pacific' almost dwarfed the 'Castle', and the comparison was accentuated by the eight-wheeled tender of the 'Pacific'. What then of the board displayed before the 'Castle' proclaiming it to be the most powerful passenger engine in Britain?

Fortunately for later LNER locomotive history, the idea of putting the claim to the test occurred to other people than the exhibition visitors and the amateur railway fraternity. The suggestion for an exchange of locomotives seems to have been made by Sir Felix Pole, the General Manager of the

G

'*Pendennis Castle*', alongside the Gresley Pacific '*Flying Fox*' at King's Cross, April 1925

GWR, to his opposite number on the LNER; when asked about this at a later date Pole was reticent, but this may have been because he regretted the ill-feeling which was later caused by the exchange. Gresley is said to have been unenthusiastic as he was not yet fully satisfied with the performance of his 'Pacifics', but to those close to him he gave the impression of welcoming an opportunity for an interchange of technical information.

The proposal was accepted by the Boards and managements of the two companies, and it was arranged that a 'Castle' should work on the LNER for a week, and a Gresley 'Pacific' on the GWR. Coal and water consumptions would be measured but, unfortunately, although both railways had dynamometer cars they were not used.

On the GWR the test engines worked the up and down 'Cornish Riviera Express'; on the LNER they worked on alternate days on the 10.10 a.m. from King's Cross to Grantham and the 1.30 p.m. from King's Cross to Doncaster, returning on the 3.7 p.m. and 6.21 p.m. trains from those towns. On the GWR, loads in the down direction decreased gradually from 530 tons on leaving Paddington to 310 tons from Exeter to Plymouth. In the up direction they varied from 310 tons from Plymouth to Exeter to 345-380 tons from Exeter to Paddington. On the LNER 475-485-ton loads were normal. The exchange was held between 27 April and 2 May 1925, and was preceded by a week of preparatory running for the visiting drivers and firemen to learn the roads. On the GWR, No. 4474 was tested against *Caldicot Castle*. On the LNER, No. 4079 *Pendennis Castle* was compared with No. 2545.

The general running of *Pendennis Castle* on the Great Northern main line equalled anything which had been recorded at that time by the Gresley 'Pacifics' with similar loads, and it included a

number of sectional times which were without precedent. The first five minutes of the first down journey revealed one of the most notable characteristics of the engine—its ability to make clean

LNER 1.30 p.m. KING'S CROSS TO DONCASTER				
Date: 30/4/25				
Engine: 4079 *Pendennis Castle*				
Load: 16 cars, 453 tons tare, 475 tons full				
Driver: Young (Old Oak Common)				
Fireman: Pearce (Old Oak Common)				
Dist. Miles		Sch. Min.	Actual m. s.	Speeds m.p.h.
0·0	KING'S CROSS .	0	0 00	
2·6	Finsbury Park .		5 45	40
5·0	Wood Green .		8 50	56½
9·2	New Barnet .		13 50	49
12·7	Potters Bar .		18 20	48
17·7	HATFIELD .	25	23 25	70
22·0	Welwyn North .		27 25	
25·0	Knebworth .		30 45	52
28·6	Stevenage .		34 15	
31·9	HITCHIN .	39	37 15	
35·7	Three Counties .		40 20	77½
41·1	Biggleswade .		45 00	eased
44·1	Sandy .		47 40	
47·5	Tempsford .		50 50	
51·7	St. Neots .		55 05	53
56·0	Offord .		59 30	
58·9	HUNTINGDON .	64	62 35	57
62·0	*Leys Box* .		66 25	44
69·4	Holme .		73 15	79
72·6	Yaxley .		75 55	70½
75·0	*Fletton Junction* .		78 00	65
76·4	PETERBORO' .	83	80 05	
3·1	*Werrington Junc.* .		5 55	57½
8·4	Tallington .		11 20	65
12·2	Essendine .		15 00	60
15·8	Little Bytham .		18 40	54
20·7	Corby .		24 30	48
23·7	*Stoke Box* .		28 25	44½
29·1	GRANTHAM .		33 55	eased
43·7	NEWARK .		47 40	
62·2	RETFORD .		67 45	
79·6	DONCASTER .	88	86 20	

'Pendennis Castle', ready to leave King's Cross with the 1.30 p.m. Leeds express

starts through the notoriously difficult Gas Works and Copenhagen tunnels. On every run Finsbury Park was passed in less than six minutes, and on the five successive runs in the test week proper the time to Finsbury Park varied between no greater limits than 5 min. 42 sec. and 5 min. 57 sec. These times were about a minute less than was normal with 'Pacifics' hauling similar loads, and were achieved with only the slightest trace of slipping on one run. Experienced observers had in mind the greater proneness of 'Pacifics' to slipping than 4—6—0s having the same adhesive weight; *Pendennis Castle* demonstrated this advantage clearly. The impression made on sceptical LNER officials on King's Cross platforms was profound.

LNER 3.7 p.m. ex-GRANTHAM—KING'S CROSS
Date: 1/5/25
Engine: GWR No. 4079 *Pendennis Castle*
Load: 463 tons tare, 485 tons full
Driver: W. Young (Old Oak Common)

Dist. Miles		Actual m. s.	Speed m.p.h.
0·0	PETERBOROUGH .	0 00	
1·4	*Fletton Junction* . .	3 09	
3·8	Yaxley . . .	6 03	
7·0	Holme . . .	9 04	69
12·9	Abbots Ripton . .	14 28	56½
14·4	*Milepost 62* . .	16 04	
17·5	HUNTINGDON . .	18 54	77
20·4	Offord . . .	21 13	
24·7	St. Neots . .	24 50	66½
28·9	Tempsford . .	28 36	70½
32·3	Sandy . . .	31 33	
35·3	Biggleswade . .	34 18	57
39·4	Arlesey . . .	38 24	62
40·7	Three Counties .	39 41	
44·5	HITCHIN . . .	43 37	56½
47·8	Stevenage . . .	48 02	43
51·4	Knebworth . .	52 18	
54·4	Welwyn North . .	55 33	
58·7	HATFIELD . . .	59 18	70½
63·7	Potters Bar . .	64 14	56½
67·2	New Barnet . .	67 45	
		p.w.s.	
71·4	Wood Green . .	72 15	
73·8	FINSBURY PARK .	74 38	
76·4	KING'S CROSS .	78 58	

The uniformity of the ascents to Finsbury Park was representative of the work of Driver Young on the LNER. The variation between runs was slight, and points of particular note were spread throughout the runs. The log of the down run of 30 April is tabulated. Of the four runs made with the full load of 475-480 tons, this had the best time to Arlesey, but the greatest variation between any of the runs on this section was only 80 sec., and by Tempsford the variation was only 35 sec. Thereafter the engine was eased by varying amounts as it was ahead of schedule. One run ended with a fast entry into Peterborough, and the overall time was 78 min. 30 sec.; for the other runs it was 80 min. 5 sec., 80 min. 37 sec. and 80 min. 45 sec. The maximum speed on any run was 83½ m.p.h., sustained for 1½ miles near Three Counties. The fastest sustained speed was an average of 71.2 m.p.h. from Hitchin to Huntingdon, 22 min. 45 sec. for 27.0 miles.

On the second stage of the down journey the interest lay in the climb to Stoke. The run tabulated gave the best time on this section, with a maximum of 65 m.p.h. at Tallington, and minima of 48 before Corby and 44½ at Stoke summit. On another run the minimum at Stoke was 46, and the lowest minimum on any run was 43 m.p.h. After Stoke the engine was eased to avoid excessive gaining of time.

On the up runs *Pendennis Castle* had little in hand as far as Grantham, and actually dropped ½ min. on one run, but again it was the uniformity of running under strange conditions which stood out, rather than the small differences. The best time from Doncaster to Grantham, on 2 May, was 55 min. 51 sec., but full details of the speeds on this run were not recorded.

Of the final stages of the up journeys one run, that on 1 May, stood out above the others, mainly because of a very vigorous start from Peterborough. The log of this run is also shown. On Abbots Ripton bank speed fell from 69 to 56½ m.p.h., and a maximum of 77 at Huntingdon contributed to even time being reached by St. Neots, and maintained from there to Hitchin. On 28 April the train was stopped for three minutes by signals at Tempsford, and after a moderate start speed rose to 63 m.p.h. at Three Counties. The minimum at Stevenage was 45, followed by 60 at Langley, 54 at Woolmer Green, 73 at Hatfield, and 57½ at Potters Bar. The load was 475 tons.

Cecil J. Allen was able to quote runs recorded by 'Pacifics' at other times which in parts equalled those of *Pendennis Castle*; but as mentioned above, some of the times recorded were without precedent. During the actual test running the 'Pacifics' fell below their usual form, possibly encouraged by the drivers' attempts to restrain the coal consumption. If this was so, it availed little, for both on the LNER and on the GWR the 'Castle' showed a significant saving. On the round trips to Grantham, the 'Castle' burned 55.7, 55.9 and 59.2 lb. per mile (on the third trip there was a severe gale), and the 'Pacific' burned 59.6, 58.1 and 59.2. On the longer Doncaster runs the 'Castle' averaged 49.8 and the 'Pacific' 55.3 lb. per mile. These figures not only showed the greater thermal efficiency of the 'Castle' but also dispelled the theory that Swindon engines could only show a superiority over other engines when burning Welsh coal. On the GWR, No. 4474 burned 50.0, 48.8 and 52.4 lb. per mile on successive down runs (the gale mentioned above affected the third run), and *Caldicot Castle* burned 44.1, 45.6 and 46.8 lb. per mile (the rise on the third day was explained by the exceptional effort made on that run). On the up runs, No. 4474's figures were

50.9, 45.2 and 40.2, and *Caldicot Castle's* were 40.6, 36.8 and 37.9 lb. per mile. Overall therefore the 'Castle' bettered the 'Pacific' by 12½ per cent on the GWR with Welsh coal, and by 6½ per cent on the LNER with Yorkshire coal. The performance of the 'Castle' on its own line is discussed in Chapter 9.

There is little doubt that the LNER management regarded the results of the tests as information private to the two companies, but in the *Great Western Railway Magazine* of June 1925 there appeared an account of the trials, presented more like the results of an international sporting contest than of a friendly exchange of technical information. The figures showed that on both lines the 'Castle' had a clear lead over the 'Pacific' in coal consumption. The GWR account of the trials emphasised the time which had been lost by the 'Pacifics', but did not mention that some of the lateness of arrival ascribed to the engine had been incurred before the test engine took over the train. The publication of the account, with its element of unfairness towards the LNER engine, brought a letter of complaint from the LNER to the GWR General Manager; but he replied that as Cecil J. Allen, an LNER employee, had broadcast an account of the trials which, it was claimed, showed partiality towards the LNER, the GWR felt justified in presenting its side of the story. However the results were interpreted, they were a complete triumph for the GWR. As if to rub salt into the wounds, the GWR sent *Pendennis Castle* to stand next to *Flying Scotsman* at the second Wembley Exhibition from May to October 1925.

One of the first 'Stars' rebuilt as a 'Castle' No. 4009 'Shooting Star', with tall safety valve bonnet and large tender

No. 4000 'North Star' rebuilt as a 'Castle', hauling a Weymouth express near Southcote Junction

In May 1925 there appeared the second batch of 'Castles', Nos. 4083-92. These differed from the first batch in the omission of bogie brakes. The saving in weight by their omission has never been recorded on the official engine diagrams.

The names of this batch were:

No.	Name
4083	*Abbotsbury Castle*
4084	*Aberystwyth Castle*
4085	*Berkeley Castle*
4086	*Builth Castle*
4087	*Cardigan Castle*
4088	*Dartmouth Castle*
4089	*Donnington Castle*
4090	*Dorchester Castle*
4091	*Dudley Castle*
4092	*Dunraven Castle*

The rebuilding of 'Stars' to 'Castles' began in April 1925, with the conversion of No. 4009. Three more were rebuilt between then and June 1926, after which the only further conversion until 1937 was the odd engine, No. 4000, which was dealt with in November 1929. These were all true 'rebuilds' in that the original frames were retained, with an extension of 1 ft. at the back. As previously mentioned, No. 4000 lost its 'scissors' valve gear, but retained its non-standard footplating. New cylinders and cabs were fitted which, with the boiler, constituted the main differences between the 'Stars' and 'Castles'. In September 1924 another rebuild had produced a 'Castle' from *The Great Bear*. Here also the original frames were retained, but with more modifications at the rear. A new section was fitted from behind the middle coupled wheels.

The third batch of 'Castles' appeared from May 1926. In accordance with Great Western practice of using the second digit of the number to indicate the wheel arrangement or some other characteristic of a type, the numbers followed on from 4099 to 5000. Their names are given on page 102.

This batch introduced a change in a detail of construction which had been a visible characteristic of all the GWR four-cylinder locomotives so far. The position of the inside cylinders opposite the

No.	Name
4093	*Dunster Castle*
4094	*Dynevor Castle*
4095	*Harlech Castle*
4096	*Highclere Castle*
4097	*Kenilworth Castle*
4098	*Kidwelly Castle*
4099	*Kilgerran Castle*
5000	*Launceston Castle*
5001	*Llandovery Castle*
5002	*Ludlow Castle*

leading bogie wheels made it necessary to provide clearance for the movement of these wheels. This was done by setting the frames in, or 'joggling' them, from a section just to the rear of the leading bogie wheels. This reduced the distance between the frames from 4 ft. 1 in. to 3 ft. 5½ in. by curves of 6 in. radius. The vertical fold or joggle in the frame was clearly visible in a three-quarter view of the locomotives. From No. 4093 the frames were continued straight to the buffer beam, with a hollow 'dished' in the frame to allow of the translation of the bogie wheels. The effect of the change was that the cylinder casting was made wider, and the greater width was apparent. The line of rivets by which the buffer beam was attached to the frames by an angle iron was nearer to the buffers. The omission of the joggle remedied a weakness in the frames; the reaction of the thrust in the inside cylinders was transmitted through this part of the framing, and this thrust imposed an alternating bending action on the curves of the joggle. The greater piston thrust of the 'Castle' compared with the 'Star' was causing fatigue cracks to appear at the joggle, on account of the alternating stress. The elimination of the joggle also simplified construction, as the accurate fitting of joggled frames to the

No. 4037 'Queen Philippa' converted to 'Castle' class, and fitted with experimental A.T.C. pick-up

inside cylinder casting had always been a difficult operation.

As the alteration in the frames did not affect the leading dimensions as shown on the standard GWR engine diagram, it was not acknowledged by the issue of a new diagram. The straight frames were fitted to all subsequent new four-cylinder locomotives, and one 'Star' conversion, No. 4037, later acquired them. In the later years of the 'Castles' they were fitted to a number of earlier engines of the class, when the front section of the frames was renewed.

In 1926 there appeared a small number of enlarged tenders. These could be distinguished, when attached to 'Castles', by the bottom edge of the flared top being in line with the bottom of the cab windows. On the original tenders this edge was well below the cab windows. These tenders were a step towards the introduction of a much improved design with the water capacity increased from 3,500 gallons to 4,000 gallons. The tanks of the new tenders were entirely above the footplating and frames, whereas in the 3,500-gallon tenders a portion of the tank had been in a well between the frames. The new tanks were thus simpler to construct and to maintain, and some improvements in the framing were possible. The coal space was given a sloping floor, so that the coal tended to feed

No. 4082 'Windsor Castle,' hauling the GWR Royal Train at the Railway Centenary celebrations 1925

No. 5000 'Launceston Castle' entering Euston during the 1926 trials on the LMSR

locomotives, and by 1930 the 'Castles' originally fitted with small tenders had acquired the larger pattern. It may be mentioned here, out of chronological order, that an experimental eight-wheeled tender with a rigid frame was built in 1931. It weighed 49 tons 3 cwt., and ran behind a number of 'Halls', Stars' and 'Castles'.

The earlier 'Castles' were fitted with Automatic Train Control, but Nos. 4096-9, 5000-2 ran for a time without it. All later engines received it when built, and the omission from these engines was soon remedied. Engines from No. 5000 were built with whistle deflector shields; Nos. 4082-5 had received them earlier, and by 1936 all the earlier engines had received them.

Early in its life, No. 5000 took part in the last of the loans to other railways, when it worked for five weeks on the West Coast main line of the LMSR, being stationed at Crewe North shed. The exact administrative procedure by which the loan was effected has never been fully explained, but it originated in the division of responsibility for LMSR motive power between the Chief Mechanical Engineer, who designed, built and overhauled the engines, and the Operating Department, who, through the Superintendents of Motive Power, operated and serviced them. Midland influences predominated on the operating side and, in accordance with the Midland 'small engine' policy, large numbers of Midland compound 4—4—0s were ordered. By 1925, when Sir Henry Fowler succeeded George Hughes as Chief Mechanical Engineer, he realised that a larger engine than a 4—4—0 would be needed sooner or later. It was therefore natural to propose a 4—6—0 version of the compound. Before this design had proceeded far, Fowler was attracted by the work of the compound 'Pacifics' in France. The 4—6—0 was therefore dropped in favour of a four-cylinder compound

towards the front; this made the tender almost self-trimming, and eliminated much of the need to rake the coal forward. There were improvements in the springing; straight leaf springs were used for the first time on the GWR, and the spring hangers were supported from the framing by rocking washers instead of pins. In the earlier 4,000-gallon tenders the spring hangers were long, and the rocking washers were just below the level of the tender frame. In later tenders the hangers were shorter, and the force between the hanger and frame was transmitted through a rubber block.

The new tenders weighed 46 tons 14 cwt. loaded against 40 tons for the smaller tenders. The first appeared behind No. 5000 *Launceston Castle* in September 1926, and 4093 soon acquired one; 5002-3 were supplied with them new, after which 5004-12 appeared with small ones. Thereafter only the larger tenders were fitted to four-cylinder

A very rare picture showing No. 5000 entering Crewe from the south, and passing an unidentified LNWR 2—4—0 'Jumbo' on the left

'Pacific', and work proceeded as far as the casting of some cylinders, and in the experimental conversion of a Hughes 4—6—0 to compound working. The Operating Department saw no attractions in this proposal; some memories of the Webb compounds still remained on the LNW section; there was opposition to the use of a 4—6—2 if a 4—6—0 would suffice, and to the use of four cylinders if three would suffice.

Such was the disagreement between the ideas of the Operating Department and those of the C.M.E. that the Operating Department persuaded the management to borrow a 'Castle'. This was known to be a first-class specimen of the wheel arrangement (unlike any of the existing LMSR engines), and it was hoped to establish that a 4—6—0 would do all that was required on the West Coast main line, and do it economically without the complications of compounding. As on the LNER in 1925, the 'Castle' showed itself a master of all that it was given to do. The tests began on Monday 25 October with a series of runs from Crewe to Euston returning on alternate days. No. 5000 was driven by Young, of Old Oak Common shed, who had worked 4079 on the LNER, and he made a good start on the first day by gaining at least 14 min. on a 175-minute schedule from Crewe to Euston with 410 tons. Over the two weeks of this series of trials the load was progressively increased to 510 tons, but the 'Castle' kept time every day. After a week's rest, a second series of trials was run between Crewe and Carlisle, on Anglo-Scottish expresses which left Euston and Glasgow respectively at 10 a.m. Over the two weeks the loads were progressively increased from 300 tons to 450 tons, and with this maximum load Shap had to be climbed one day in a gale of wind and rain.

The accompanying tables show the logs of two of the runs. The first one is the final up run from Crewe, with a 17-coach train of 489 tons tare, and 510 tons full. The start from Crewe was leisurely, and after a fall to 37½ m.p.h. on Madeley bank, Whitmore was passed 3½ min. late. Recovery of time began at once, and without exceeding 72 m.p.h. Young had time comfortably in hand when he was stopped by signals at Rugby No. 7. Recovery of the time lost by this check was more energetic, and after a minimum of 57 at Roade, speed reached 75 m.p.h. at Castlethorpe. After a fall to 63½ between Wolverton and Bletchley, speed rose to 68. There was then a gradual fall to 60 at Cheddington, and the climb to Tring ended with a minimum of 52½ m.p.h. Continued fast running brought the train through Watford 3½ min. early, and there was ample reserve to allow for a permanent-way slack

			LMSR 10.30 a.m. CREWE—EUSTON Date: 27/10/26 Engine: GWR No. 5000 *Launceston Castle* Load: 17 cars, 489 tons tare, 510 tons full Driver: Young (Old Oak Common)		
Dist. Miles			Sch. Min.	Actual m. s.	Speed m.p.h.
0·0	CREWE		0	0 00	
4·7	Betley Road	.		10 00	40½
7·9	Madeley	.		14 55	37½
10·4	Whitmore	.	15	18 25	
14·6	Standon Bridge	.		22 45	64½
19·1	Norton Bridge	.	24	26 55	70½
24·4	STAFFORD		30	31 45	slack 40
28·6	Milford	.		37 00	55½
33·7	Rugeley	.	40	42 20	65
37·0	Armitage	.		45 25	59
41·7	LICHFIELD	.	48	50 05	
48·0	TAMWORTH	.	55	55 35	72
51·5	Polesworth	.		58 55	58½
55·7	Atherstone	.		63 15	55
60·9	NUNEATON	.	69	68 40	62
64·5	Bulkington	.		72 40	52½
70·0	Brinklow	.		78 20	63½
				sig. stop	0
75·5	RUGBY	.	85	87 10	
77·7	*Hillmorton*	.		90 45	45
82·7	Welton	.		97 05	
88·3	Weedon	.		102 25	72½
95·2	BLISWORTH	.	107	108 40	
98·1	ROADE	.	110	111 40	57
103·2	Castlethorpe	.		116 20	75
105·6	Wolverton	.		118 20	63½ min. after
111·3	BLETCHLEY	.	124	123 40	68
117·8	Leighton Buzzard	.		129 50	62
121·9	Cheddington	.		133 55	60
126·3	TRING	.	141	138 50	52½
130·0	Berkhamsted	.		142 40	68
133·5	Hemel Hempstead	.		145 40	72
137·0	King's Langley	.		148 35	76½
140·5	WATFORD JN.	.	155	151 30	72½
155·7	Hatch End	.		155 10	68
146·6	Harrow	.		156 50	72
149·9	Wembley	.		159 35	77½ p.w.s. 35
152·6	WILLESDEN JUNCTION	.	167	163 45	slack 25/70
156·9	*Camden No. 1*	.		169 25	
158·0	EUSTON	.	175	173 25	
	Net time: 166½ min.				

to 35 m.p.h. between Wembley and Willesden, together with the slack to 25 m.p.h. through Willesden Junction station, which was imposed throughout the trials because of limited cylinder clearance. The time to the arrival at Euston was 173 min. 25 sec., a gain of 1½ min. on schedule. The net time was 166½ min.

A second table shows the run of 16 November when, with a gross load of 415 tons, No. 5000 gained 8 min. on the 167-minute schedule from Crewe to Carlisle, despite a loss of 2½ min. by two permanent-way slacks. The climb to Coppull summit was good, with minima of 46 m.p.h. at Boar's Head, and 47½ at milepost 11½. The running from Garstang to Carnforth was fast, with speed not falling below 65 m.p.h., and reaching 71½ at Hest bank. With nearly 6½ min. in hand there was no call for a vigorous climb to Shap, but with minima of 26½ m.p.h. at Grayrigg and 20 at Shap summit, with a recovery to 66 m.p.h. at Tebay, running time was just kept from Carnforth to Shap summit. On the return journey on the following day with the same load time was gained more rapidly. A speed of 36 m.p.h. was maintained both on the 1 in 131 from Carlisle to Wreay and on the long 1 in 125 to Shap station. This gave a gain of

No. 5000 'Launceston Castle' at Durran Hill shed (former Midland Railway) Carlisle in 1926

7½ min. to Shap summit. The descent was lively, with speeds of 86½ m.p.h. at Scout Green, and 80½ at Hay Fell. By Oxenholme the train was 11 min. ahead of schedule, and despite signal checks at Burton and Lancaster, the gain had increased to 14 min. by Wigan. Signal stops at Bamfurlong and Winsford reduced the gain to 7¾ min., and the actual time to Crewe was 168 min. 15 sec.; the net time was 157 min., the same as the actual time on the northbound run.

With 450 tons on the following day, Young had the added difficulty of a westerly gale and heavy rain. On exposed stretches of line north of Preston the engine began to slip, and the gravity sand gear could not force the sand under the wheels before it was swept away by the gale. Some time was lost between Preston and Tebay, but on Shap itself less trouble was experienced, and time would have been bettered by Carlisle but for a signal stop at Penrith. This run was a severe test for the engine and its crew, but Young and his fireman Pearce had already proved their ability to master a strange road, and were to survive an even more severe test in America in the following year.

The times achieved in these runs were good, but not unprecedented; what was revealing was, in E. S. Cox's words, the way the 'engine performed with quiet mastery all the work on which the "Claughtons" . . . made the welkin ring with their reverberating exhaust'. Furthermore, the coal consumption per drawbar horsepower hour was less than had been recorded with any LMSR engine, although greater than had been recorded in the 1924 'Castle' tests. The trials made a profound impression, and the Operating Department was able to prevail upon the management. Work on the compound 'Pacific' was stopped, and it was decided

LMSR 1.10 p.m. CREWE TO CARLISLE (10 a.m. EUSTON TO GLASGOW)

Date: 16/11/26
Engine: GWR 5000 *Launceston Castle*
Load: 57 axles, 400 tons tare, 415 tons full
Driver: W. Young (Old Oak Common)

Dist. Miles		Sch. Min.	Actual m. s.	Speeds m.p.h.
0·0	CREWE . .	0	0 00	
4·8	Minshull Vernon		8 20	58½
8·7	*Winsford Junction*	10	12 00	71½
14·4	Acton Bridge .		16 50	72½
16·2	Weaver Junction .	18	18 25	65*
21·2	Moore . .		22 50	74
22·3	*Acton Grange Junc.*		23 50	64½
—			p.w.s.	25*
24·0	WARRINGTON	28	26 25	48/55½
29·8	*Golborne Junction* .		33 10	50½
33·2	Bamfurlong .		36 45	64
35·8	WIGAN . .	41	39 15	57½
38·0	Boar's Head .		41 50	46
39·1	Standish . .	45	43 10	50
41·6	Coppull . .		46 15	47½/71½
45·5	*Euxton Junction* .	53	49 40	65*/ 67
50·9	PRESTON . .	61	55 35	25*
52·2	*Oxheys Box* .	64	58 20	35
55·7	Barton . .		62 50	55½
60·4	Garstang . .	72	67 30	65
67·6	Galgate . .		74 10	67
70·8	*Lancaster No. 1 Box*		77 10	65
71·9	LANCASTER .	84	78 10	68
75·0	Hest Bank .		80 50	71½
78·2	CARNFORTH .	90	83 40	65
82·7	Burton . .		88 20	50½
85·5	Milnthorpe .		91 00	59
91·0	OXENHOLME .	104	97 30	43½
94·5	*Hay Fell Box* .		103 00	34½
98·1	Grayrigg . .		110 00	26½
104·1	TEBAY . .	122	116 40	66
107·1	*Scout Green Box* .		120 20	32
109·6	*Shap Summit* .	133	126 40	20
118·9	Clifton . .		135 55	79
123·1	PENRITH . .	147	139 40	57*
133·6	Southwaite .		149 20	70½
136·1	Wreay . .		151 35	64*
—			p.w.s.	
141·0	CARLISLE .	165	157 00	

*Speed reduced by brakes.
Net time: 154½ min.

that the new engine should be a 4—6—0. The Operating Department, despite its inclination towards three cylinders, was so impressed that it would have accepted the 'Castle' design as it stood, and an approach was actually made to the GWR, by way of a 'feeler', to find whether Swindon would build 50 'Castles' for the LMSR. Somewhat naturally this request was declined, as was also the subsequent request for a set of drawings. The LMS in its extremity then looked elsewhere.

Although not a strict part of Great Western locomotive history, it may be mentioned that in 1923 and 1924 the Chief Mechanical Engineer of the Southern Railway was faced with the problem of designing a passenger engine capable of working 500-ton trains at average speeds of 55 m.p.h. over the principal routes of the system. A 'Pacific' and a 4—6—0 were considered, but before a decision was reached J. Clayton, Personal Assistant to the C.M.E. of the Southern, made a footplate trip on No. 4076 on the down 'Cornish Riviera Express' on 1 October 1924. Ten days later he made a trip on a Gresley 'Pacific'. He was thereby confirmed in his opinion that a 4—6—0 would do the job, and the *Lord Nelson* was the outcome. The design of the *Lord Nelson* owed much to the association of Maunsell's assistant, James Clayton, with Church-ward during the latter part of World War I, when proposals for new standard locomotive designs were being worked out by certain prominent members of the Association of Railway Locomotive Engineers. As Clayton came to realise the genius that lay behind Churchward's practice on the GWR he became a most fervent admirer of it, and it influenced all his subsequent design work on the Southern Railway. This was a continuation of the Swindon influence that had commenced at Ashford in 1914, when Maunsell had recruited some of his new staff on the SECR from former Great Western men. For the GWR, the important point about the *Lord Nelson* when it appeared in 1926 was that the tractive effort of 33,500 lb. was nearly 2,000 lb. in excess of that of the 'Castle'. As the GWR had chosen to equate tractive effort with power in its publicity, it could not complain when the Southern claimed to have Britain's most powerful passenger engine.

Reverting to the story of the 1926 trials with *Launceston Castle*, when the Chief Mechanical Engineer of the LMSR had been instructed to get 50 powerful 4—6—0s built ready for the summer traffic of 1927, after the failure to obtain drawings of the 'Castle' the Southern Railway was approached, and a set of drawings of the *Lord Nelson* sent to Glasgow for helping the North British

'Pendennis Castle', with intermediate type tender, hauling an up mail train circa 1926

Locomotive Company who had been awarded the contract for building the new engines. Swindon influence, not only through *Launceston Castle* but also through the *Lord Nelson*, was thus brought to bear in the design of the 'Royal Scots'. It is interesting to recall that in all the earlier LMS correspondence about these engines they were referred to as 'Improved Castle type' !

For three successive years the month of May saw the appearance of a new batch of 'Castles'; in 1927 it was the fourth series, Nos. 5003-12. These were:

No.	Name
5003	*Lulworth Castle*
5004	*Llanstephan Castle*
5005	*Manorbier Castle*
5006	*Tregenna Castle*
5007	*Rougemont Castle*
5008	*Raglan Castle*
5009	*Shrewsbury Castle*
5010	*Restormel Castle*
5011	*Tintagel Castle*
5012	*Berry Pomeroy Castle*

As has been mentioned, No. 5003 had a 4,000-gallon tender when new, but the others ran for up to three years with 3,500-gallon tenders. Before the completion of No. 5012, the first 'King' had been completed; a heavier axle loading had been accepted, an engine larger than the 'Improved Star'

No. 4086 'Berkeley Castle' on down stopping train near Twyford

The Cornish Riviera Express (530-ton load) passing Twyford East hauled by engine No. 4086
'Builth Castle'

of 1919 had materialised, and the 'compromise' appeared to have completed its role. In fact, only a quarter of the 'Castles' had yet been built, and five years later construction was to be resumed.

Engine No. 5001 of the 1926 batch of 'Castles' was the subject of an experiment in connection with the design of the 'Kings'. From December 1926 to March 1928 it ran with a set of driving wheels turned down to 6 ft. 6 in. After a period it was reported that there was no significant difference in its performance, but this was scarcely surprising as the normal 'Castles' wheels of 6 ft. $8\frac{1}{2}$ in. dia. could be turned down a total of nearly 4 in. overall, and the minimum diameter before the tyres were scrapped was 6 ft. $4\frac{7}{8}$ in.

The first 40 'Castles' were originally allocated to Old Oak Common, Newton Abbot and Laira thus:

Old Oak Common	4073-83/9-94/7-9
	5000-2/5/6/10
Newton Abbot	5003/11/2
Laira	4084-8/95/6, 5004/7-9

These are the original allocations; by the time 5012 had appeared, some of the others had changed sheds. In the late nineteen-twenties, after the building of the 'Kings', the 'Castles' were dispersed over the system, and in 1932, before construction was resumed, the 40 pure 'Castles' and six conversions were distributed as follows:

Old Oak Common 19, Bristol 2, Exeter 1, Newton Abbot 8, Laira 6, Wolverhampton 2, Cardiff 6, Chester 2.

Engine No. 4079 'Pendennis Castle', photographed at Old Oak Common soon after construction

'CASTLES' NOW PRESERVED

'Caerphilly Castle', at Old Oak Common in 1923, during the first running trials

CHAPTER 9

PERFORMANCE OF THE 'CASTLES'

In the previous chapter, dealing with the inception of the 'Castle' class locomotives, and the remarkable results of certain dynamometer-car test runs that were communicated to the World Power Conference of 1924 in a paper by C. B. Collett, the influence of the design on other railways was also described, and the fine runs made during the respective Interchange Trials commented upon. These were inevitably special occasions, when the locomotives concerned were in first-class condition, and supplied with good coal. They were also handled by specially chosen enginemen. To judge the performance of the 'Castles' in their early days by these runs alone would be to gain a misleading impression. It is important to recall also that the 'Castles' held the position of premier passenger locomotive class of the Great Western Railway for barely four years. *Caerphilly Castle* was turned out in the summer of 1923, and *King George V* followed in 1927. Furthermore, in that period came the General Strike of 1926, followed by the prolonged coal strike, during which latter the railways of this country had to rely on large quantities of imported coal.

My own first experiences of these engines were in 1925 and 1926 and were anything but impressive, time being lost by engines on the 5.42 p.m. Exeter to Paddington; on the 4.15 p.m. Paddington to Swindon, and on the 3.30 p.m. Paddington to Exeter. The last two runs were made in 1926 and both showed all the symptoms of poor steaming; but the first of the three was in the summer of 1925, when performance on the West of England service was at a remarkably high level generally. This to some extent is anticipating, because the first really comprehensive account of 'Castle' performance was published by Cecil J. Allen in *The Railway Magazine* for December 1924, when full details of three runs on the 'Cornish Riviera Express', with maximum winter load, were tabulated. On one of the runs Allen rode on the footplate, with Chief Locomotive Inspector George Flewellyn keeping a close watch on all the proceedings. The engine was the celebrated No. 4079 *Pendennis Castle,* and the fully-documented record of this run provides a most valuable example of current standards of maximum performance. The booked point-to-point times were carefully observed, except where certain anomalies in the timings had remained unchanged over many years; but while the performance was impeccable in this respect it is important to realise that it was not always so.

No. 4074 'Caldicot Castle', with large tender, at Shrewsbury

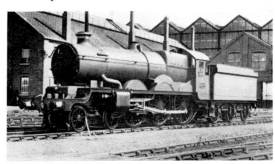

One of the later 'Castles', No. 5070 'Sir Daniel Gooch' at Swindon

THE DOWN 'CORNISH RIVIERA EXPRESS'

	1	2
Run No.	1	2
Date	13/10/24	2/5/25
Engine	4079	4074
Load: cars, tons tare/full		
To Westbury	14 495/530	14 498/530
To Taunton	12 423/455	12 426/455
To Exeter	10 360/390	10 363/390
To Plymouth	7 255/275	8 292/310
Driver	W. Young	E. Rowe
Fireman	Chellingworth	H. Cook

Dist. Miles		Sch. Min.	Actual m. s.	Speed m.p.h.	Reg. opening	Cut-off %	Actual m. s.	Speed m.p.h.
0·0	PADDINGTON	0	0 00		½	75	0 00	
1·3	Westbourne Park		3 15		¾		3 15	42
5·7	Ealing		9 20		"	30	9 08	
9·1	SOUTHALL	11	13 00	61	"	26	12 42	59
13·2	West Drayton		17 00	65	"	"	16 44	65½
18·5	SLOUGH	20	21 45	69	"	"	21 26	68
24·2	Maidenhead	25½	26 55	65	"	"	26 36	66½/65
36·0	READING	37	37 50	slack 45	"	"	37 25	slack
44·8	Aldermaston		47 05	62½	"	"	46 20	62
53·1	NEWBURY	56	55 45	57½	"	"	54 38	60
58·5	Kintbury		61 05	61	"	27	60 05	60½
61·5	Hungerford		64 10	57	"	"	63 12	55½/60½
66·4	Bedwyn	69½	69 15	60	"	29/30	68 17	57
70·1	Savernake		73 25	48	"	20	72 25	46
75·3	Pewsey		78 30	74	small port	20	77 26	72
81·1	Patney		83 20	71½	"	17	82 16	70
86·9	Lavington		88 05	80½	"	"	87 00	77½
95·6	WESTBURY	97½	95 35	slack 35	¾	25	94 40	slack
98·5	*Milepost 112¾*		99 10		"	"	98 13	52
101·3	FROME		103 00	slack 35	"	22	101 40	slack/51½
106·6	Witham		109 50	48½	"	23	108 03	50
108·5	*Milepost 122¾*		112 30	39½	small port	17	110 24	46
111·9	Bruton		115 55	74	"	"	113 25	72½/76
115·3	CASTLE CARY	120	118 55	slack 64	"	"	116 18	75
120·2	Keinton Mandeville		123 15	70½/64	"	"	120 26	72½
125·7	Somerton		128 25	68	"	"	125 28	64
127·9	Long Sutton		130 35	60	"	"	127 30	
131·0	*Curry Rivel Jc.*		133 20	71½	"	"	130 09	72
137·9	*Cogload Junction*	143	139 35	65	¾	20	136 06	68
142·9	TAUNTON	148	144 25	60	"	"	140 30	64
144·9	Norton Fitzwarren		146 25	60	"	"	142 22	67
150·0	Wellington		152 10	50½	"	30	147 17	58
151·8	*Milepost 172*		154 30	40½	"	35	149 19	41
152·8	*Milepost 173*		156 15	31	"	35	150 42	41
	Whiteball Tunnel		p.w.s.	25	"			40
153·8	*Whiteball Box*		158 28		small port	17	152 12	45
158·8	Tiverton Junction		163 35	75	"	15	156 46	75
161·1	Cullompton		165 35	69	"	"	158 38	76½
170·2	Stoke Canon		173 10	76½	"	"	166 00	72/74
173·7	EXETER	179	176 30	slack 30	½	"	169 10	
178·4	Exminster		182 10	65	"	"	174 40	
188·7	Teignmouth		193 15	57½	small port	"	184 54	
			p.w.s.	10				
193·9	NEWTON ABBOT	203	200 30		full	20	190 25	
195·0	*Aller Junction*		202 00	50	"	"	192 25	p.w.s.
196·7	*Milepost 217*		204 15	35	"	42 max.		
197·7	*Dainton Box*	209½	206 25	24½	shut	15	197 40	
202·5	Totnes	215½	211 55	57½	full	41	203 00	
205·3	*Tigley Box*		215 50	27	"	33	206 55	30
207·1	*Rattery Box*	223	219 20	33	"	25	210 25	35
209·4	Brent	225	222 40	49	"	22	213 28	56
211·6	Wrangaton		225 25	50	small port	15	215 40	
219·0	*Hemerdon Box*	237	233 40	53	shut	"	223 10	
221·7	Plympton		236 35	64½ max.	"	"	226 55	72
			p.w.s.	25			p.w.s.	
224·2	*Lipson Junction*	245	240 20	23	"	25		
225·7	PLYMOUTH	247	244 00				231 58	

The three runs just mentioned all conveyed gross loads of 515 to 525 tons behind the tender from Paddington to Westbury, and of 440 to 450 tons from Westbury to Taunton. At that time the scheduled allowance over the 95.6 miles from Paddington to Westbury was 97½ min. and the three engines took 103 min. 10 sec., 99 min. 54 sec. and 95 min. 35 sec. The second train, which was hauled by engine No. 4077 *Chepstow Castle*, had lost about 2 min. through a permanent-way check; but the first run, on which nearly 5¾ min. were lost, was unchecked, as was the third run with *Pendennis Castle*. Despite some fast subsequent running with the reduced load, the first run did not recover all the lost time by Exeter, which was passed ¾ min. late. Furthermore, on Cecil J. Allen's return run from Plymouth on the following day, with the same engine and crew, the performance had little of the sparkle that had so distinguished it on the down journey. But as an example of 'Castle' working at its best, that down journey is worthy of special study. The times and speeds, together with the regulator openings and cut-offs, are shown in the accompanying table.

The details of engine working, which were the first ever to be published regarding GWR locomotives in *The Railway Magazine*, created almost as great an impression as Collett's paper to the World Power Conference had done some eight months earlier. At that time the idea of a 4—6—0 locomotive hauling a train of 525 tons at 69 m.p.h. on level track and working in 26 per cent cut-off was unheard of, among followers of Allen's monthly articles. Actually, by GWR standards it was very hard work. On ordinary express passenger duties the usual working for the four-cylinder locomotives was in 17 or 18 per cent, and rarely as much as 20 per cent for fast work on the level. It depended upon whether the drivers worked with an absolutely full regulator opening or, as on Allen's footplate trip, had the regulator open only about ¾ full. This was preferred by many of the men. The driver of *Pendennis Castle* was William Young of Old Oak Common shed, who later became one of the most widely experienced express drivers in Great Britain. He had the distinction of working *Pendennis Castle* between King's Cross and Doncaster; *Launceston Castle* between Euston and Carlisle; and then, in 1927, he was selected to take the *King George V* to the U.S.A. and drive it on test over the Baltimore and Ohio Railroad.

Careful analysis of the performance of *Pendennis Castle* on this 1924 run on the 'Cornish Riviera Express' indicated that the engine was being steamed at approximately 24,000 lb. per hour be-

No. 4078 'Pembroke Castle' on up express near Reading

tween Paddington and Savernake, and that the coal rate was somewhat over 3,000 lb. per hour. In his account of the trip Allen laid emphasis on his impression that between Paddington and Westbury there had been nothing to suggest that the engine was being thrashed. Actually this was very far from being the case. When scientific train timing methods were introduced by the nationalised British Railways, and point-to-point timings were closely reconciled with the capacity of the locomotives, a firing rate of 3,000 lb. per hour was fixed as the very maximum that could be expected on a hand-fired locomotive for any length of time; so that on this run of *Pendennis Castle* in 1924, even if the boiler was not steamed to its absolute limit, the engine was being worked almost to the limit of the fireman. This provides ample explanation why performance of the standard put up on this journey was not consistently achieved in the working of the down 'Cornish Riviera Express'. Drivers preferred to drop a little time to Westbury, and get it back afterwards where the point-to-point timings did not make such severe demands.

On Allen's run, having passed Westbury 2 min. early, the subsequent proceedings were a 'cake-walk' by comparison—at any rate until Newton Abbot was reached. For example, No. 4075 *Cardiff Castle*, which had lost 5¾ min. to Westbury, gained 4 min. on *Pendennis* between there and Stoke Canon. The accompanying log reveals the very easy steam under which *Pendennis* was worked for most of the way between Westbury and Taunton. It is significant that on the last day of the 1925 Interchange Trial with the London & North Eastern, when Driver Rowe, on No. 4074 *Caldicot Castle*, was given instructions to make the fastest time he could, that in the early stages the only appreciable advantage he gained on *Pendennis Castle*, as shown in the log adjoining, was by a liberal interpretation of the speed restrictions at Reading. The engine was again being steamed up

Up Ocean Mail special in Sonning cutting: engine No. 4094 'Dynevor Castle'

to the limit of the fireman's capacity, as far as Savernake. *Caldicot Castle* began to draw ahead when *Pendennis Castle* was being run easily.

On the journey recorded by Cecil J. Allen, some interesting details were published of the engine working on the difficult stretch of line between Newton Abbot and Plymouth. It was only here, on climbing the steep gradients, that an absolutely full opening of the regulator was used. On Dainton bank from a maximum speed of 50 m.p.h. at Aller Junction cut-off was gradually increased from 20 per cent up to a maximum of 42; and this took the train over Dainton summit at a minimum speed of $24\frac{1}{2}$ m.p.h. On Rattery bank full regulator was again used throughout from Totnes, and the maximum cut-off employed was 41 per cent. The speed fell from $57\frac{1}{2}$ m.p.h. through Totnes to 27 at Tigley Box, which point marks the end of the steepest part of the bank. Although there was a permanent-way slack to 25 m.p.h. between Tavistock Junction and Laira Junction, the arrival in Plymouth was 3 min. early. The net times were $175\frac{1}{2}$ min. to passing Exeter, and 239 min. to Plymouth.

On this occasion the load conveyed beyond Exeter was one of seven coaches, whereas the 'Castles' were permitted to take eight on the fastest schedules over the South Devon line; but the run showed a comfortable margin in hand on every stage of the journey after Westbury and emphasises the uneven nature of the booking, which required inordinately hard work over the first 70 miles from Paddington to Savernake. The inspector estimated that $3\frac{1}{2}$ tons of coal had been burned, giving an average of 35 lb. per mile, but in the early stages the consumption was nearer 50 lb. per mile. By the tender gauge there were 3,250 gallons of water in the tank at Paddington, and this was supplemented by 1,500 gallons at Aldermaston troughs, by 1,700 at Westbury, 900 at Cogload, and 1,100 gallons at Starcross. The total water consumption was about 6,900 gallons, or 30 gallons per mile. Both these figures for consumption were very good, the coal figure being particularly notable as there was appreciable slack in the coal. No figures of boiler pressure are shown in the table, for Allen observed that only twice did the pressure fall perceptibly below 225 lb. per sq. in. For two short periods, when slack in the coal was causing trouble, it fell to 215 lb. per sq. in.

On the very fast run made by engine No. 4074, on the last day of the Interchange Trials in 1925, the general running beyond Newton Abbot was well above that of No. 4079, despite the extra coach. This sustained effort near to the end of a four-hour journey was notable, though the broad indications are that the steaming rate of the engine was considerably less throughout from Savernake than the effort sustained in that first 70 miles. Time was also gained first at Reading and then by a liberal interpretation of the speed restrictions along the coastal section from Starcross to Teignmouth. Permanent-way checks impeded the running at Aller Junction and again near Plympton, but the train nevertheless reached Plymouth in $231\frac{3}{4}$ min. giving an arrival a little over 15 min. early. Although this was the fastest run on record with a 'Castle' hauling the full load of the down 'Cornish Riviera Express'—an appreciably faster run than the earlier runs of the test series—the coal consumption was only slightly greater than on the earlier runs, on which 44.1 and 45.6 lb. per mile had been consumed. On the very fast run made on the last day the consumption was 46.8 lb. per mile and the very substantial advance over the estimated consumption on Cecil J. Allen's trip namely 35 lb. a mile, is a clear indication of the extra effort being put forth on this notable occasion. It might be added that despite the very hard effort put forward the coal consumption on this trip was less than on any of the rival LNER 'Pacific' journeys, when the overall time from Paddington to Plymouth was about a quarter of an hour longer.

In general, the working of the up 'Cornish Riviera Express' was a much easier task. The load was unchanged between Exeter and Paddington, and as only the Cornish resorts and Plymouth were provided for the tonnages were generally lighter than the gargantuan down train. The normal load of the up service was usually about 350 tons; but holiday workings could provide more interesting occasions, and two of these are set out in the accompanying table. They display the work of the same two drivers whose work has just been discussed on the down train—E. Rowe and W. Young. The first of these two runs was made on the first day of the Interchange Trials 1925, when by obvious arrangement with the Traffic Department, the 'Cornish Riviera Express' was run very much harder than the schedule required and arrived in Paddington 15 min. early. As a piece of stage management in a publicity campaign it was superb; as a piece of

Down West of England express at Twyford: engine No. 4090 'Dorchester Castle'

locomotive running it was extremely good though, of course, no traffic man could honestly commend the idea of a train arriving at its destination a quarter of an hour ahead of time. So far as the performance of the 'Castle' class engines was concerned, however, the run provides an extremely interesting and important piece of data, because it is probably the fastest time ever actually recorded between Exeter and Paddington. There was a steady gain of time throughout the journey; but perhaps the finest individual feat was the acceleration, after Westbury slack, to 69 m.p.h. on the level before Lavington and the subsequent minimum speed to 61 m.p.h. up 4 miles of 1 in 222 gradient. Time was gained by speed somewhat in excess of the limits through Reading, and the finish was very fast. Despite the hard work throughout, coal consumption was only 40.6 per mile.

The companion run with engine No. 4077 *Chepstow Castle*, driven by W. Young, was particularly interesting because it was made in the summer of the long coal strike, with the engine burning low-grade imported fuel. In the circumstances it was no mean task to have to haul a load

Engine No. 4032 'Queen Alexandra' rebuilt as a 'Castle'

THE UP 'CORNISH RIVIERA EXPRESS'

Run No.		1		2	
Date		27/4/25		19/8/26	
Engine		4074		4077	
Load: cars, tons, tare/full		10 358/380		12 431/465	
Driver		E. Rowe		W. Young	
Fireman		H. Cook		Chellingworth	

Dist. Miles		Sch. Min.	Actual m. s.	Speed m.p.h.	Actual m. s.	Speed m.p.h.
0·0	EXETER	0	0 00		0 00	
3·5	Stoke Canon		6 14		6 11	50
7·2	Silverton				10 32	52
12·6	Cullompton		15 33		16 35	53½
14·9	Tiverton Junction				19 43	44/51
19·9	*Whiteball Box*		23 31	47½	26 10	37½
23·7	Wellington		26 54		29 52	80
28·8	Norton Fitzwarren				33 32	88
30·8	TAUNTON	33	32 12		34 58	80
35·8	*Cogload Junction*	38	36 30		38 58	slack 55
43·8	Langport				46 30	60
48·0	Somerton				50 57	55
53·5	Keinton Mandeville				56 22	62
58·4	CASTLE CARY	61	56 10		60 55	62
61·9	Bruton		59 11		64 35	50½
65·2	*Milepost 122¾*		63 09	46	69 10	34½/72
72·4	FROME		70 00	slack	76 35	slack 30
78·1	WESTBURY	83	76 14	slack	83 25	slack 30
82·3	Edington		81 00	61		
86·8	Lavington		85 21	69/61	93 13	61
91·7	*Milepost 82*		p.w.s.		98 48	50
92·6	Patney		92 10			
94·9	Woodborough		94 34	57		
98·4	Pewsey		98 00	64/65	105 50	59
103·6	Savernake		102 57	62	111 22	55
107·3	Bedwyn	112			114 55	66
112·2	Hungerford				118 58	72
120·6	NEWBURY	124	117 19		125 55	72
127·0	Midgham				131 16	70
135·8	*Southcote Junction*		129 59		139 10	
137·7	READING	142	132 10	slack	141 35	slack 50
142·7	Twyford		136 58		147 23	64
149·5	Maidenhead	153½			153 35	68
155·2	SLOUGH	159	147 09		158 45	67½
164·6	SOUTHALL	168	155 01		167 45	65
168·0	Ealing				170 54	
172·4	Westbourne Park		161 27		175 12	56
					sigs.	
173·7	PADDINGTON	179	164 01		179 05	

Net times, min.:		162	178¼

of 460 tons from Exeter to Paddington in 179 min., particularly as at that time the by-pass lines at Frome and Westbury had not been constructed, and severe speed restrictions to 30 m.p.h. were in force at both places. The engine was being very skilfully handled, so as to avoid having to steam the boiler hard on any section. Throughout the journey time was lost on uphill stages and regained by very free running downhill. A maximum speed of 88 m.p.h. at Norton Fitzwarren will be particularly noted.

The impression one gains is that on the heaviest trains of the West of England service the 'Castles' were overloaded. When all conditions were favourable they could handle maximum load trains to time; but they could not be relied upon in all circumstances. This became even more apparent on the Birmingham route, although these engines never came into general use on the line in the same way as the 'Stars' had done previously, and the 'Kings' did subsequently. All the 'Castles' of the first batch were stationed at Old Oak Common, and consequently it was at first only on the one London single-home turn—the 9.10 a.m. down, and the 2.35 p.m. up from Wolverhampton—that one sometimes found a 'Castle'. A few engines of later batches were stationed at Stafford Road, but the finest work recorded by 'Castles' on the Birmingham service came, curiously enough, after the introduction of the 'Kings', when the smaller engines were deputising for the larger ones on the very difficult 6.10 p.m. down. For a time in 1930 engine No. 4088 *Dartmouth Castle* was at Wolverhampton and she was on the most difficult turn of the day for weeks on end. This turn was of course the 11.35 a.m. up (12 noon from Birmingham) and the 6.10 p.m. down.

During this period, which included the Whitsun holiday, I was able to travel by the train when the first portion was loaded to 14 coaches. The slip coaches were carried on the second part, so that the gross tonnage of 475 had to be conveyed through to Wolverhampton. A very dependable driver was on the job, A. Taylor of Stafford Road shed; the running throughout was of a very high standard, and Leamington was reached in a net time of 89¼ min. A slight signal check after Westbourne Park caused a loss of half a minute, making the train exceed the allowance of 7 min. to Old Oak Common West Junction by 20 sec. From that junction the adherence to point-to-point times was remarkable, the only further loss being between High Wycombe and Princes Risborough. The fall by only 1½ m.p.h., from 52½ to 51 m.p.h. in the 4.3 miles from Gerrards Cross to Beaconsfield, including 3½ miles at 1 in 254, was outstanding. The climb to Saunderton was aided by a speed of 50 m.p.h. through High Wycombe, where the limit is 35 m.p.h., but even so the minimum speed of 42 at milepost 22 was excellent with this load. The high standard of work was maintained to Leamington. Between Leamington and Birmingham timekeeping was impossible with such a load, and the net time, after allowing for a permanent-way slack approaching Snow Hill, was nearly 3 min. over the booking.

The ascent of Hatton bank is tackled less than a mile from the Leamington start, and despite half a mile of 1 in 109 down, there is little chance to gain momentum. No. 4088 did well to reach 45 m.p.h. before Warwick, and in passing Hatton without falling below 32 m.p.h. had equalled the best hill climbing by 'Castles' in the West of England. On the continuation of this run to Wolverhampton, Taylor actually cut the booking of 20 min. to 18¼ min., with speeds of 35½ m.p.h. on the climb to Handsworth Junction and an unusual maximum of 64 m.p.h. before the Wednesbury slack. That time should be gained with an abnormally heavy train on this very difficult section of the route was an indication of the crew's determination and skill.

6.10 p.m. PADDINGTON—BIRMINGHAM
Load: 14 coaches, 440 tons tare, 475 tons full
Engine: 4088 *Dartmouth Castle*
Driver: A. Taylor (Stafford Road)

Dist. Miles		Sch. Min.	Actual m. s.	Speed m.p.h.
0·0	PADDINGTON .	0	0 00	
1·3	Westbourne Park	3	3 55	
			sigs.	
3·3	*Old Oak Common West Junction* .	7	7 20	slack
7·8	Greenford . .		12 55	57½
10·3	Northolt Junction	15½	15 35	54½
14·8	Denham . .		20 05	63½
17·4	Gerrards Cross .		22 55	52½
21·7	Beaconsfield .		27 50	51
24·2	*Tylers Green* .		30 05	70½
26·5	HIGH WYCOMBE	32	32 15	slack 50
28·8	West Wycombe .		35 05	47
31·5	Saunderton .		38 45	
32·3	*Milepost 22* .		39 45	42
34·7	PRINCES RISBOROUGH	41	42 30	70½
40·1	Haddenham .		46 40	83½
44·1	*Ashendon Junction* .	49	49 40	slack 58
47·4	Brill . . .		52 55	
50·4	Blackthorn . .		55 35	70½
53·4	BICESTER . .	58	58 15	62
57·2	Ardley . .		62 15	52½/69
62·4	*Aynho Junction* .	67	67 15	slack 64½
64·0	King's Sutton .		68 45	65½
67·5	BANBURY .	72	71 55	67
71·1	Cropredy . .		75 15	57½
76·3	Fenny Compton .		80 15	76½
81·2	Southam Road .		84 15	74/78
87·3	LEAMINGTON	91	89 50	
2·0	Warwick . .		3 45	45
6·2	Hatton . .		10 15	32
10·4	Lapworth . .		15 20	58
12·9	Knowle . .		18 05	54½
16·3	Solihull . .		21 40	60½
20·1	Tyseley . .		25 00	68
			p.w.s.	
22·2	Bordesley . .		27 10	
23·3	BIRMINGHAM .	26	29 30	

Net times, min.: Paddington—Leamington 89¼
Leamington—Birmingham 28¾

*Nameplate of No. 4037 (rebuilt from Star)
after renaming, from 'Queen Philippa'*

One of the later 'Castles', No. 5046 'Earl Cawdor', originally 'Clifford Castle'

By the year 1928, with the introduction of the 'Kings', sufficient 'Castles' were available at Old Oak Common for them to be drafted on to duties additional to the West of England, and the one Wolverhampton 'single-home' job. They were, for example, put on to some of the South Wales trains. But those worked by Old Oak shed were not normally the heaviest on the service and the trains which were loaded most heavily were still 'Saint' workings. Amongst trains which were 'Castle' turns was the 3.55 p.m. down. This train was allowed 140 min. for the 133.4 miles to Newport, including a conditional stop at Badminton, which was usually made. A series of runs published in *The Railway Magazine* on this train gave, on one run, a net time of $92\frac{3}{4}$ min. for the 100.0 miles to Badminton, with 325 tons, and on another run a net time of 99 min. with 385 tons. There were a number of other runs of little less merit than these. The observer who timed these runs remarked that on undelayed runs some drivers seemed to saunter out of Paddington as if they had all day before them; but when hindered by enforced slowings they 'stirred their engines to mighty feats of acceleration'. Enforced slowings were common, particularly on the congested line through the Severn Tunnel and amidst the coal traffic of South Wales.

On the run which achieved the net time of $92\frac{3}{4}$ min., the engine was No. 4090 *Dorchester Castle*. Even time was reached by Reading, which was passed at $74\frac{1}{2}$ m.p.h.; Didcot, 53.1 miles out, was passed in 50 min. 20 sec. at $75\frac{1}{2}$ m.p.h., speed having fallen in between to 70 at Goring. A distance of 43 miles had been covered at an average of $71\frac{1}{2}$ m.p.h. when a signal check to 43 m.p.h. at Wantage

Road cut progress short. After a slow recovery to Swindon the driver opened his engine out, and from a speed of 76 m.p.h. at Little Somerford he stopped at Badminton, 10.3 miles away, in 9 min. 45 sec. Up the long gradient at a nominal 1 in 300 speed fell to 66 m.p.h. and then recovered to 68, and was still rising when steam was shut off for the Badminton stop. The actual time to Badminton was 96 min. 20 sec. As the train was ahead of schedule, signal checks followed, and there was a permanent-way slack before Newport, but Newport was reached a minute early.

The second run mentioned above was unchecked and the actual time to Badminton was 99 min. 5 sec. The start was leisurely, and nearly 4 min. were dropped to Slough, but running then became more lively. Speed reached 70 m.p.h. at Maidenhead and 74 at Goring, on the level. The minimum at Uffington was 66 m.p.h. and there was an increase to 69 at Shrivenham. For 36 miles the average was 70 m.p.h. High speeds down to the Severn Tunnel were uncommon, and the maximum in the tunnel itself was usually 60-65 m.p.h., with a fall to 30-32 m.p.h. on the 1 in 90 climb to Severn Tunnel Junction. On one run, however, No. 4083, with 385 tons, was allowed to reach 80 m.p.h. in the tunnel, and surmounted the 3 miles of 1 in 90 at a minimum of 45 m.p.h. The distance of 5.5 miles from Severn Tunnel East Box to Severn Tunnel Junction were covered in the unusual time of 5 min. 15 sec.

The last service on which the work of the 'Castles' at this period is worthy of record was the 3.45 p.m. from Swindon, the 'Cheltenham Flyer'. In 1929 the schedule was cut to 70 min., a figure

116

Torquay – Bradford express on the sea wall near Teignmouth: engine No. 4098
'Kidwelly Castle'

which had already been shown to leave a sufficient margin for out-of-course delays. The work of the 'Castles' on the new schedule soon showed that further acceleration was possible, but the most spectacular run during the period of the 70-minute booking was made by a 'Star', as recounted in Chapter 6. Two good 'Castle' runs that I logged personally are shown in the accompanying table. In both of these the start was, by 'Flyer' standards, leisurely. No. 5003 *Lulworth Castle,* with an eight-coach train, had a slight signal check after Shrivenham, and the driver then extended his engine to

The Cheltenham Flyer near Uffington: engine No. 5043 then named 'Banbury Castle', but later 'Earl of
Mount Edgcumbe'

'THE CHELTENHAM FLYER'

Run No.		1	2
Date		1929	1930
Engine		5003	4090
Load: tons, tare/full		254/275	265/280

Dist. Miles		Sch. Min.	Actual m. s.	Actual m. s.
0·0	SWINDON	0	0 00	0 00
5·8	Shrivenham		7 40	7 38
			sigs.	
10·8	Uffington		11 55	11 50
13·4	Challow		14 00	13 55
16·9	Wantage Road		16 35	16 37
20·8	Steventon	19	19 25	19 34
24·2	DIDCOT	22	21 50	22 09
28·8	Cholsey		25 05	25 46
32·6	Goring		27 45	28 45
35·8	Pangbourne		30 00	31 22
38·7	Tilehurst		32 05	33 40
41·3	READING	36½	34 00	35 45
46·3	Twyford		37 55	39 48
53·1	Maidenhead		43 10	45 00
58·8	SLOUGH	51	47 35	49 25
64·1	West Drayton		52 05	53 30
68·2	SOUTHALL	59	55 35	56 50
71·6	Ealing		58 20	59 31
			sigs.	
76·0	Westbourne Park		63 15	63 18
			sigs.	
77·3	PADDINGTON	70	67 15	65 38
Net time, min.:			64¼	65⅝

good effect. Speed crossed the 'eighty' line near Challow, and reached 86½ m.p.h. at Didcot. From there to Reading it was held between the limits of 83½ and 86½ m.p.h. After Reading there was a decided easing of the engine, but nevertheless the net time was only 64¼ min. On the second run No. 4090 *Dorchester Castle*, with a nine-coach train of somewhat lighter stock, encountered no checks. and with no station-to-station average reaching 80

m.p.h., stopped in Paddington 4¼ min. early. These runs showed that a further cut in the schedule would be quite practicable if the condition of the engine and the quality of fuel could be assured. However, the publicity value of the 'Flyer' was clearly established, and the early 1930s were to see an astonishing demonstration of the capacity of the 'Castle' for high-speed running on track which was little better than level.

Engine No. 5010 'Restormel Castle', as originally built with small tender

Foretaste of the 1930s: No. 5016 'Montgomery Castle', with special headboard. The engine in the background is the 'North Star'

Nameplate of engine No. 5069, destined to achieve the all-time steam record for an Ocean Mail special from Plymouth to Paddington

CHAPTER 10

INTRODUCTION OF THE 'KINGS'

In 1919 Churchward proposed to fit to the 'Star' chassis a boiler of maximum diameter 6 ft. and with a firebox of length 10 ft., giving a grate area of 30.3 sq. ft. This design of boiler fitted later to the 47XX 2—8—0 resulted in a 4—6—0 of $82\frac{1}{2}$ tons, with a maximum axle load of $20\frac{1}{2}$ tons. The civil engineer could not accept this, and the resultant compromise, four years later, was the 'Castle', with a boiler of maximum diameter 5 ft. 9 in., but with the same size of grate as had been proposed in the 1919 scheme. The reduction in the size of boiler held the total engine weight to 79 tons 17 cwt, and the axle loading to 19 tons 14 cwt.

Whether or not the 1919 proposal would have given a locomotive significantly better than the 'Castle' is doubtful, as the grate area would have been the same. It is, however, unlikely that its introduction would have eliminated the need for a still larger engine as soon as a relaxation of Civil Engineering limitations allowed an increase in axle loads. In 1926 Stanier, then Principal Assistant to the C.M.E., had the idea of a compound version of the 'Castle' and got F. W. Hawksworth to have this interesting proposition sketched out in outline. Compared with the simple 'Castle', the most conspicuous difference in the compound would have been that the outside high-pressure cylinders, with a diameter of 17 in., would have been ahead of the trailing bogie wheels. The wheelbase of the bogie was increased by 1 ft. to 8 ft. and the bogie centre was moved forward by 1 ft. 10 in. This would have placed the leading bogie wheels ahead of the inside cylinders, which could thus have had a diameter of 25 in. The inside cylinders would have been slightly inclined, a proposal which Churchward would never have countenanced. The starting tractive

No. 6000 'King George V' as originally built, in photographic grey

*After the triumphant return from the U.S.A. No. 6000 posed alongside Nos. 5010
and 4004 at Old Oak Common*

effort would have been 35,700 lb. The engine would have had greater cylinder volumes than the larger Frenchmen, but a smaller grate.

The outcome was vividly described to me by Hawksworth himself. The scheme had progressed far enough for Stanier to suggest it was time to show it to Collett. They went in to see him, and as Hawksworth put it: 'In about five minutes we were out again!' So much for compounds in the post-war era on the GWR.

In 1919 the Government set up a committee to investigate the stressing of railway bridges. The committee was to review the methods of calculating the stresses in bridges, with particular reference to the allowance to be made for impact loading, that is, the effect of a locomotive and train running on

'A' shop at Swindon, during the building of the 'Kings'

121

to a bridge at speed. An important influence on the impact loading is the method of balancing the reciprocating parts of the locomotive. The inertia effect of the reciprocating parts (that is, the piston, crosshead, part of the weight of the connecting rod, and, with Walschaert's valve gear, parts of the valve gear) tends to produce fore-and-aft forces on the locomotive, which may be transmitted through the drawbar to the train. The only completely satisfactory way of balancing these effects is by equal and opposite reciprocating parts. The effects can, however, be partially offset by adding additional balance weights to the driving wheels, in such positions that the centrifugal forces which they apply to the axles are directly opposite to the inertia forces of the reciprocating parts when these forces are at their greatest values (that is, approximately, when the balance weights are at the same height above the rails as the axles). These additional balance weights, over and above what is required to balance the rotating parts, are commonly called 'overbalance'. Unfortunately, at each revolution of the wheels the centrifugal forces which these balance weights produce tend to lift the axles and then to press them harder on the rails. This varying vertical force on the rails is called 'hammer-blow' or 'dynamic augment', and in some two-cylinder locomotives as conventionally balanced it exceeded 10 tons. It thus effectively increased the maximum axle load by this amount.

In a four-cylinder engine with the cranks equally spaced the hammer-blow can be eliminated entirely if all four cylinders drive on to one axle, as in the LNWR 'Claughtons'; but if the drive is on two axles, as in the GWR 'Stars' and 'Castles', other factors have to be taken into account. The Bridge Stress Committee tested a total of 39 types of locomotive on 42 bridges in many parts of the country, and certain of the results were unexpected, to say the least of it. It was shown, for example, that a four-cylinder engine is not inherently better than a two-cylinder, and it was with Churchward's locomotives that this was demonstrated. Until that time on the 'Stars' it was the practice at Swindon to balance a proportion of the reciprocating parts separately for the inside and outside cylinders, in the leading and middle pairs of coupled wheels respectively. Although the balance applied to the leading coupled axle was opposed to that of the middle one, and the total engine hammer-blow was relatively small, the hammer-blow from each of the individual axles actually exceeded that of the two-cylinder 'Saint' class! During the course of the Bridge Stress Committee's work the method of balancing was revised, and the

relative figures for the 'Saint', 'Star' and 'Castle' classes were then as follows:

| Engine Class | Max. Axle Load tons | Speed at 6 r.p.s. m.p.h. | Hammer-blow at 6 r.p.s. | | Max. Combined load at 6 r.p.s. tons |
			Whole engine tons	Axle tons	
'Saint'	18.4	86	17.9	6.9	25.3
'Star'	18.6	86	3.7	3.7	21.5
'Castle'	19.7	86	3.5	3.5	23.1

Until the work of the Bridge Stress Committee civil engineers had not made any concession in the maximum axle load limits imposed. The limits had been based on dead weight. The classic case had been that of the LNWR 'Claughtons', on which restriction was placed on the size of the boiler, to avoid increasing the axle-load, whereas the maximum combined load imposed upon the track at 6 r.p.s. was only $19\frac{3}{4}$ tons, compared with $33\frac{1}{4}$ tons of the 4—4—0 'George the Fifth' class.

Two major factors, and an incidental one, helped to hasten the course of events on the GWR. Taking the incidental one first, the scrapping of *The Great Bear* caused a considerable stir at Paddington. Sir Felix Pole, so it is said, was surprised to learn how the workings of the 'Pacific' engine had been restricted by its axle-loading; but a matter of more serious concern was that the 'Castles', despite their inherent excellence, had very little in reserve on maximum West of England loadings, and the period of the Coal Strike in 1926 had shown how quickly that reserve could be used up when fuel conditions were not ideal. Within the limit of a 20-ton axle-load, however, there was little that could be done about it, and then, of course, the second major factor intervened—the construction of the Southern Railway 'Lord Nelson' class 4—6—0 with a nominal tractive effort of 33,500 lb. The publicity folks at Waterloo immediately proclaimed, by poster and other means, that their new engine was the most powerful in Great Britain—which it was on the basis of nominal tractive effort—and the Great Western, which had taken immense pride in possessing that distinction up to that time, in the 'Castle', had cause for much concern. The deliberations of the Locomotive Committee of the directors under the enthusiastic and well-informed chairmanship of Sir Aubrey Brocklebank made a strong plea for the relaxation of the 20-ton axle-loading and as the strength of bridges imposed the limitation on axle load, the Civil Engineer should prepare diagrams to show what each bridge could carry. The

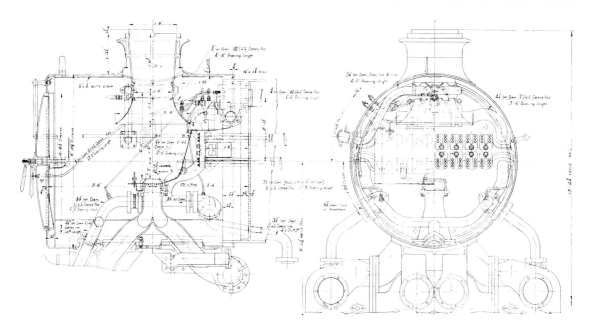

Smokebox arrangements on the 'King' Class

Civil Engineer, J. C. Lloyd, was called in, and he agreed to produce the information. He was also asked what axle load was now provided for in new bridges, and he replied that for 22 years all new bridges had been designed for a nominal axle load of 22 tons. Because of the hammer-blow in GWR two-cylinder engines, the static axle load had been limited to 19½ tons; but in the light of the Bridge Stress Committee's work he could now agree to a static axle load of 22 tons for four-cylinder engines on bridges which had been rebuilt to these standards.

This increase in bridge strength had been agreed between the then Civil Engineer, J. C. Inglis, and the Civil Engineering Committee of the Board. Such, however, was the narrow departmentalism of the GWR in the early years of the twentieth century that, although Inglis later became General Manager, neither his successors as General Manager, nor the Chief Mechanical Engineer, knew of the development. Lloyd was then asked if he could allow a further concession to 22½ tons for four-cylinder engines, and to this he agreed.

Pole then instructed Collett to prepare the design of a locomotive with 22½ tons axle load, and to have the first engine ready for the summer traffic of 1927. The Civil Engineer was instructed to have the Paddington-Plymouth route ready for the increased axle loading, and it was found that only four bridges remained to be strengthened. In commissioning this new design, Pole was as much

concerned with prestige as with meeting traffic requirements, for the introduction of the *Lord Nelson*, with a tractive effort of 33,500 lb., had enabled the Southern Railway to publicise it as the most powerful passenger engine in the country. As the GWR had seen fit to equate tractive effort with power in its publicity, the only answer which it could make to this claim was the introduction of an engine with a still higher tractive effort. The 1926 exchange had shown that a larger passenger engine could be expected on the LMS, and Collett was therefore instructed to get the tractive effort up to 40,000 lb., a figure which was unlikely to be exceeded on other railways for some time.

The importance which Pole attached to this numerical distinction was shown by a statement which he made in the *GWR Magazine*, beginning: 'Not only GWR employees, but a wide circle of well-wishers and enthusiasts, have anxiously enquired whether the GWR Company would surrender the honour of possessing the most powerful passenger locomotive in the country...'

Each dimensional factor contributing to the tractive effort formula was considered:
(a) diameter and stroke of cylinders
(b) coupled wheel diameter
(c) boiler pressure
In the event each one of the four was altered from the 'Castle' figures, and it is interesting to see how much each change contributed to the increase in nominal tractive effort from the 31,625 lb. of the

'Castle' to the 40,300 lb. of the new engine proposed.

Dimension	'Castle'	'Super-Castle'	Increases in Nom. T.E. lb.
Cyl. dia. in.	16	16¼	990
Cyl. stroke in.	26	28	2560
Boiler pressure p.s.i.	225	250	3980
coupled wheel dia. ft. in.	6—8½	6—6	1145

Of these, on the engines as first built the increase in cylinder diameter was no more than nominal. Only the first six engines were built new with 16¼ in. cylinders. The rest were bored to 16 in., but of course they would be increased with successive reborings on overhaul, and the dimension of 16¼ in. was regarded as the official figure for purposes of calculating the nominal tractive effort. The two major factors contributing to the enhancement of power were the increase in cylinder volume, and the raising of the boiler pressure. One gathers that Collett would have been satisfied to use the standard diameter of coupled wheels, and avoid the cost of making new patterns, and of subsequent design changes that were occasioned at the front end. With 6 ft. 8½ in. wheels the nominal tractive effort of the new engine would have been 39,100 lb. But Sir Felix Pole was most anxious to have at least 40,000 lb. and so 6 ft. 6 in. coupled wheels were adopted, with the attendant problems they introduced. Many years later that celebrated model engineer, the late J. C. Crebbin, who was a most intimate friend of Sir Felix, told me how Pole had once confided to him the very high capital cost of

introducing the new engines, in patterns, tools and special machinery. Crebbin added that a good deal of this cost would have been avoided if insistence had not been placed upon topping the 40,000 lb. mark.

Set out like this, it is relatively easy to lay down basic dimensions contributing to nominal tractive effort, but those basic dimensions had to be backed up by a boiler that would make the 'nominal' figure a reality. The detail design of the new engine was due to F. W. Hawksworth, who was then Chief Draughtsman, and a remarkable piece of design work it was, to build a locomotive of such tractive capacity, with an overall weight of no more than 89 tons.

The boiler was to be longer than that of the 'Castle', and this, together with the greater weight, called for an increase in wheelbase. The spacing of the coupled wheels was increased by 1 ft. 6 in. and the bogie wheelbase by 8 in., the distance from the rear bogie wheels to the leading coupled wheels remaining unchanged. Except for changes resulting from these increases in length, the motion remained unchanged from the previous four-cylinder locomotives. Adhering to Churchward's insistence on horizontal inside cylinders meant that the use of smaller driving wheels reduced the clearance under the inside cylinders. This could have been met by adopting Churchward's early practice of having the cylinder centre line offset from the centre of the driving axle, but in fact the wheel diameter of the bogie was reduced from the previous standard figure of 3 ft. 2 in. to 3 ft., and the bogie was redesigned.

At about this period there were a number of failures of Churchward bogies through rivets breaking, and it was felt that a plate-framed bogie would be stronger. The late A. W. J. Dymond was given the job of designing such a bogie, and he soon

The first five 'Kings', lined up at Old Oak Common shed

124

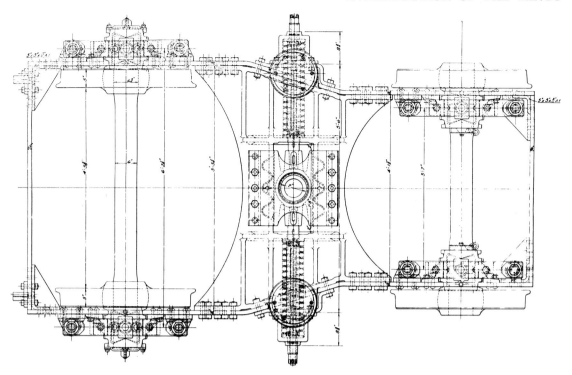

Plan view of the bogie, 'King' class locomotives

found that it was very difficult to fit inside plate frames under the inside cylinders, consistent with making the frame of adequate depth. He therefore arrived at a design in which the frame abreast of the leading bogie axle was outside the wheels, and the rear part of the frame inside the wheels. This curious arrangement was submitted to Collett who, to the designer's surprise, immediately accepted it.

Later investigation showed that the weakness of the Churchward bogie lay not in the strength of its frames, but in inadequacy of diagonal bracing. A proposal to fit plate-framed bogies to the 'Halls' was therefore abandoned in favour of inserting additional diagonal bracing in the standard bogie. Had this decision been reached a little earlier, the 'Kings' would probably have had a standard Churchward bogie.

The equalising bar arrangement was abandoned, and the new bogie had individually-sprung axles. At first the only springing for the axleboxes was short laminated springs with rigid hangers. To mitigate the effects of the longer engine wheelbase, the trailing coupled axleboxes were given one inch of lateral play under the control of inclined slides, like the Cartazzi slides of the standard GWR pony truck. The trailing section of the coupling rods had spherical bushes to accommodate the translation of the trailing axle.

The boiler, designated Standard No. 12, was the largest narrow-firebox boiler in Britain, but its design followed closely on previous Swindon practice. Before the boiler was designed, the locomotive inspectors were asked which type of boiler was the most dependable steamer, and they all replied that it was the No. 1 boiler. As the new boiler was not hampered by the restrictions which were imposed on the 'Castle' boiler, it was possible to make the main ratios much nearer to those of the No. 1 boiler than were those of the 'Castle'. It was thus said that the 'King' boiler was a true enlargement of the Standard No. 1. Some boiler ratios for the 'Star', 'Castle' and 'King' are shown in the following table:

COMPARISON OF BOILER RATIOS

Ratio	Star	Castle	King
Firebox heating surface/grate area	5·72	5·42	5·66
Total evaporative heating surface/grate area . . .	6·45	6·78	6·45
Superheating surface/grate area	9·69	8·66	9·14

The maximum diameter was 6 ft., as in the No. 7 boiler, and the firebox length 11 ft. 6 in. The barrel

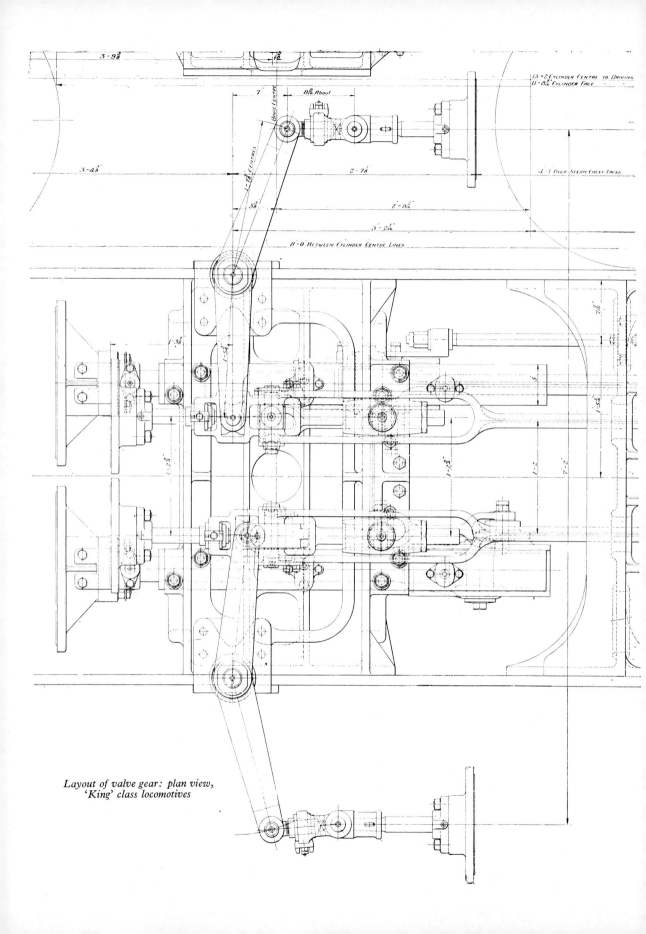

*Layout of valve gear: plan view,
'King' class locomotives*

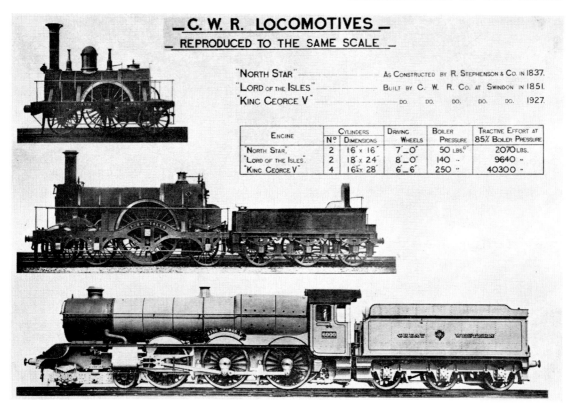

Development of GWR locomotive power: 1837 to 1927

length was 16 ft., an increase of 1 ft. 2 in. on the No. 1 boiler. The grate area was 34.3 sq. ft., an increase of $16\frac{1}{2}$ per cent on the 'Castle'. This was balanced by an increase of 18 per cent in the firebox heating surface, and of 19 per cent in the superheating surface. To distribute the weight of the boiler evenly over the rear section of the engine frame, flat leaf springs about 8 in. long were fitted in grooves in the boiler carrying brackets beneath the firebox.

The increase of 27 per cent in the nominal tractive effort was not fully matched by the increase in the size of boiler, and thus, even more so than in the previous four-cylinder engines, short cut-off working would be required.

Collett's part in the day-to-day design work was less than Churchward's had been, and the detailed design work owed much to the fine team of senior draughtsmen working under the direction of F. W. Hawksworth.

The class was initially dubbed a 'Super-Castle', and it was rumoured that the engines were to be named after cathedrals. The plan to send the first engine to America led to the choice of a more striking name, and the decision to name them after Kings of England was taken before the first engine

had been completed. Unlike the 4021-30 series of 'Stars', which omitted the numbers of individual monarchs, the 'Kings' were named after individual Kings of England, starting with King George V and running in reverse order to King Stephen. Whether this arrangement was of greater assistance to railway enthusiasts in teaching them the order of the English Kings, or in helping them to remember the numbers of the 'King' class engines, is not recorded.

The striking appearance of the 'Kings' came from a combination of their generally massive size and specific details of the design. The chimney was shorter and of larger diameter than those of the 'Castles'; the outside bearings of the bogie and the conspicuous front stretcher of the bogie frame implied solidity, and the straight diagonal top line of the main frames adjoining the inside cylinder, together with the box-like steam chest cover, gave a more thrusting appearance ahead of the smokebox than in the 'Stars' and 'Castles'.

The measure of improvement in train loading which the 'Kings' brought to the West of England services is shown by the following summary of the maximum loadings with which an unassisted engine was expected to keep time.

	Paddington to Taunton	Taunton to Plymouth
Saint	392 tons	252 tons
Star	420	288
Castle	455	315
King	500	360

The most important gain was the additional 45 tons from Taunton to Plymouth, which enabled much double-heading to be avoided between Newton Abbot and Plymouth with the summer loading of the West of England expresses. Furthermore, even with the increased loading, it was possible to reduce the time of the 'Cornish Riviera Express' from its long-standing 247 min. to an even 4 hours from Paddington to Plymouth. The 'Kings' were allowed initially to work only between Paddington and Plymouth, and between Paddington and Wolverhampton via Bicester. This restriction was indicated on the engine route map as 'hatched red', and was indicated on the engine by two red discs. No power classification was given to them in GWR days.

No. 6000 appeared in June 1927 and, after some trial running, it reappeared from Swindon fitted with Westinghouse brake. It was soon revealed that this did not presage a brake revolution on the GWR but was in preparation for a visit to America. The idea of the visit originated in 1925. Daniel Willard, the President of the Baltimore & Ohio Railroad, was already considering how his Company would celebrate its centenary in 1927. He therefore commissioned an eminent railway enthusiast, Edward Hungerford, to attend the centenary celebrations of the Stockton & Darlington Railway, and to report his observations. During his stay in England,

Hungerford met Pole, and from their conversation emerged the idea that an English engine (that is, for Pole, a GWR engine) should take part in the celebrations. When the decision to build the new engine was taken, it was clear that this was the engine which must go to America, though at first this was not appreciated in Swindon Works. K. J. Cook, then Assistant Locomotive Works Manager, has told how the general outline of the new class was known, but that very few drawings had yet reached them. Then one day he was called into his chief's office; Stanier was there, and Cook began to explain how he was planning to have the first engine of the new class completed by the end of September. But Stanier cut him short by saying, 'Young man, she's got to be in the USA by August!' The task was achieved with sufficient margin for the engine both to complete the necessary trial trips, and to be exhibited at a number of stations in aid of the GWR 'Helping Hand' fund, which aided members of the staff in time of need. At Paddington, on 1 July, nearly 3,000 people inspected the engine, and many were turned away disappointed. On 20 July the engine worked the down 'Limited' for the first time, and made an excellent run.

The expedition to the U.S.A. was in the personal charge of Mr. W. A. Stanier, as he was then, in his capacity of Principal Assistant to the Chief Mechanical Engineer. The engine arrived at Roath Dock, Cardiff, on 2 August 1927, and was loaded on the S.S. *Chicago City* on the following day. It was accompanied by the replica broad-gauge engine *North Star*. The boiler was loaded separately from the chassis on the deck of the ship, no crane capable of lifting the locomotive in one piece being available. It reached Locust Point, Baltimore, on

The two locomotives that visited the U.S.A. in 1927: 'King George V' and the replica 'North Star'

Engine No. 6000, ready for the American visit fitted with Westinghouse brake

21 August, and was taken thence to the Mount Clare shops of the Baltimore & Ohio. The fineness of its detailed work compared with contemporary American locomotives immediately attracted attention.

The exhibition was open from 24 September to 15 October, and was visited by a quarter of a million people. No. 6000, handled by Driver W. Young and Fireman Pearce of Old Oak Common, led the procession each day, and attracted great interest. An oval track had been laid in the exhibition grounds, and a procession of locomotives paraded round the track past the viewing stands. There was a gentle slope approaching the grandstand, and Young allowed No. 6000 to coast down it. The engine moved past the stand in complete silence, whereas the American engines, even new ones, groaned, squeaked and clanked. Never was the excellence of Swindon workmanship shown up more strikingly. Amongst the visitors who were allowed to ride on the engine was Henry Ford I, who took many photographs, and announced his intention of making a model of the engine.

Two days after the close of the exhibition, No. 6000 was given a test run on the Baltimore & Ohio railroad. Starting from Baltimore, the engine ran to Washington (36 miles), and then made a trip to Philadelphia ($132\frac{1}{2}$ miles); finally it returned to Baltimore. The load comprised a dynamometer car and six coaches which, in the heavyweight American stock of the day, weighed 544 tons tare. The task set Driver Young and Fireman Pearce was thus formidable. The load was as great as was handled on the West of England trains, but instead of the progressive shedding of load by the 'Limited' on its four-hour journey, this load was to be hauled over 272 miles, with a total running time for the day of seven hours. Instead of the familiar soft Welsh coal, the engine was burning hard gas coal, which formed large quantities of clinker, and was better suited to grates of twice the size of that of *King George V*. Added to this was the Westinghouse brake, a strange road, the different feel of the roadbed, the need for additional vigilance on a railway without fencing, and the general unfamiliarity of all the lineside equipment. And to crown all, the work of the engine was being studied in the dynamometer car by senior officers of three American railroads.

A 'Star' and two 'Castles' had previously maintained the honour of the Great Western when tested on two 'foreign' lines in England. Now, under much more severe conditions, *King George V* and its crew ably maintained the honour not only of Swindon but of British locomotive engineering generally. Pearce's contribution was notable; despite the difficult fuel, pressure was never below 205 lb. per sq. in., and on the last leg of the test

129

Front end of No. 6000, with 'Britannia' (Miss Bruhl) showing also the original bogie springing

station, speed rose to 23 m.p.h., and the drawbar pull was nearly 9 tons at one point. The equivalent drawbar pull, corrected for gradient, was nearly 60 per cent of the nominal tractive effort. The cut-off was recorded as 55 per cent; in the 1953 tests of No. 6001 this tractive effort at 23 m.p.h. required a steam flow of 28,000 lb./hour and a cut-off of 50 per cent.

Although the Baltimore & Ohio had water troughs, the water level was lower than on the GWR and No. 6000's scoop was ineffective. Two stops were thus needed for water, one at Camden station, Baltimore, and the other at Elks Mills. The start from Elks Mills was on a 1 in 115 gradient, and it was here that the drawbar pull of 5 tons at

was maintained at 235-245 lb. per sq. in. There was an almost complete absence of black smoke from the chimney, in contrast to the American engines both at the exhibition and in ordinary service. At the request of the railroad officials speed did not exceed 74 m.p.h., and for much of the test was limited to 65, but the general running was up to the standards maintained on the home railway. The gradients varied down to 1 in 79. Amongst notable figures recorded was a drawbar pull of 5 tons sustained at 48 m.p.h. on a gradient of 1 in 115; the equivalent drawbar horsepower was nearly 1,700.

The accompanying table shows the log of the second leg of the journey, from Washington to Philadelphia. It was on the early stages of this run that the worst trouble with fuel was experienced. Cut-off was 25 per cent up the bank towards Muirkirk, 20 per cent on the undulating section to Camp Meade Junction, and 15 per cent on the falling gradients towards Halethorpe, where a maximum speed of 73 m.p.h. was reached. On the 1 in 79 gradient, which extends for 2½ miles out of Camden

BALTIMORE AND OHIO RAILROAD, WASHINGTON—PHILADELPHIA
Date: 17/10/27
Engine: GWR No. 6000, *King George V*
Load: Dynamometer car + 6 cars, 544 tons tare
Driver: W. Young (Old Oak Common)

Dist. Miles		Actual m. s.	Av. speed m.p.h.
0·00	NEW YORK AVENUE	0 00	
0·57	'F' Tower .	2 30	13·6
4·68	Alexandria Junction	8 20	42·4
7·49	Berwyn . . .	12 00	46·0
12·83	Muirkirk . . .	17 55	54·0
16·45	Laurel . . .	21 45	56·5
19·87	Camp Meade Junction	25 00	63·4
24·37	Dorsey . . .	29 10	66·4
28·79	Relay . . .	33 30	61·4
30·54	Halethorpe . .	35 50	44·9
34·42	Carroll . . .	40 55	45·6
36·00	CAMDEN .	44 55	
0·00		0 00	
1·44	Mount Royal .	5 10	16·7
2·47	Huntington Avenue .	8 25	18·3
3·40	Waverley . . .	10 50	23·2
6·79	Bay View . . .	15 40	41·8
13·14	Poplar . . .	22 40	54·6
15·67	Cowenton . . .	25 10	57·9
19·69	Bradshaw . .	30 15	47·3
21·34	C.N. Tower . .	32 40	41·3
23·62	Van Bibber . .	35 10	54·3
27·33	Belcamp . . .	38 50	60·7
32·23	Aberdeen . . .	43 50	58·8
36·93	Havre de Grace .	48 50	57·6
39·35	Aiken . . .	53 40	30·1
47·80	Leslie . . .	63 10	53·5
52·56	Childs . . .	69 05	48·3
	Elks Mills: water stop 6 min. 40 sec.		
59·36	Newark . . .	85 55	
65·34	Stanton . . .	92 40	53·2
67·69	W. J. Tower . .	96 05	41·5
68·51	Wilsmer . . .	97 50	28·1
69·63	Elsmere . . .	98 55	62·0
71·48	Wilmington . .	102 05	35·1
76·12	Silverside . . .	108 20	44·5
82·42	Feltonville . .	114 40	59·7
95·02	East Side . .	133 15	
96·51	PHILADELPHIA (Chestnut St.) .	137 45	

The pageant of locomotives at the Baltimore and Ohio centenary celebrations

48 m.p.h. was recorded. The American officials were very impressed with the riding of the engine, but, as is recorded later, the engine might well have given a different impression. The engine was fitted with a bell for its trial run, and retained this for the remainder of its life. It bears an inscription: 'Presented to the locomotive *King George V* by the Baltimore and Ohio Railroad in commemoration of its centenary celebrations, September 24—October 15, 1927.' Two medals were also fixed to the cab sides. The clean lines of the engine created a great impression in the United States, and a number of express engines on the Baltimore & Ohio and other railroads appeared with cleaner external lines and, in some cases, with copper-capped chimneys.

The first twenty 'Kings' were ordered on the same Lot number, but they appeared in two batches, the first six by July 1927, and the remain-ing fourteen between February and June 1928. Soon after the first engines entered traffic, reports were received of rough riding, and as wear developed in the axleboxes, the engines developed alarming motions, nosing at the front and lurching from side to side at the rear. On 10 August 1927, the bogie of No. 6003 was partially derailed whilst travelling at speed near Midgham on straight track. Fortunately the derailment did not spread to the train, and the results were not serious. They were, however, alarming, not only because there was no obvious reason why this derailment should have occurred on good track, but also because No. 6000 was about to be tested in America, where the track might be well below GWR standards.

There is a story, possibly apocryphal, that Collett visited the scene of the derailment, and poking his umbrella into several sleepers, found that the metal

The two plaques presented to the GWR in commemoration of the American visit, affixed to the cab sides of engine No. 6000

View of bogie and front end 'King' class locomotive, showing finalised arrangement of bogie springing

tip penetrated. He therefore blamed the Civil Engineer for the derailment, on the grounds that the track was defective.

Nevertheless, an immediate investigation was made into the riding of the 'Kings' and, as suspicion fell on the bogie springs, a section was cut from the head of a rail on the weighbridge at Swindon. This allowed one wheel to drop, and it was found that a drop of $1\frac{1}{2}$ in. relieved the wheel of all load. There was thus little margin for defects in the track consistent with the wheel loads remaining sufficiently great to ensure adequate flange control. Coil springs were therefore introduced into the spring hangers to soften the springing. Plates were also inserted in the trailing axleboxes to reduce the lateral clearance to $\frac{1}{16}$ in., in place of 1 in., and the inclined slides were later removed. From the seventh engine onwards the slides were omitted, but the spherical bushes were fitted to all the engines of the class. It was not until the mid-fifties that it was realised that these were no longer required, and they were then replaced by cylindrical bushes.

These changes eliminated the rolling of the

Engine No. 6004 'King George III' with intermediate arrangement of bogie springing

No. 6021 'King Richard II' on West of England express near Reading

*The Cornish Riviera Express near Shaldon bridge, Teignmouth: engine
No. 6012 'King Edward VI'*

engines, but fracturing of bogie springs continued, and after some months the trailing coupled wheel springs were redesigned to make them softer (33 plates at $\frac{3}{8}$ in. and one at $\frac{1}{2}$ in., in place of 21 at $\frac{7}{16}$ in. and one at $\frac{1}{2}$ in.). This cured the trouble, and the 'Kings' then gained the reputation of being amongst the best-riding engines in Britain.

After the Midgham derailment, Stanier received a cable from Collett telling him that No. 6000 was not to be run on a main line until permission was received from Swindon. When the modifications to the bogie springing had been agreed, details were sent to Stanier, and he was able to arrange with the Baltimore & Ohio Company for the necessary work to be done in their shops. Fortunately the engine was not troubled by the rolling which

affected other members of the class at this time. The 'Kings' soon established themselves as powerful engines, and they showed mastery over the West of England workings. Their introduction was heralded by the usual blaze of publicity, including the publication of a book entitled *The King of Railway Locomotives*. The high tractive effort was exploited to the full, as Pole intended.

A further batch of ten 'Kings' was built in 1930 and appeared between May and August. They displayed a few visible changes from the earlier engines. In September 1930, No. 6029 travelled to Manchester for the centenary celebrations of the Liverpool & Manchester Railway, and was serviced at Agecroft shed on the former L & YR. This was the furthest north ever reached by a 'King'.

*The Midgham incident: the Cornish Riviera Express halted, with the bogie of engine No. 6003
derailed*

133

CHAPTER 11

THE 'KINGS' AT WORK

SIR Felix Pole's promise that the first engine of this new class should be exhibited and run during the centenary celebrations of the Baltimore & Ohio Railroad in August 1927 set the target for production of the 'King' class, and the pioneer engine was completed at Swindon in June of that year, followed by five more in July. It was essential that No. 6000 should be fully run-in before leaving England, because it was not only to be exhibited but also run out on the line. The ordinary running-in turns were successfully performed and on 20 July 1927, No. 6000 worked the down 'Limited' non-stop from Paddington to Plymouth. The day was a Wednesday, and at mid-week in the period of the summer service the load was no more than moderate, namely 425 tons gross as far as Westbury

and 350 tons beyond. But the particular point of interest was that for the first time ever a load of 338 tons was taken from Newton Abbot to Plymouth without assistance.

The tare load for the new engines over this section was fixed at 360 tons; but no more than two days were to elapse before there was a still more convincing demonstration. On the Friday of that same week engine No. 6001 *King Edward VII* was put on to the train; the load was one coach heavier throughout, and crowded with passengers; and the load taken unassisted over the South Devon line was no less than 375 tons tare, 400 tons full behind the tender. Skeleton logs of these two inaugural runs are shown on the next page.

The potential of the 'Kings' was exploited

Engine No. 6003 on down West of England express near Reading, a week before the Midgham derailment

quickly; in the winter timetable of 1927, 7 min. were cut from the schedule of the down 'Limited'. But despite the publicity that accompanied the introduction of the 'Kings', and the magnificent appearance of the new engines, there was definitely something about them that left the more thoughtful of outside observers slightly unimpressed. By the year 1927 the slight recession in Great Western locomotive performance that had followed the Coal Strike of 1926 had largely disappeared, and both 'Stars' and 'Castles'—not to mention the trusty old 'Saints'—were back on top form. And when vast new locomotives were introduced to do work that the older engines had done so brilliantly, when conditions were favourable, the need for so great an advance was questioned. The publicity was inclined to be regarded purely as publicity. After all, it was argued, if *Knight of the Grand Cross* could take 530 tons out of Paddington on the down 'Limited', and with appropriate reductions of load at Westbury, Taunton and Exeter bring the train into North Road 3 min. early, was there really a need for locomotives of 40,300 lb. tractive effort, in order to cut a mere 7 min. off the schedule? In any case the Interchange Trial of 1925 had shown that a 'Castle' could cut 15 min. off that schedule!

The inaugural runs of engines Nos. 6000 and 6001 on the 'Cornish Riviera Express' included nothing that was really significant in the way of performance. If the 'Stars' had taken 288 tons over the South Devon line, on the proportions of tractive

effort to load the 'Kings' ought to have had 410 tons, not 360. It only needed news of the derailment at Midgham to give a slightly jaundiced view of the new locomotives. Neither was the first detailed account of their working any more reassuring. Following his very successful footplate run from Paddington to Plymouth on a 'Castle' in the autumn of 1924, Cecil J. Allen was accorded a similar privilege on a 'King' in October 1927, with results that led to a good deal of controversy in the columns of *The Railway Magazine*! All the arguments that had centred around the differences in boiler design between Swindon and Doncaster practice were revived, and the instances of bad steaming of GWR engines during the period of the 1926 Coal Strike were recalled.

The engine was No. 6005, and the loads on the four successive stages of the journey were much the same as on Allen's footplate run with *Pendennis Castle*, three years earlier, namely 525, 450, 380 and 270 tons gross behind the tender. The tender had been loaded with indifferent coal, however, and although having a nominal tractive effort vastly greater than that of a 'Castle' the engine was never master of the schedule until the load was reduced to 7 coaches at Exeter. By Slough 1 min. 40 sec. had been dropped, and speed was only $62\frac{1}{2}$ m.p.h. A permanent-way slack to 40 m.p.h. caused further delay, and the lateness rose to $3\frac{1}{2}$ min. There was a further permanent-way slack at Aldermaston, and speed did not rise above $57\frac{1}{2}$ m.p.h. until Savernake

CORNISH RIVIERA EXPRESS

Date			20/7/27	22/7/27
Engine No.			6000	6001
Engine Name			*King George V*	*King Edward VII*
Load: tons E/F				
To Westbury			410/425	447/480
To Plymouth			338/350	375/400

Dist. Miles		Sch. Min.	Actual m. s.	Actual m. s.
0·0	Paddington	0	0 00	0 00
—			p.w.s.	p.w.s.
9·1	Southall	11	16 19	13 03
18·5	Slough	20	24 53	21 15
36·0	Reading	37	41 57	36 55
53·1	Newbury	56	59 18	55 25
66·4	Bedwyn	69½	72 18	68 35
95·6	Westbury	97½	98 58	95 55
101·3	Frome		105 44	103 32
115·3	Castle Cary	120	120 11	118 45
142·9	Taunton	148	146 20	143 30
153·8	*Whiteball Box*		159 04	157 28
173·7	Exeter	179	176 43	176 15
225·7	Plymouth	247	242 26	246 59

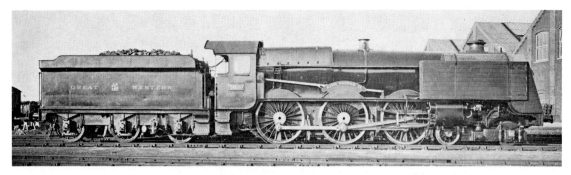

*Engine No. 6005 'King George II' with indicator shelters ready for
dynamometer car trial runs*

had been passed 6 min. late. There was a gradual recovery, and by Taunton lateness was under 2 min., but with only 380 tons a further minute was lost by Exeter. However, there was no difficulty in recovering this loss after Exeter, and Plymouth was reached in 237 min. 50 sec., or 233½ min. net. Much work with the pricker had been needed, and the interest of the run lay in the fireman's efforts to combat difficulties which at that time were not frequent on the GWR. The publication of this run, in very extended detail, caused something of a sensation among students of locomotive performance, and there were some, with no particular partisan feelings, who were inclined to the view that Swindon design practice, in enlarging the 'Star' to the proportions of the 'King', had over-reached itself, and that for locomotives of 40,000 lb. tractive effort the large boiler and wide firebox favoured by Doncaster was preferable.

In any event, Allen was offered another trip, and at the second try he was favoured with an immaculate performance from the locomotive point of view, though the incidence of no fewer than *eight* permanent-way checks prevented the end-to-end schedule being maintained. The steaming was as near perfect as made no matter, and there appeared

in print for the first time details of a run on the GWR when the working cut-offs for fast, high output running on level track were less than 20 per cent. Between Paddington and Reading, where *Pendennis Castle* had needed 26 per cent cut-offs, *King James I* was doing equal or slightly faster work on 18 per cent. Of course cut-offs of this order were nothing new on the Great Western. They had been a commonplace for many years on 'Stars' and 'Castles' when those engines were working under optimum conditions. It was only in the haulage of 500-ton trains on the 'Limited' and similar duties when so loaded that the driving had to be much harder. Complete details of this run are given in the accompanying table.

It must nevertheless be emphasised that although the 'King' class engines, in good working conditions, were completely master of any task the traffic department liked to put to them, their ultimate capacity, like that of the 'Castles', was the ability of the fireman to shovel coal. On that day in May 1925, when *Caldicot Castle* brought the 'Limited' into Plymouth 15 min. ahead of time, neither the front-end limit nor the grate limit of the engine had been reached. Whether the engine was a 'King' or a 'Castle' the same amount of steam had to be

*No. 6000, with presentation bell, on up
Bristol express near Swindon*

*No. 6018 'King Henry VI' on up West
of England express*

THE DOWN 'CORNISH RIVIERA EXPRESS'

Load to Westbury 14 cars 492/525 tons   to Exeter   10 cars 337/380 tons
to Taunton 12 cars 421/450 tons   to Plymouth 7 cars 253/270 tons
Engine: No. 6011 *King James I*
Driver: Wright: Fireman: Hounslow

Dist. Miles		Sch. Min.	Actual m. s.	Speed m.p.h.	Regulator Opening	Cut-off %	Boiler pressure lb./ sq. in.
0·0	PADDINGTON	0	0 00		½	75	230
1·3	Westbourne Park		3 05		¾	23	240
5·7	Ealing		9 10		¾	20	240
9·1	SOUTHALL	11	12 45	59	full	18	245
13·2	West Drayton		16 55	65	,,	18	245
18·5	SLOUGH	20	21 35	70½	,,	18	245
24·2	Maidenhead	25½	26 40	66	,,	18	245
36·0	READING	37	37 30	slack 40			245
44·8	Aldermaston		46 55	65	,,	20	245
53·1	NEWBURY	55½	54 55	61	,,	18	240/235
58·5	Kintbury		60 10	62½	,,	18	240
61·5	Hungerford		63 15	57½/61½	,,	20	240
66·4	Bedwyn	68½	68 15	58½	,,	20	230
68·6	*Grafton Curve Junction*		70 50	p.w.s. 20	,,	30	240
70·1	Savernake		73 55		,,	18	240
75·3	Pewsey		79 05	71½	,,	18	225
81·1	Patney		83 50	77½/80½	½	16	235
86·9	Lavington		88 35	p.w.s. 20	full	20	240
95·6	WESTBURY	96	98 35	slack 35	,,	20	240
98·5	*Milepost 112¾*		102 05	54	,,	20	245
101·3	FROME		105 30	slack 35	,,	20	250
106·6	Witham		112 00	53½	,,	20	245
108·5	*Milepost 122¾*		114 15	50½	½	16	240
111·9	Bruton		117 15	77½/83½	1st port	16	245
115·3	CASTLE CARY	118	120 00	slack 50	½—¾	16	245
120·2	Keinton Mandeville		124 55	67	¾	16	245
125·7	Somerton		129 45	75	full	16	240
131·0	*Curry Rivell Junction*		134 05	79	½	16	240
137·9	*Cogload Junction*	140	140 55	p.w.s. 10	full	20	245
142·9	TAUNTON	144½	147 45	58½	,,	20	240
144·9	Norton Fitzwarren		149 45	62½	,,	20	240
147·5	*Milepost 167¾*		152 10	64	,,	20	240
150·0	Wellington		154 40	58½	,,	25	240
152·8	*Milepost 173*		157 55	42½	,,	30	235
153·8	*Whiteball Box*		159 25	44	full ½	16	230
158·8	Tiverton Junction		164 05	76½	½	16	240
161·1	Cullompton		165 55	80½	½	16	240
170·2	Stoke Canon		173 05	76½	1st port	16	240
173·7	EXETER	174½	175 55	70	full	16	240
178·4	Exminster		179 40	82	shut	20	240
				p.w.s. 10	½	20	245
188·7	Teignmouth		195 25	slack 40/65	½	20	245
193·9	NEWTON ABBOT	198½	201 25	slack 25	full	20	245
195·7	*Milepost 216*		204 13	50½	,,	25	245
197·7	*Dainton Box*	204½	207 50	24½/60	shut	35 (max.)	240
202·5	Totnes	210½	213 35	53	full	20	245
204·7	*Milepost 225*		216 49	31½	,,	30	245
205·3	*Tigley Box*		217 50	29	,,	35	245
207·1	*Rattery Box*		221 15	36	,,	25	245
209·4	Brent	219½	224 10	54	,,	25	245
211·6	Wrangaton		226 40	p.w.s. 25	shut	20	245
219·0	Hemerdon Box	231	235 55	60/68	½	20	240
221·7	Plympton		238 30	50	½	20	235
225·4	Mutley		sigs.			20	
225·7	PLYMOUTH	240	245 35			20	

Net times, Paddington to Exeter   167¾ min.
Paddington to Plymouth 228 min.

*The down Cornish Riviera Express: a photograph taken near Reading West showing the full
14-coach load: engine No. 6000 'King George V'*

put through the cylinders. The 'Kings' did not represent any advance in locomotive design technique or practice. They were, rather, a very ingenious enlargement of the 'Star', and embodying all the principles established by Churchward in years before World War I.

Nevertheless, as the engine crews became thoroughly used to the workings of these great machines, and learned the art of exploiting the vast tractive power without causing an undue drain upon the boiler, the standards of performance on the West of England line positively soared, and the reputation of the 'Kings' as the really great locomotives they were became established. Their tractive effort was no mere paper figure, because they enjoyed that immunity from slipping that was characteristic of all Great Western 4—6—0s, and that tractive effort could be used with confidence for lifting heavy loads smartly away from rest or climbing steep gradients.

Three exceptionally fine runs of the 1929-30 period are clearly shown in the accompanying table—all on the 'Cornish Riviera Express', after some adjustments had been made in the intermediate timing. Allen had remarked that an allowance of 37 min. to Reading seemed unnecessarily severe; but the new time was 36 min., and runs 1 and 2 show that it was quite practicable with trains of 500 tons gross. Exeter was booked to be passed in $171\frac{1}{2}$ min., an allowance which was at that time one of the fastest bookings in the world over such

a distance, if not the fastest.

Run No. 1 shows a good all-round performance by No. 6000 in July 1929, when only the Weymouth slip portion was carried. By Slough the train was almost on time, and even time was reached by Twyford. The time of 35 min. 15 sec. to Reading was notable, but the slack was evidently treated lightly. Up the Kennet Valley more time was gained, and Savernake was passed in 68 min. for 70.1 miles. A permanent-way slack to 15 m.p.h. at Woodborough spoiled the descent, but there was a recovery to 82 m.p.h. at Edington, and the time to Westbury was 92 min. 40 sec. Running beyond Frome was similar to that of No. 6011, except that Castle Cary was passed at the full 60 m.p.h. which was allowed. Despite signal checks before and after Cogload, Taunton was passed at 57 m.p.h. in 139 min. 51 sec., and speed fell to 26 m.ph. at Whiteball Box. The train was a minute early at Exeter. The continuation of this run is shown in a separate table and is discussed later.

The second run was notable for the very quick start, probably the fastest ever recorded with so great a load. To be within 36 sec. of the Southall booking and 18 sec. ahead of the Slough booking was remarkable for a 500-ton train, and showed the advantages to the operating authorities of the tractive effort of the 'Kings'. A speed of $76\frac{1}{2}$ m.p.h. at Slough was also notable with this load. The passing time at Reading was thus 1 min. 45 sec. inside the new booking, and running of a similar

THE DOWN 'CORNISH RIVIERA EXPRESS'

Run No.		1		2		3	
Date		7/29		1930		1/9/30	
Engine No.		6000		6020		6013	
Load: cars, tons, tare/full							
To Westbury		14 479/510		14 — /505		16 543/580	
To Taunton		11 378/405		12 — /430		13 443/475	
To Exeter		11 378/405				13 443/475	

Dist. Miles		Sch. Min.	Actual m. s.	Speed m.p.h.	Actual m. s.	Speed m.p.h.	Actual m. s.	Speed m.p.h.
0·0	PADDINGTON	0	0 00		0 00		0 00	
1·3	Westbourne Park		2 55		2 37		3 40	
5·7	Ealing				8 13		10 10	52½
9·1	SOUTHALL	11	12 00	60	11 36	63	13 55	59
18·5	SLOUGH	20	20 20	73	19 42	76½	22 35	71½
24·2	Maidenhead	25	25 00	72	24 28	71½	27 35	68
31·0	Twyford	30½	30 50	69	30 03	74	33 30	73
36·0	READING	36	35 15	slack	34 15	slack 45	37 55	slack 50
37·8	*Southcote Junction*		37 20	56			39 50	
44·8	Aldermaston				43 25	68	46 50	61
53·1	NEWBURY	54	51 35	62	50 58	62½	55 10	58½
58·5	Kintbury				55 58	67	60 45	
61·5	Hungerford				58 54	61	63 55	58½
66·4	Bedwyn	67	64 05	64	63 31	65	68 45	59
70·1	Savernake		68 00	52	67 19	53	73 05	45½
75·3	Pewsey		72 55	75	72 03	77½	78 10	72½
78·8	Woodborough		76 10	p.w.s. 15				
81·1	Patney		80 05	55	76 42	70½	82 55	75
86·9	Lavington				81 13	79	87 35	83½
91·4	Edington		89 00	82			91 10	74
95·6	WESTBURY	94	92 40	slack	89 24	slack	95 00	slack 40
101·3	FROME		99 30	slack	p.w.s.		102 00	slack 40
106·6	Witham					51	108 15	49½
108·5	*Milepost 122¾*		108 45	50/82	108 26	49	110 40	45
111·9	Bruton				111 38	82	113 50	82
115·4	CASTLE CARY	116	114 35	slack 60	114 29	slack 60	116 35	slack 69
120·2	Keinton Mandeville				118 57			
125·7	Somerton		124 00	72 max.	123 54	65	125 40	64½
129·9	Langport		127 39		127 39	77½	129 20	75
137·9	*Cogload Junction*	137	sigs. 134 45	55	134 41	70½	136 15	65
142·9	TAUNTON	142	sigs. 139 55	57	140 57*		140 55	60
144·9	Norton Fitzwarren						143 00	63½
150·0	Wellington		147 25	54			148 25	
153·8	*Whiteball Box*		153 20	26			154 35	28
158·8	Tiverton Junction		158 25	72			159 30	74
161·1	Cullompton						161 35	76½/79
170·2	Stoke Canon		167 30	81 max.			sigs. 169 25	
173·7	EXETER . pass	171½	170 20	slack 60			sigs. 173 10	

Net time, min.:							
To Taunton				138*			
To Exeter		166				172½	

*Arrival of slip coach

standard to that of the previous run, but un-impeded by checks, brought the train through Westbury in 89 min. 24 sec., 5½ min. early. The Taunton slip portion came to rest in 140 min. 57 sec., or 138 min. net.

On the third run No. 6013 had a formidable load of 16 coaches, 543 tons tare, and 580 tons full, reduced only to 475 tons by the slipping of three coaches at Westbury. The new booking proved to be too severe for this loading in the earlier stages, but with 43 tons over the full load for standard timekeeping, Driver Wimhurst was quite entitled

Down Cornish Riviera Express near Twyford: engine No. 6004 'King George III'

to a few extra minutes. Nevertheless, he was ahead of time by Cogload Junction, and it was only signal checks before Stoke Canon and Exeter that prevented him from passing Exeter on time. Speed passed the seventy line twice before Reading, with 71½ m.p.h. at Slough and 73 at Twyford. Up the Kennet Valley No. 6013 managed to reach 61 m.p.h. at Aldermaston, and the fall from 59 m.p.h. at Bedwyn to 45½ at Savernake was creditable with this load. This run gave the highest speed on the descent to Westbury of any of the 'King' runs so far described, with 83½ m.p.h. at Lavington. Another fine climb followed after Frome, with a fall from 49½ m.p.h. at Witham to 45 at the sum-

A scene in Sonning Cutting, with No. 6011 'King James I' overtaking No. 4085 'Berkeley Castle'
on a stopping train

Up Cornish Riviera Express near Reading: engine No. 6002 'King William IV'

mit. As the train was ahead of time at Taunton, Whiteball could be taken gently, and speed fell from $63\frac{1}{2}$ at Taunton to 28 m.p.h. at the summit. A brisk run down to Exeter, with a maximum of 79 m.p.h. after Cullompton, was interrupted by the signal checks mentioned previously.

A separate table herewith shows the continuation to Plymouth of the run by No. 6000 shown on page 139. With 18 tons more than the maximum unassisted load, the driver carried on to Plymouth without assistance, and cut 50 sec. from the allowance from Exeter to Plymouth. Along the coastal stretch 3 min. were gained, and this allowed for some loss of time on the banks. On Dainton there was a fall from 45 to 20 m.p.h.; but the climb to Rattery was excellent for a load of 405 tons. The speed at Totnes was only 52 m.p.h., but Tigley was passed at 25 m.p.h. and there was a good recovery to 32 m.p.h. at Rattery. A clear run into Plymouth gave an arrival 3 min. early.

The debut of the 'Kings' on the Birmingham line was not auspicious. Engines 6017, 6018 and 6019 were sent new to Wolverhampton in the summer of 1928, and a run clocked by myself on the 6.10

THE DOWN 'CORNISH RIVIERA EXPRESS'

Date: July 1929
Engine: 6000 *King George V*
Load: 11 cars, 378 tons tare, 405 tons full
All distances and times are measured from Paddington

Dist. Miles		Sch. Min.	Actual m. s.	Speed m.p.h.
173·7	EXETER . pass	$171\frac{1}{2}$	170 20	slack 60
178·4	Exminster . .		174 45	68
188·7	Teignmouth .		185 30	slack 47
193·9	NEWTON ABB.	$195\frac{1}{2}$	191 20	slack
195·7	*Milepost 216* .		194 10	45
196·7	*Milepost 217* .		195 55	32
197·7	*Dainton Box* .		198 25	20
202·5	Totnes . .		204 40	52 max.
205·3	*Tigley Box* .		210 20	25
207·1	*Rattery Box* .		214 05	32
209·4	Brent . .	218	217 35	45
219·0	*Hemerdon Box* .	230	228 30	60
223·8	*Laira Junction* .		233 20	68/48
225·7	PLYMOUTH .	240	237 00	

Net time: Paddington to Plymouth $232\frac{1}{2}$ min.

p.m. from Paddington on 3 August, with No. 6019 *King Henry V,* showed a net loss of 3 min. on

Engine No. 6013 'King Henry VIII' at Old Oak Common

sign that things were going well on the footplate, that speed restrictions were scrupulously observed. There was no need to snatch the odd seconds by 'cutting' the limits, and at Ashendon Junction speed was reduced to 52 m.p.h. The recovery from this slack was immediate and vigorous. Blackthorn was passed at 75 m.p.h., but after detaching the Bicester slip portion one minute early and being relieved of 55 tons of load the engine was justifiably

schedule from Paddington to Leamington. The load was 480 tons gross to Bicester, 450 tons to Banbury and 385 tons onwards. Generally it can be said that the uphill work was poor, and despite very fast downhill speeds the lost time could not be recovered. This run indicated that the 'Kings' required getting used to, because the Wolverhampton top link of that period included some of the most capable enginemen that have ever served the GWR, and in later years, indeed they did wonderful work with the 'Kings'. Another journey that I made at Whitsun 1929 on the same train, also with engine No. 6019, was much better, as a net time of 90 min. from Paddington to Leamington was made with a load of 475 tons. The train was divided and no slips were included in the first portion. But taken all round, this run was completely eclipsed by the experience I enjoyed on the same train at Whitsun 1930, when a 'Castle' was used instead of a 'King'. The remarkable performance of *Dartmouth Castle* on that later occasion is detailed in Chapter 9.

A much finer run with a 'King' on the Birmingham line was that set out in the accompanying table, with engine No. 6008. The start was inclined to be slow, with an unusually leisurely exit from Paddington itself, and speed not rising above 58 m.p.h. at Greenford. But after a maximum of 63 m.p.h. at Denham, some magnificent performance developed. Up the 1 in 175 to Gerrard's Cross speed did not fall below 54½ m.p.h. and it recovered to 59 m.p.h. on the 1 in 254 to Beaconsfield. There was no more than a slight excess over the speed limit of 35 m.p.h. through High Wycombe, and then the hill climbing to Saunderton was very fine with a minimum speed of 50 m.p.h. at the summit.

From the subsequent work it is evident that these strenuous uphill efforts had been achieved without any mortgaging of the boiler. Fast work followed to Ashendon Junction, with a top speed of 83½ m.p.h. at Haddenham, and it was a sure

2.10 p.m. PADDINGTON–BIRMINGHAM
Engine: 6008 *King James II*
Load: To Banbury: 16 cars, 457 tons tare, 490 tons full
To Leamington: 14 cars, 405 tons tare, 435 tons full
To Birmingham: 13 cars, 370 tons tare, 400 tons full
Driver: Brunsdon (Stafford Road)

Dist. Miles		Sch. Min.	Actual m. s.	Speed m.p.h.
0·0	PADDINGTON .	0	0 00	
1·3	Westbourne Park .		4 02	
3·3	*Old Oak Common*			
	West Junction .	7	7 33	slack 40
4·6	Park Royal . .		9 17	
7·8	Greenford . .		13 03	58
10·3	Northolt Junction .	15½	15 37	58
14·8	Denham . .		20 05	63
17·4	Gerrard's Cross .		22 45	54½
21·7	Beaconsfield .		27 27	59
24·2	*Tylers Green* .			69
26·5	HIGH WYCOMBE .	32	31 50	slack 42
28·8	West Wycombe .		34 45	
31·5	Saunderton .		37 58	50½
32·2	*Milepost 22* .		38 46	50
34·7	PRINCES			
	RISBOROUGH .	41	41 18	70
40·1	Haddenham .		45 27	83½
44·1	Ashendon Junction .	49	48 36	52
47·4	Brill . . .		52 02	69
50·4	Blackthorn . .		54 30	75
53·4	BICESTER .	58	56 55	67½
57·2	Ardley . .		60 32	59½/68
62·4	*Aynho Junction* .	67	65 20	slack 60
64·0	King's Sutton .		66 55	
67·0	*Milepost 85¾* .		70 27	sig. stop
67·5	BANBURY .	72	77 00	stop
71·1	Cropredy . .		6 20	51
76·3	Fenny Compton .		11 35	73½
81·2	Southam Road .		17 30	81
86·3	*Milepost 105* .		19 35	
87·3	LEAMINGTON .	91	21 28	
2·0	Warwick . .		3 20	54½
6·2	Hatton . .		8 12	46
10·2	Lapworth . .		12 24	64
12·9	Knowle . .		14 51	63
16·3	Solihull . .		17 57	68
20·1	Tyseley . .		20 58	75
22·2	Bordesley . .		22 40	
23·3	BIRMINGHAM .	26	24 35	

Net times, min.: Paddington—Leamington 87¾
Leamington—Birmingham 24½

Cornish Riviera Express, with Centenary Riviera stock (1935) in Sonning Cutting: engine No. 6020 'King Henry IV'

eased a little, and speed fell off to 50½ m.p.h. at Ardley summit. Unfortunately the driver was denied a clear run through Banbury, and a lengthy signal stop outside made it necessary to stop in the station in order to detach the slip portion.

A very smart run was made onwards to Leamington, and then after shedding another coach and continuing with a load of 405 tons, a very hard run followed into Birmingham. The usual very rapid start was made out of Leamington, with no more than 3 min. 20 sec. taken for the first 2 miles, to Warwick. Then on the 3½ miles of 1 in 104 to

Hatton speed fell only from 54½ to 46 m.p.h., giving the fast time of 8 min. 12 sec. to Hatton station. Thereafter speed ruled high, and one can note particularly the almost precipitate entrance into Birmingham, with no more than 3 min. 37 sec. for the last 3.2 miles from Tyseley to the stop in Snow Hill station. This, however, was not peculiar to this run. It was quite typical of the way the Wolverhampton drivers used to run in. With a good track, a clear road, and a very long platform in the station itself there was no risk involved in these very rapid approaches.

A 16-coach summer holiday load near Somerton (Somerset)

CHAPTER 12

SOME TECHNICAL DETAILS

THE general proportions of the Churchward standard boilers were settled by 1903 when 4—6—0 No. 98 appeared. Various small changes were made subsequently in the dimensions of the fireboxes, but the only notable change was the extension of the coning of the barrel. As previously mentioned, the first coned barrels had the taper on the second ring only, whereas the boiler fitted to No. 40 had the taper extending over the full length of the barrel. The drawing opposite shows the boiler fitted to 4—6—0 No. 100 in 1902 and that fitted to No. 98 in 1903. These diagrams show clearly the tapering water spaces between the inner and outer firebox in the later boiler, together with the slope of the crown of the firebox. It also shows the outline of the No. 1 boiler as it appeared on a drawing dated July 1904. Apart from the first two boilers built in 1903, the main dimensions of the No. 1 boiler did not vary by more than $\frac{3}{16}$ in., although there were numerous small changes in the number of firetubes and, later, in the length of the superheater elements. These changes affected the areas of heating surface commonly published.

Two dimensions remained standard throughout the development of the Churchward boiler. There was a clear space of 2 ft between the crown of the inner firebox and the crown of the firebox casing. This provided a large space for the collection of steam, and the steam at the top of the space was sufficiently dry for there to be no advantage in fitting a dome. In the first Churchward boilers, with parallel barrels, the crown of the firebox casing was 9 in. above the top of the barrel; this dimension remained in the taper boilers, although it then referred to the front of the barrel only.

The boilers in the upper two illustrations opposite show the position of the feed as originally arranged, at the bottom of the barrel. At a later date top feed was adopted as standard as described in Chapter 4.

The tapered form of the barrel and firebox resulted from increasing the width of the water space at the cross-section of the boiler where the rate of heat release was greatest, that is, at the front of the firebox. It ensured adequate circulation of the water at that section. It gave a further advantage in that, compared with a boiler of equal volume but without taper, there was less change of level of water over the inner firebox when the engine breasted a steep gradient, or when the brakes were applied fully. The slope of the firebox roof from front to rear was introduced to minimise the change of water level under these conditions.

All corners of the firebox had large radii to minimise the stresses set up when the boiler distorted under pressure and heat. For the same reason, stays were not brought to the edges of the firebox plates; this allowed flexibility at the corners. All stays were as nearly as possible at right angles to the surfaces which they connected; this may be seen on page 147. This shows a No. 7 standard boiler, but apart from the numbers of tubes and flues this is almost identical in appearance with the boilers fitted to the 4—6—0s.

A total of 924 No. 1 boilers were built between 1903 and 1944. Of these, 132 were originally saturated, but, apart from a few early ones, these were all fitted later with superheaters. Between 1914 and 1919, 108 boilers were fitted with superheaters having four element groups per flue, but apart from these and the experimental superheaters mentioned later in this chapter, all the boilers of this group were built or rebuilt with the standard Swindon No. 3 superheater, with three element groups per flue. The boilers with three-row superheaters which appeared from 1944 onwards were not fitted to 'Stars', but boilers of the other variations could be, and were, used on the class. For use on the 'Stars' the boilers required the special smokebox, which, although of the same dimensions

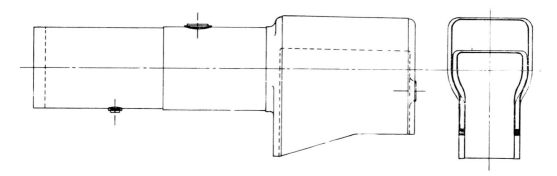

Std. Boiler No. 1 February 1902

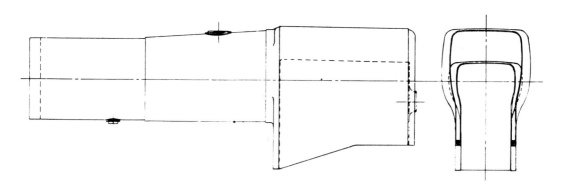

Std. Boiler No. 1 February 1903

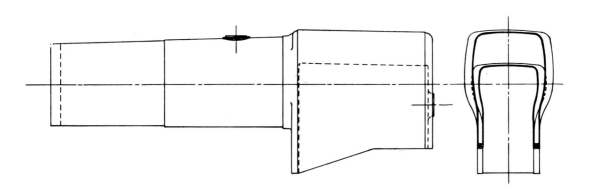

Std. Boiler No. 1 July 1904

Development of the No. 1 standard boiler

145

K

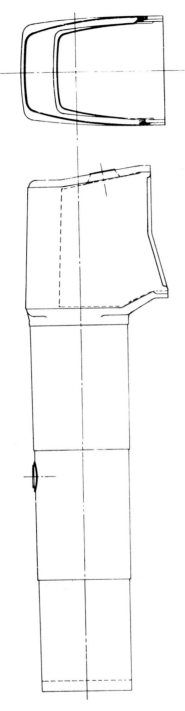

Boiler of The Great Bear

as the one used on the two-cylinder engines, was not interchangeable. Changes of smokebox were, however, made at overhaul, and boilers originally fitted to two-cylinder engines could at a later date appear on 'Stars'. By this means some short-cone boilers originally fitted to 'Saints' were fitted to 'Stars' between 1909 and 1920.

The boilers of the 'Castles' and 'Kings' were not, of course, fitted to any other classes. A total of 60 No. 8 boilers were made between 1923 and 1927 with the original large grates. These met the needs of the first 46 'Castles'. For the 'Kings' 34 boilers were made to the original design.

The diagram immediately below shows the automatic 'jumper' blastpipe top—another Swindon speciality. With heavy loads, and the corresponding admission of a maximum amount of steam to the cylinders, excessive back pressure can occur if the capacity of the blastpipe is designed to give a free exhaust in normal conditions. By automatically increasing the capacity of the blastpipe, by the rising of the jumper ring, a free exhaust is obtained in both normal and maximum working conditions.

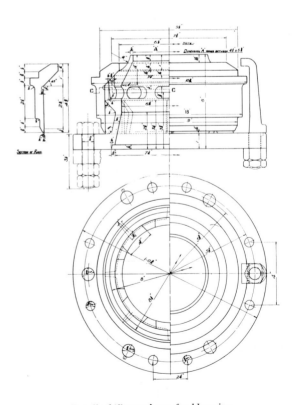

Detail of 'Jumper' top for blastpipe

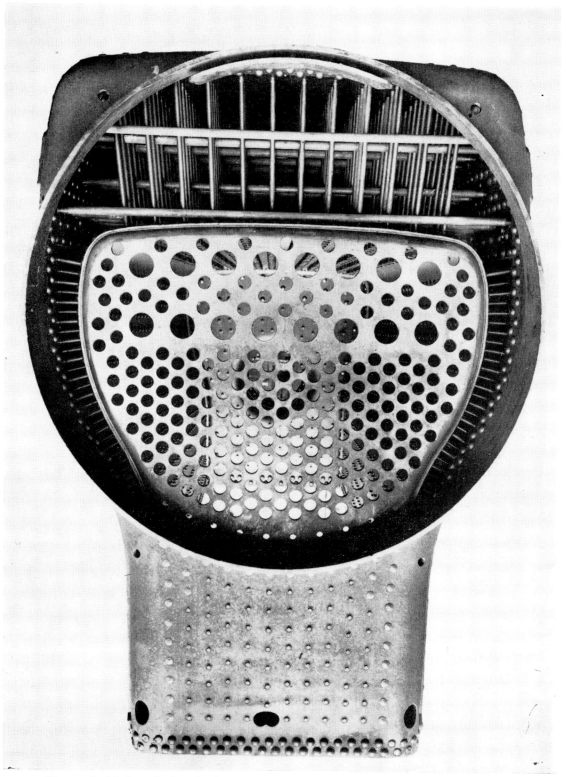

Photograph of firebox tubeplate, showing the careful rounding of corners to avoid stress concentrations, and the arrangement of stays

1. DAMPER CONTROLS.
2. COAL WATERING COCK.
3. EXHAUST INJECTOR CONTROL:
4. FLAP PLATE.
5. FIREHOLE DOORS.
6. WATER GAUGE.
7. STEAM HEATING PRESSURE GAUGE.
8. "   "   VALVE
9. BOILER STEAM PRESSURE GAUGE.
10. EXHAUST INJECTOR LIVE STEAM VALVE.
11. RIGHT HAND "   "   "   "
12. VACUUM GAUGE.

13. EJECTOR STEAM VALVE
14.   "   AIR   "
15. BLOWER VALVE.
16. REGULATOR HANDLE.
17. LUBRICATOR.
18. REVERSING HANDLE.
19. TIP-UP SEAT.
20. SANDING GEAR LEVERS
21. AUDIBLE SIGNALLING APPARATUS.
22. CYLINDER COCK LEVER.

Cab-layout, 'King' class engines

The standard pattern of exhaust for the blower and ejector adopted by Churchward consisted of a ring inserted between the base of the chimney and the petticoat. The ring had two annular passages, to the lower of which the blower exhaust was led, and to the upper the ejector exhaust. The steam was exhausted from the annular passages into the chimney by inclined holes. This arrangement of 'blower ring' was later adopted by the LMS and SR.

The regulator valve of the GWR locomotives was a slide valve designed to give very gradual opening to steam. Movement of the valve through half its travel gave an area of opening to steam of one-eighth of the full opening. The use of a smokebox regulator and a small superheater made GWR engines much more sensitive to changes of regulator opening than engines with dome regulators and large superheaters, because there was less steam contained between the regulator valve and the cylinder. This was of importance at starting, for it resulted in slipping of the wheels being checked very quickly when the regulator was shut. It was found that the 'Kings' were more prone to slipping at starting after they had been fitted with larger superheaters, for there was a greater volume of steam to be drawn from the superheater before pressure in the steamchest dropped sufficiently for a slip to be checked.

GWR cabs were notable for the height of the footplate from rail level, and for the nearness of the firehole door to the cab floor. The main firehole door consisted of two sliding plates, operated by a single handle and links. There was also a hinged flap, attached below the main door, which could be raised by a chain to cover most of the door. The common technique for firing the engine was for the flap to be lowered before each shovelful was fired, and to be raised again immediately afterwards. This reduced the ingress of cold air to the minimum, but it was a complicated operation, and could well have been assisted by arranging a balance weight and treadle, so that the fireman could operate the flap by light foot pressure.

A single water gauge was provided, with test cocks for use in case of failure of the gauge. Two whistles were provided, one for normal and one for emergency use.

There were no cab doors, and this, combined with the height of the footplate, made the cabs exposed. Some enginemen maintain that the short Churchward cabs, in conjunction with the low tender, were less draughty than the side-window cabs with high tenders.

Cab and tender, showing exposed layout on early Churchward engines. The early 'Stars' were like this

The exposed sides of a 'Castle' footplate, even after introduction of the large tenders

VALVES

Churchward realised at an early stage that the cylinder performance at which he was aiming could be attained only by the use of piston valves. Slide valves could not give the areas of port opening, unless they were of such a size that friction losses would be prohibitive. In 1903 he said: '. . . they [piston valves] are undoubtedly one of the most troublesome pieces of mechanism with which any-one can have to deal. I have set before myself the task of curing the defects, if possible. . .'

His first piston valves, used on the 2—4—2Ts, were of the solid plug type; that is, they were solid discs with three narrow grooves round the periphery. Theoretically, these valves produced no friction, for they were smaller than the bore of the valve liner, and should have made no contact, but in fact distortion of the valve liner due to heat caused binding, wear and excessive leakage. An American valve with L-shaped spring rings, and a flat 'bull' ring clamped between them, was then tried. This did not prove entirely satisfactory, but when another American design, known as the 'semi-plug' valve, appeared Churchward acquired the manufacturing rights, and soon adopted it as his standard pattern.

The construction of the valve is shown alongside. The main seal is provided by a side serrated ring, which is split and normally closes up so that it does not touch the valve liner. When steam is admitted to the steam chest, it enters the valve head through holes, and acts on the inside surface of the serrated ring, thus pressing it tightly against the valve liner. The serrated ring is held by the exhaust snap rings, which are also split, and have cover plates over the splits to seal them. Inside the valve head is a wedge ring, which, by pressing against two other wedge-shaped rings (the wall rings) presses the exhaust snap rings tightly against the outer lips of the valve head. The whole assembly is locked solid whilst steam is on; when steam is shut off, the pressure inside the valve head falls, and all the split rings close up, allowing the valve to float freely in the valve liner.

The construction of the valve is complicated, and when it was first produced at Swindon considerable hand fitting was needed. Gradually the accuracy of the machining processes was improved, and the production of the valves was established as a mass-production process. All work on the valves was done at Swindon; running sheds changed complete valve heads. The performance of the valves was very good, steam leakage being small, but the development of solid valve heads with from four to

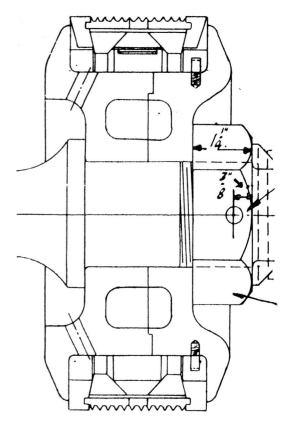

GWR standard piston valve arrangement, as applied on the 'Castle' class from the '5000' series onwards

six narrow rings provided a cheaper and equally satisfactory valve, and Stanier did not include the semi-plug valve amongst the 'Wiltshire wisdom' which he conferred on Derby.

The passage of the steam through the valve was controlled by the outer edges of the snap rings. On modern narrow-ring valves, with the outermost ring set well in from the edge of the valve head, the body of the valve forms a restriction when the valve first opens. In the GWR valves the body of the valve was well clear of the steam edge of the snap rings, and offered no restriction. This was a good feature. It was the unrestricted flow at the instant of opening which gave the GWR engines their characteristic bark at starting, and the machine-gun crack of the exhaust when working hard at speed. It also explains why, when some GWR engines were fitted with BR valves, it was found necessary to work them at a longer nominal cut-off than usual.

A locomotive valve gear must allow for the effect of the angularity of the connecting rod. With the

A set of Walschaert's valve gear set out for inspection in Swindon Works

crank in its mid-position, the crosshead is 0.7 in. to the rear of its mid-position, because of the inclination or angularity of the connecting rod. Thus when the piston is moving backwards, it is at $53\frac{1}{2}$ per cent of its stroke and when the piston is moving forwards, it is at $46\frac{1}{2}$ per cent of its stroke. The piston thus has a 'bias' towards the rear of the cylinder, and its motion is not symmetrical. If steam is to be cut off at the same position of the piston at each end of the cylinder, the valve must be given a similar non-symmetrical motion: otherwise the cut-off at the rear of the cylinder will be less than that at the front.

In a Walschaert's gear the non-symmetrical motion of the valve is produced partly by the inclination of the eccentric rod, and partly from the point of attachment of the eccentric rod to the expansion link being to the rear of the centre line of the link. As with the piston, the effect of the correction is to give the motion of the valve a 'bias' to the rear. If a straight rocker is used to drive the outside valve of the four-cylinder engine from the inside, the 'bias' is reversed by the rocker, and the outside valve thus has a bias towards the front of the steam chest, whereas the outside piston has a bias towards the rear of the cylinder. With the figures given above, if the inside valve is given the necessary bias to produce equal cut-off of 50 per cent at both ends of the cylinder, the outside

valve will be displaced in the wrong direction, and the error in the outside cut-off is doubled, that is, the cut-off at the front will be about 57 per cent and that at the rear about 43 per cent. This error is partially corrected in the Swindon valve gear by the cranking of the rocker lever.

The correction of the outside valve events by this method was a compromise; if the outside cut-offs were made exactly equal, the points of release to exhaust at the front and back of the cylinders would not be exactly equal. Great importance was attached at Swindon to synchronisation of the exhaust openings, as this was considered to contribute to the good steaming of the engine by maintaining an even blast. The setting of the outside valves was therefore arranged to favour the points of release more than the points of cut-off. The only published figures of actual valve setting of the GWR four-cylinder engine (a 'Castle') are given in Phillipson's *Locomotive Design: Data and Formulae*. When the front and back cut-offs for the right inside cylinder were 20.8 per cent and 20.4 per cent, the figures for the right outside cylinder were 26.9 per cent and 19.1 per cent. The points of release were 70.9 per cent and 68.5 per cent for the inside cylinder and 72.3 per cent and 67.6 per cent for the outside cylinder. The differences in release for the four valve heads were thus less than the differences in cut-off.

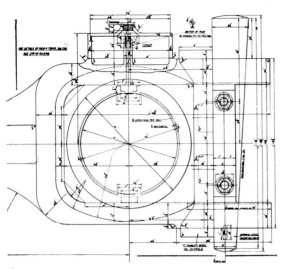

Big-end of inside connecting rod French type

classes, and trouble with what had been the 'Achilles heel' of those famous engines was virtually eliminated.

No less important and successful was the Swindon design of driving axlebox. The version of this used on the 'Castle' class is shown in the accompanying drawing. Its outstanding feature is the use of a cast-steel body, with a relatively thin gunmetal bearing having a thin, continuous white-metal lining. The effectiveness of Great Western practice in axlebox design became widely appreciated after Stanier went to the LMSR. On that line the 'Royal Scots', with driving axleboxes of standard Midland design, had a bad record with heating troubles. They were of solid manganese bronze, with three gunmetal inserts between which the white-metal was applied. In the relatively light working conditions that had been traditional on the Midland Railway this type of axlebox had given reasonable service; but in heavy express duty, and long non-stop runs such as were required from the

From the time of Churchward, Great Western locomotives have been noted for their freedom from heating troubles, and this has been due in large measure to the highly-developed designs of connecting rods and axleboxes used. With outside cylinder engines it had been the practice to make the connecting rod big-ends adjustable, so that allowance could be made in erection and maintenance for slight inaccuracies in the engine itself. But Churchward, by insisting on greater precision and uniformity in the building of his engines, was able to adopt solid big-ends for the outside cylinders, with far greater simplicity in design, and a relatively trouble-free job in service. But, of course, a solid big-end cannot be used for inside cylinders, and as became well known in more recent times the inside big-end could be a source of weakness in a locomotive developing high power outputs. No such trouble beset the Great Western Railway. The inside big-ends on the four-cylinder engines followed very closely upon the de Glehn design incorporated in the three French compounds. The forked end arrangement can be seen from the accompanying reproduction of the Swindon working drawing. It was adopted, with only slight detail changes on the Stanier 'Pacifics' of the LMSR, and a later and most interesting application was due to K. J. Cook when he was Chief Mechanical and Electrical Engineer of the Eastern and North Eastern Region of British Railways. What could be termed the 'de Glehn-Swindon' big-end was substituted for the original Doncaster design on the inside connecting rods of the Gresley 'Pacifics' of both 'A3' and 'A4'

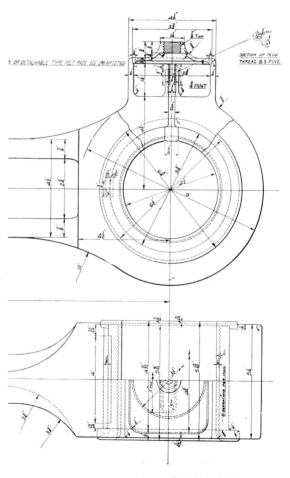

Outside connecting rod solid big-end

'Royal Scots', the inserts tended to work loose, and there were many failures. The substitution of the Swindon type of axlebox made a vast difference.

Associated with the design of bearings in maintaining the excellent reputation of Great Western locomotives for freedom from heating troubles was the design of the lubrication system. Swindon Works, like Crewe, designed most of their own fittings, and the various parts of the lubrication system were all 'home made'. A sight-feed lubricator of high capacity was mounted on the firebox backplate, within easy reach of the driver, as can be seen from the illustration on page 148. While the driver could regulate the amount of feed the supply of oil to the cylinders was initiated automatically by the opening of the regulator. The cam and linking arrangement which opened the oil feed valve can be seen above the quadrant plate of the regulator itself.

The first steam to reach the cylinders on starting the locomotive comes through an auxiliary steam pipe and brings with it a supply of oil. The shape of the cam slot in the link is such that the lubricator controlling the oil feed valve is not opened until the regulator has moved about $\frac{3}{4}$ in. from the 'shut' stop. The 'jockey' valve of the regulator does not admit steam to the cylinders until the handle has been moved about $\frac{3}{4}$ in. from

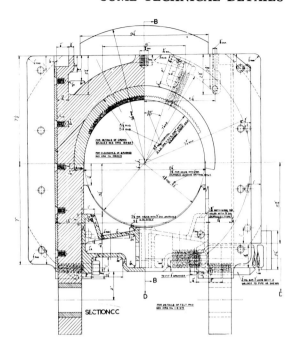

SECTION CC

Detail of driving axlebox

the stop, but it is arranged that the oil feed valve is opened just before the jockey valve of the steam regulator opens.

ENGINE LOADINGS

The following note appeared in the GWR Service Timetable before the tables of loading of trains:

The loads given in the tables represent the capacity of the engine if the standard point-to-point timing is to be maintained. On sections where gradients will permit, these loads may be exceeded with a suitable increase in the point-to-point timing, but in sections where there are steep rising gradients it will be necessary to provide an assistant engine.

The following figures were current at the end of the period covered by this book.

	King	Castle	Star
Paddington—Westbury—Wellington	500	455	420
Wellington to Whiteball	455	420	392
Whiteball to Newton Abbot	500	455	420
Newton Abbot to Rattery or Brent (with a clear run through Aller Junction)	360	315	288
Rattery or Brent to Plymouth	455	420	392
Plymouth to Hemerdon (with a clear run through Plympton) .	360	315	288
Hemerdon to Newton Abbot	385	350	315
Newton Abbot to Paddington	500	455	420
Reading—Bristol—Taunton (up and down) . . .	500	455	420
Paddington to Cardiff (up and down)	—	455	420
Paddington to Wolverhampton (up and down) . . .	500	455	420
Paddington to Birmingham (special loading for 2-hour trains, up and down)	400	355	320

CHRONOLOGY: 1902 to 1930

February	1902	Engine No. 100 completed
June	1902	G. J. Churchward became Loco. Superintendent
March	1903	Engine No. 98 completed
December	1903	Engine No. 171 completed as a 4—6—0
October	1903	De Glehn compound *La France* delivered
June	1905	French engines Nos. 103 and 104 delivered
April	1906	Engine No. 40 *North Star* built
February	1907	First 4-cylinder 4—6—0 No. 4001 built
February	1908	*The Great Bear* built
August	1910	Interchange trials with LNWR
-	1913	15 in. cylinders standardised on 'Stars'
December	1921	G. J. Churchward retired
January	1922	C. B. Collett appointed Chief Mechanical Engineer
May	1922	'Abbey' class engines built
August	1923	*Caerphilly Castle* built
March	1924	Trials of *Caldicot Castle*
-	1924	C. B. Collett's paper to World Power Conference
January	1924	Conversion of *The Great Bear* to 4—6—0 begun
-	1924	British Empire Exhibition
April	1925	Interchange trials with LNER
Autumn	1926	Interchange trials with LMSR
June	1927	*King George V* built
August	1927	Visit of *King George V* to U.S.A.

ACKNOWLEDGEMENTS

The author and publishers wish to express their thanks to the following for permission to use illustrations:

P. J. T. Reed Esq.: p.16, 20 top, 28 bottom left, 35, 47, 149 left.

M. W. Earley Esq.: p.64, 72 top, 76, 101, 106 top and bottom, 107, 111, 112, 132 top, 134, 138, 140 top and bottom, 141, 143 top.

F. J. Arthur Esq.: p.79.

E. D. Bruton Esq.: p.117 top.

F. R. Hebron Esq.: p.103 top, 143 bottom.

O. S. Nock Esq.: p.113 bottom, 116.

K. H. Leech Esq.: p.149 right.

E. S. Cox Esq.: p.103 bottom, 105.

Real Photographs Co. Ltd: p.27 bottom right, 32 bottom, 33 left and right, 40 top left and right, 41 top, 44 top and bottom, 53 top and bottom, 54, 55, 58 left and right, 60, 65, 68, 69 bottom, 72 bottom, 73 bottom left and right, 75 top, 78 right, 85 top, 88, 89 bottom, 93 bottom, 99, 100, 102 bottom, 109 left and right, 113 top, 115, 117 bottom, 119 bottom, 132 bottom right, 136 bottom left and right.

The Locomotive Publishing Co. Ltd: p.27 top, 77, 84 bottom.

Acknowledgement is also made of photographs loaned from the author's collection taken by the following:

The late F. E. Mackay: p.19, 29, 57, 59 top and bottom, 66, 69 top.

By the late W. J. Reynolds: p.41 bottom, 62, 75 bottom, 78 left, 89 top, 91 top and bottom, 98, 108 top and bottom, 118, 121 top, 132 bottom left, 142.

By the late E. Little: p.84 top.

By R. Brookman Esq.: p.20 bottom.

For the remainder of the photographs, 52 in all, indebtedness is expressed to British Railways, also for the drawings from which most of the diagrams have been reproduced.

Indebtedness is also expressed to Prof. W. A. Tuplin for loan of the blocks from which the diagrams on pages 26 and 52 have been prepared.

The coloured frontispiece is from a water-colour painting by V. Welch.

INDEX

BIBLIOGRAPHY

The late G. J. Churchward's *Locomotive Development*. K. J. Cook. (Proc. Inst. Loco. Engineers 1950)

Locomotives of the Great Western Railway. (R.C.T.S. Publications)

Large Locomotive Boilers. G. J. Churchward. (Proc. Inst. Mech. Engineers 1906)

An Outline of G.W.R. Locomotive Practice. H. Holcroft

Fifty Years of Western Express Running. O. S. Nock

Great Western Steam. W. A. Tuplin

Modern Locomotive Practice on the G.W.R. F. W. Brewer. (*The Railway Magazine* 1928-1930)

British Locomotive Practice and Performance. C. Rous-Marten and Cecil J. Allen. (*The Railway Magazine* 1905-1935)